BURT FRANKLIN: BIBLIOGRAPHY & REFERENCE SERIES 373
American Classics in History & Social Science 151

HISTORY

OF THE

GOVERNMENT PRINTING OFFICE,

GOVERNMENT PRINTING OFFICE BUILDING, showing the new addition now (June, 1881) in course of erection.

HISTORY

OF THE

Government Printing Office,

(AT WASHINGTON, D. C.)

WITH A BRIEF

RECORD OF THE PUBLIC PRINTING

FOR

A CENTURY

1789–1881.

By R. W. KERR.

BURT FRANKLIN
New York, N. Y.

Z
232
U6
K4
1970

Published by LENOX HILL Pub. & Dist. Co. (Burt Franklin)
235 East 44th St., New York, N.Y. 10017
Originally Published: 1881
Reprinted: 1970
Printed in the U.S.A.

S.B.N.: 8337-19157
Library of Congress Card Catalog No.: 77-132811
Burt Franklin: Bibliography and Reference Series 373
American Classics in History and Social Science 151

CONTENTS.

4   *Contents.*

LIST OF ILLUSTRATIONS.

6   *List of Illustrations.*

INTRODUCTION.

THE original design of this book was simply to furnish something which would answer as a guide to the many visitors who yearly inspect the different departments of the Government Printing Office. It was not intended to elaborate it with any allusion to the early printing for the Government; to embody in it the laws relating to the subject of public printing; to supply any data of the former business of the office; nor to illustrate it as it now appears. It was intended only to recapitulate, in as brief a manner as possible, the present dimensions and capacity of the office, with a reference to the machinery in use, the number of hands engaged, the style of work produced, the manner of its execution, etc. But it has grown greatly beyond its first conception, and my own intention and expectation; and whether the present design be good or bad, I have no apology to make, as I believe the many historical and other incidents contained in its pages will prove of some value and interest; although possibly not presented in the most attractive form.

But few persons outside of a printing office, or those having daily business with printers, have any idea of the numerous processes through which written matter must pass before it becomes a finished, printed book. Printing is a slow and tedious business at best, notwithstanding the many and diversified improvements which have been invented to facilitate the rapid production of printed matter.

That the reader—if he be not a printer—may form some conception of the magnitude of the undertaking, I will endeavor to give, without the use of trade terms where they can be avoided, the many different and devious processes, in the order of their occurrence, involved in the production of a simple public document, from the time of its entry into the Government Printing Office until it reaches the Capitol for distribution to Senators and Representatives as a completed, printed volume.

The first operation, and perhaps the most important one, at least to the author, after the receipt of the manuscript in the office, is to see that it is arranged in the order in which it is supposed to have been

7

written. It not unfrequently happens that the document has been
kicked from pillar to post at the committee-rooms of the Capitol for
days, or pulled to pieces by a dozen different correspondents in their
eager hunt for news; and, nine times out of ten, when it reaches the
Public Printer it is in the reverse order of its original production, or
so badly "mixed up" by the displacement of pages, that it would be a
mass of nonsense if printed as received at the office. But here it falls
into the hands of careful and conscientious workmen, to whom the
authors of Government literature owe a debt of gratitude of great
magnitude, who exert a "rectifying" influence over this rumpled
monstrosity that smooths its future career, and places the author in the
first ranks of modern writers. When the order of its being has thus
been determined by these experts, it is carefully read over, page after
page, by the same individuals, who seek to harmonize the many incon-
sistencies found, and by a series of hieroglyphic pencil-marks, only
intelligible to printers, indicate the particular type in which each head-
line or portion of the text is to appear. Each page of the manuscript
is then numbered, from the first to the last, to prevent any confusion
in its subsequent career.

It is now ready for another process : It goes to the person having
charge of the mechanical branch of the Document Room (for instance), where it is parceled out to the compositors, who reproduce
the original in type. If it is an extensive publication, perhaps a
hundred or a hundred and fifty men will be engaged upon it at once,
and in an hour from the time the copy reaches the compositors' hands,
the proof-slips are passing into the Proof Room to be read. When a
certain number of lines have been set in the composing-stick, the
composed matter is dexterously lifted out, and placed on a frame with
brass bottom and wooden sides lined with brass, and called a
"galley," in which it is securely fastened by the aid of a piece of
beveled wood, called a side-stick, and small wooden wedges or quoins.
When a number of these galleys, filled with type, are ready, they are
removed to a proof-press, and impressions taken, which is called a first
proof, and with these printed proofs the manuscript is sent to the
Proof Room, where it is given out to, perhaps, as many different readers
as there are galley-proofs, the manuscript being separated to correspond in quantity precisely with the matter on each proof-slip. The
reader now looks over the printed impression, marking the errors
detected as he proceeds, in a manner peculiar to the craft, while a
"copy-holder" by his side reads aloud every word and figure or
peculiar mark or character found on the original copy. The effort of
this reader is to produce an exact counterpart of the manuscript, for
sometimes the value of an official document depends as much upon its

peculiarities of construction as it does upon the faithful production of the language used.

It is next passed to another reader, who is termed a "silent reader," and he goes over it to detect any errors of "omission or commission" on the part of the first reader. He also refers frequently, in case of doubt, to the original copy, but does not have an assistant like the first reader.

These proof-slips, which, perhaps, from the number of pencil corrections on the margin, would lead one to believe that a first-class epidemic of small-pox is raging in the office, are now transferred to the compositors for further manipulation, who proceed to correct the proof; *i. e.*, to change letters in wrongly-spelled words, or to substitute the proper words, and sometimes whole sentences, for those which have been incorrectly deciphered. After this operation is completed, a second impression, in "galley" form, is made, which is called a "revise," and this is carefully compared by a proof-reviser with the first proof, to see that no errors have been neglected by the compositors. This second or revised proof is now again sent to the compositors, and they proceed as before to correct any remaining errors. This process of revising, in the more important scientific publications, is frequently repeated three and four, and sometimes five and six times, to insure the utmost accuracy in the future book.

The matter is now ready to be "made up" into pages, which is done by means of a gauge, of the exact length of the pages in the proposed book; and, when so cast off into proper lengths, is securely tied up with a strong cord to facilitate the handling of the four or five thousand little pieces of metal which go to make up a page of matter. It is now arranged on an imposing-stone, in such a manner that when printed the pages will follow in regular order; and when a sufficient number of pages—usually sixteen—are made up and so arranged, a chase—a light frame-work of iron, divided by bars into four equal sections—is placed around them, and they are tightly wedged or "locked up."

If the matter is to be stereotyped, the pages of type, before they reach this stage of progress, are sent to the Stereotype Foundry.

These several pages are now called a "form," or a "signature," from which another proof or revise is taken, which is again sent to the reviser, who goes over the headings of each page carefully, and whose duty it is to scrutinize the general make-up or arrangement of the whole, and to see that the pages have been correctly imposed; *i. e.*, arranged in the proper numerical order, etc. When any errors found in this form revise have been corrected, it is lowered into the Press Room by steam power.

Here it is taken in charge by one of our "colored brethren," and placed upon the bed of the press; the irregularities in the surface of the type planed down by the pressman, and it is now ready for the clean white paper. The young lady who is to manipulate these snowy sheets with her delicate taper fingers, now ascends to the raised platform at the side of the press, and by a peculiar push and pull separates a single sheet from the pile of paper at her elbow, and gently lowers it within reach of the steel fingers of the press, which clutch it viciously, and drag it into a dark abyss. A single revolution of the huge cylinder carries it over the waiting form beneath, and elastic tapes convey it to the rear of the press, where it appears transformed into a printed "signature" of the future book.

There are now three ways of treating these printed sheets before they are gathered into books, all of which, however, when done, have about the same effect, viz, to remove any irregularities in the surface of the printed signature: 1st, they may be "dry-pressed," in the old-fashioned way, by placing three or four sheets between hard, smooth pieces of pasteboard, and subjecting them to powerful pressure in a hydraulic press; 2d, or they may be passed through Gill's Hot Rolling or Calendering Machine, which not only removes all irregularities from the printed signature, but imparts a pleasant, glossy surface to the paper; 3d, or they may be permitted to lie in sheets a day or two, and then folded and pressed in bundles in Jones' Hydraulic Sheet Pressing Machine. When either the first or the second of these operations has been consummated, the sheets are ready to be transported by elevators to the Folding Room on the fourth floor.

When these pressed sheets reach this room, the many signatures are divided among the lady folders, and each sheet is folded separately, so that the first and last pages of the signature are on the outside. They may, however, be folded by machinery. The process of machine folding is fully described elsewhere, and need not be stated here.

The next operation is termed "gathering"; *i. e.*, gathering the sheets or signatures into books. The folded sheets of the book are laid out along the edge of the gathering table in the regular numerical order of the signatures, and the "gatherer" then commences at the last sheet or signature, taking one from that pile, one from the next, and so on until the first sheet or title of the book is placed upon the top of all the others. This completes a set of the signatures in the coming book. This operation is, of course, repeated as many times as there are volumes printed. These gathered signatures are now examined, or "collated," as the process is called, to see that the sheets have been collected in their proper alphabetical or numerical order.

If the book is to be delivered unbound, it is then passed—if it is a hurried document—to the stitchers, twenty, or forty, or a hundred of whom can be put at it instantly, and the work rushed out with great rapidity. But if it does not exceed one hundred or one hundred and fifty pages, and is not specially hurried, it may be stitched upon Thompson's Wire Pamphlet Stitching Machine. Books intended for binding are sent to the Bindery as soon as collated, as the process of sewing is, I believe, the world over, a part of the work of the binder.

It is not the intention to give here a description of the various processes or of the numerous styles of binding books in practice in the office; but to refer only to the more important manipulations books receive, and the number of machines used in the process. Cloth binding is commonly termed "cows" by the binders here, but the derivation of the term is unknown to me. Although it is one of the cheapest styles of binding, it is one which requires the use of more machinery than the more expensive bindings.

The first process the book passes through after it reaches the bindery is termed "smashing"; *i. e.*, reducing the sheets of a volume, by enormous, sudden pressure in a powerful toggle-jointed machine, to the smallest possible space, to facilitate its more convenient handling by the sewers, etc.

After being properly pressed in the smashing machine, they are "sawed out" for "sewing." The machine for this purpose has a number of circular saws, with teeth projecting about one-eighth of an inch above the top; the books are put up in bunches of six or eight, carefully knocked up evenly on the backs, and passed over the saws, which cut five grooves across the back. They are now ready for sewing. This is an important part of book-making, and has a great deal to do with the good or bad appearance of the future book, as the work is properly or poorly performed. The operation is somewhat complex and difficult to explain, but consists in securing the several signatures together in proper form, by means of a combination of peculiar stitches, with the aid of a sewing frame to hold the work as sewed. The process is also performed to a certain extent by the aid of machinery. The Wire Book Sewing Machines enjoy a monopoly of a certain class of the work, while certain other classes of the literature issued from the office are sewed exclusively by hand.

The volumes are now ready for the forwarder, who first pastes together the two outside, white, or "waste leaves," which is done to add strength to the book; they are then beaten with a hammer, to remove all surplus swell caused in the sewing, and are next put up in bunches of suitable size for cutting. They are now removed to the cutting machine, and the edges trimmed precisely according to the intended margin. The forwarder now glues the backs, and when almost dry, he rounds them. This is done by hand, no machinery having yet been invented which does the work in a satisfactory manner; and it is done by beating the backs with a hammer into a convex shape; after which they are ready to be backed. The books are now removed to the backing machine; they are placed perpendicularly between the jaws of the machine, having the back and sides exposed about one-eighth of an inch; the iron roller of the machine is now worked back and forth over the back, forming a joint or projection on each side of the book, sufficiently large to accommodate the covers. The forwarder now again takes them, and lines the back with brown paper, after which the books are ready for their cases or covers.

The cases are made by another set of operators, who are termed "case-makers." The only machinery used in this operation is a common clothes-wringer, and a gauge in the shape of a letter T, with two parallel pieces of iron forming the back, one of which works in a slot which can be moved any distance required, according to the size of the back of the book. The cloth, having been previously cut by machinery the proper size, is generously smeared with glue all over the surface; the gauge is then laid upon the cloth, two pieces of board are placed evenly against the gauge, and a strip of Manila paper inserted in the back; the gauge is then taken off, and the edges of the cloth turned over the boards, which are then passed through the wringer to make the cloth adhere to the boards. This process, simple as it may appear, requires considerable skill and experience, before a workman can become sufficiently expert to make the number of cases required as a day's work. After the cases are perfectly dry, they are removed to the embossing press, where they are embossed, and the backs lettered. These presses are the most powerful and expensive machines used in the Bindery.

The books are cased by another set of workmen, called "casers"; and after the cases are put on they are subjected to more pressure in a standing press, after which they are ready for delivery.

The public document which we set out to follow through the many processes involved in its completion as a finished book, is now ready to be lowered by elevators to the first floor, whence it is taken by wagons to the Capitol, where it is delivered in lots to the Folding Rooms or the Document Rooms of the Senate and House of Representatives; and when receipts are received for the volumes, the responsibility of the Public Printer ceases. No matter how humble or unimportant the subject treated of in this document may be, the law provides for its distribution to every State and Territory of the Union; while another law directs the distribution of a limited number, through the Librarian of Congress, to foreign Governments.

I am indebted to many kind friends connected with the establishment for valuable assistance and advice in preparing this volume, and if it is acceptable to them, and the many others who inspired me with substantial encouragement in the shape of "dollar subscriptions"— without which it would undoubtedly never have survived its conception —I will consider myself well repaid for the labor required in its preparation.

The drawings for the illustrations of the interior and exterior of the Government Printing Office building were made by Mr. C. F. TRILL, and the engraving was executed on wood by Mr. H. H. NICHOLS, the well-known Washington engraver. That they have both performed their difficult parts in a most satisfactory manner, is evident to those familiar with the many obstacles which had to be surmounted.

The excellent likeness of Mr. DEFREES, the present Public Printer, was also engraved by Mr. NICHOLS.

CHAPTER I.

SHORT HISTORY OF PUBLIC PRINTING FROM 1789 TO 1881.

THE First Congress, under the present Constitution, met in the city of New York on the 4th day of March, 1789, in pursuance of a resolution of the Congress of the Confederation of September 13, 1788, and held its first session in the City Hall in that city, and remained in session two hundred and ten days, having adjourned on the 29th day of September of the same year. The Second Session of the First Congress, which was commenced on Monday, January 4, 1790, and which terminated on August 12, 1790, was also held in New York.

The Third Session of the First Congress met in Philadelphia, December 6, 1790, and convened in Carpenters' Hall. At this session all of the original "thirteen" States were for the first time represented. Congress continued to meet in Philadelphia until the 14 of May, 1800.

The Second Session of the Sixth Congress was held in the Old Capitol Building in the city of Washington, November 17, 1800, and since that time Congress has continued to hold its sessions in Washington City.

———

The first mention of public printing found in the Annals of Congress is in relation to printing the laws, and was in the form of a report, presented by Mr. Sylvester, a member of the House of Representatives, early in the First Session of the First Congress, recommending that proposals be invited for "printing the laws and *other proceedings*" of Congress. It is presumed that this resolution covered, by "other proceedings," the printing of the bills and resolutions, and such documents and reports as were necessary in the transaction of the business of the House.

In May, 1789, several petitions were presented to the House by those engaged in the business of printing in New York, praying to "be employed in the printing for Congress," but the Annals do not give any information as to whether any of the petitioners were ever engaged by Congress or not.

A joint arrangement between committees of the two houses was entered into about this time, which provided "that 600 copies of the acts of Congress and 700 copies of the journals" should be printed, and directing the Secretary of the Senate and Clerk of the House to have the work done. This action of the joint committee was subsequently approved by both houses.

It appears that this arrangement did not give very general satisfaction, as numerous propositions looking to more expedition, accuracy, etc., in the execution of the work were presented in the House; but no change was effected for several years.

As the Senate, up to 1794, sat with closed doors, and the proceedings preserved are of very meager character, I can only judge of the nature of the rules governing the printing for that body by what is found in the proceedings of the House. It is very certain, however, that the method of doing the work mentioned above also prevailed in the Senate from the beginning of the First Congress until the Second Session of the Eighth Congress.

In an act making appropriations for the support of the Government, passed in 1794, is found the first specific appropriation for the public printing; and as the juxtaposition with other items will doubtless appear rather singular to the reader of Congressional literature of the present day, the following extract from the law is appended:

"For the expenses of *firewood, stationery*, and *printing work*, and all other contingent expenses of the two houses of Congress, ten thousand dollars."

There was appropriated, in the same law, for like purposes: for the Secretary of State, including the publication of the laws of the First Session of the Third Congress, $2,261.67; for the Treasury Department, $4,000; and for the War Department, $800.

Up to the time of the passage of this law, the printing was paid for from the contingent fund of Congress and the Departments, without being specifically mentioned in the laws.

The first proposition to appoint a printer to the House was made by Mr. Randolph, in December, 1801, during the First Session of the Seventh Congress. This proposition had, it seems, the sanction of a committee of that body; but the recommendation of the committee, owing to opposition to multiplying the offices of the House, was defeated, only about twenty members voting in favor of it.

A very lengthy discussion occurred during the Second Session of the Seventh Congress (in February, 1803) in the House, upon the propriety of printing public documents; *i. e.*, communications from the President and Executive Departments. The particular document in question was a message from the President, and accompanying papers, relating to the expenditures from the contingent fund of the Executive

Departments for several years previous. The discussion took a wide range, but the real opposition was founded upon the expense, which it was estimated would be $10,000. The proposition was finally passed by a vote of 38 to 28, and the document printed.

In 1804, in the Second Session of the Eighth Congress, a resolution was passed requiring the "Clerk of the House to advertise for proposals for supplying the House of Representatives with stationery and printing, and to award the contract to the lowest bidder." At the next session, the Clerk made a report of his action under this resolution, but the papers are inaccessible, if in existence at all, which I doubt, and I am unable to record the difficulties which he probably encountered in the first attempt at the contract system as applied to the public printing. We find that the Senate also took action on the subject in a resolution to "appoint a committee to inquire into the expediency of establishing permanent rules for the regulating and conducting the printing for the Senate." The committee to whom the resolution was referred reported favorably, and, having changed it into a concurrent resolution, it was passed.

This system—the letting of the printing to the lowest bidder, and which was the first joint attempt to have the printing for the Government executed by contract—prevailed in both houses of Congress until the passage of the resolution of 1819. The work was done in a very imperfect manner, and excited from time to time an endless amount of unfavorable criticism, and was also very expensive and unsatisfactory, owing to the delays and inaccuracies in its execution.

In December, 1818 (Fifteenth Congress, Second Session), a resolution was passed appointing a joint committee of the two houses of Congress to "consider and report whether any further provisions of law are necessary to insure dispatch, accuracy, and neatness in the printing done for the two houses of Congress." In obedience to this resolution, a committee was appointed to examine into the subject. The committee, consisting of General Wilson, a Senator from New Jersey —a practical printer, and editor of the *True American*—and General T. A. Rogers, a member of the House of Representatives from Pennsylvania, visited New York and Philadelphia, and made diligent inquiry in respect to the cost and the best method of having the work executed. On their return to Washington, the committee made a very valuable report upon the subject. This committee was the first to advocate the creation of a national printing office, as the best and most economical method of procuring the printing for the Government. A portion of their report, touching upon this point, is as follows:

"How far it is reputable for Congress to endeavor to get their work

done below a fair and reasonable price, may be a matter of doubt, but
it does not admit of a question that the compensation ought to be
adequate to the object of procuring that work to be done at a proper
time and in a suitable manner.   A second mode suggested to and considered by the committee was the establishment of a national printing
office (with a bindery and stationery annexed), which should execute
the work of Congress while in session, and that df the various Departments of Government during the recess, and should do all the binding,
and furnish the stationery, for the Departments, as well as for Congress.
To ascertain the amount of expenditures on these objects, inquiries
were addressed by the committee to the heads of Departments, Attorney-General, and Postmaster-General, and an answer received from
each.   Some of the reports were made in such a manner as not to
enable the committee to separate the accounts for printing from those
for binding and stationery; but the whole amount exceeds $41,000.
Add to this the expenditures of the Senate and House of Representatives on the same objects, namely, the former $8,000, and the latter
$15,000, and the aggregate cost of the public printing, binding, and
stationery is about $65,000 a year, of which probably one-half is for
printing; and this, it will be remembered, does not include the great
variety and number of blanks executed elsewhere than at the seat of
Government from copies furnished by the Departments of the Treasury, War, &c., and which might all be done here at a much less
expense were a national printing office established.   The committee
are of opinion that such an establishment, under the superintendence
of a man of activity, integrity, and discretion, would be likely to produce promptitude, uniformity, accuracy, and elegance in the execution of the public printing; and they are not certain that it would not
in the result, connecting with it a bindery and stationery, as already
suggested, be found the most economical."

These recommendations were made nearly half a century before the
object advocated was accomplished.

The recommendation of this committee, however, for want of
time, as was alleged, was not acted upon; but the necessity for some
legislation on the subject of the printing required by Congress was
imperative.   The country had greatly increased in population, and the
business of Congress had been so frequently interrupted or interfered
with owing to the delays and inaccuracies in the printing done, that
the resolution of March 3, 1819, was hastily framed and passed.   It
provided that each house should elect its own printer, and designated
how the work should be done, and the prices to be paid.

The joint resolution is as follows:

JOINT RESOLUTION OF 1819.

"*Resolved*, *etc.*, That the printing of Congress, unless when otherwise specially ordered, shall be done in the following form and manner, viz: Bills, as heretofore, with English type on foolscap paper. Rule or table work, in royal octavo size, when it can be brought into that size by any types not smaller than brevier; and where it cannot, in such form as to fold conveniently into the volume. All other printing with a small pica type, on royal paper, in pages of the same size as those of the last edition of the laws of the United States, including the marginal notes.

"And the following prices shall be allowed and paid for the above described work: For the composition of every page of bills, $1; of every page of small pica type, plain work, $1; of every page of small pica rule-work, $2; every page of brevier rule-work, $3.50; and for a larger form of brevier rule-work, in proportion.

"For the press-work of bills, including paper, folding and stitching: for 50 copies, 25 cents per page; for 400 copies, $1.25 per page; for the press-work of tables, other than those in the regular octavo form: for 600 copies, including as above, $5.50 per form; for the press-work of the journals, of 900 copies, including as above, $1 per page; for all other printing, in the octavo form, of 600 copies, including as above, 87½ cents per page; and for a larger or smaller number, in proportion.

"That as soon as this resolution shall have been approved by the President of the United States, each house shall proceed to ballot for a printer to execute its work during the next session of Congress; and the person having the greater number of votes shall be considered duly elected, and shall give bond, with sureties, to the satisfaction of the Secretary of the Senate and Clerk of the House of Representatives, respectively, for the prompt, accurate, and neat execution of the work; and in case any inconvenient delay should be, at any time, experienced by either house in the delivery of its work, the Secretary and Clerk, respectively, may be authorized to employ another printer to execute any portion of the work of the Senate and House, and charge the excess in the account of such printer, for executing such work, above what is herein allowed, to the printer guilty of such negligence and delay: *Provided*, That nothing herein contained shall preclude the choice of the same printer by the Senate and House of Representatives."

The custom above referred to, of printing the bills of Congress in English type, is still followed, but the size of the page has been reduced to about two-thirds the length of an ordinary foolscap sheet. Nonpareil has taken the place of brevier type for the tabular matter, and long primer has superseded small pica for the text.   Brevier type, however, is used very extensively for extracts, and in some cases for whole volumes, where the desire is to condense as much as possible.

Under this law of 1819, Gales & Seaton, so well known in after years in connection with the printing for the Government, and as the publishers of the *National Intelligencer*, were elected printers to the Senate and the House of Representatives on the 3d of March, 1819. Two years later they were re-elected by both houses; and February 25, 1823, were again re-elected printers to the House, and on the following day (February 26) were also re-elected printers to the Senate. This firm was continued as printers to the House for several years after this, having been re-elected in 1827 and 1833, and in 1835 were also again elected printers to the Senate.

In 1827, in the Senate, Messrs. Duff Green, Gales & Seaton, Peter Force, and Thomas Ritchie were nominated for election as printers to the Senate.   Under the law of 1819, a majority of all the votes cast was necessary to a choice.   Two ballots were taken, which having resulted in no choice, the election, by resolution of the Senate, was declared at an end.   At the next meeting of Congress, however, on the first day of the session, the subject was brought up in the Senate by the introduction of the following preamble and resolution:

"*Whereas*, In pursuance of a joint resolution of the Senate and House of Representatives, passed in 1819, regulating the subject of printing for the two houses of Congress, respectively, an election having been had by the Senate, during the last session, for a printer to the Senate, and Duff Green having, according to the provisions of said resolution, received the greatest number of votes: Therefore,

"*Resolved*, That in the opinion of the Senate the said Duff Green is duly elected printer to the Senate."

After a debate of considerable animation, in which Senators Eaton, Hayne, Benton, Berrien, and Woodbury advocated, and Senators Macon, Harrison, Chambers, and Robbins opposed the resolution, ineffectual attempts having been made to postpone it and lay it upon the table, it was adopted by a vote of 25 yeas to 19 nays.

Thus Messrs. Gales & Seaton were displaced by the election of Duff Green, but, as before stated, were reinstated in 1835.

Blair & Rives were first elected printers to the Senate March 3, 1837, and were re-elected February 27, 1839.

During the extra or first session of the Twenty-fifth Congress, after eleven ballots, on September 5, 6, and 7, Mr. Thomas Allen was elected House printer, and January 30, 1840, Blair & Rives superseded him. Blair & Rives were elected Senate printers February 20, 1841.

At the time of the inauguration of President Harrison (1841), Blair

& Rives were the printers to the Senate. At the Executive Session of the Senate, held after the new President had taken his seat, Mr. Mangum, of North Carolina, offered a resolution to dismiss Messrs. Blair & Rives. During the discussion of the resolution, Messrs. King, of Alabama, and Henry Clay, of Kentucky, indulged in very bitter and offensive language to each other, which resulted in a challenge under the code by Mr. King. The difficulty was amicably settled by the interposition of friends, before the gentlemen met in mortal combat. Blair & Rives were dismissed, and their official bond taken from them.

Thomas Allen was elected to take the place of the deposed firm June 15, 1846. Gales & Seaton became Senate printers again December 5, 1843; and Ritchie & Heiss, December 4, 1845. Thomas Allen was the editor of the *Madisonian.* In the House, Gales & Seaton were elected printers June 11, 1841; Blair & Rives, December 7, 1843; and Ritchie & Heiss, December 3, 1845.

The Congressional printing, up to 1839, was executed under the joint resolution of 1819, but at that time it was considered that the prices fixed by law were too high; and the whole subject having been referred to a select committee, the result of their investigation was a report recommending a reduction in the scale of prices of fifteen per cent. The minority, who were Whigs, claimed that the reduction in the prices should be still greater, some twenty per cent.

At the Extra Session of the Twenty-seventh Congress, the subject of the printers' compensation was again taken up and examined. The prices were then fixed at twenty per cent. less than those provided for under the law of 1819, under which reduction Gales & Seaton were elected printers; but subsequently—at the last session of the Twenty-seventh Congress—the same majority who had thus reduced the pay of the printers, repealed their action by adding an appropriation to the general appropriation law sufficient to make Gales & Seaton's compensation equal to the prices fixed by the resolution of 1819. The printing for the House during the Twenty-seventh Congress amounted to about $200,000.

March 3, 1845, the following clause in a general appropriation law was approved:

"And all Congressional printing executed under an order of either house, made after the 4th of March, 1845, shall be paid for at prices twenty per centum less than those fixed by the joint resolution of March 3, 1819."

Various laws relating to the printing were enacted between 1840 and 1846, some of which provided that the printing for the Departments, the Supreme Court, etc., should be done by contract; but not until 1846, when the Garrett Davis resolution became a law, was all the printing done by contract.

In 1846, when Mr. Polk was President, Thomas Ritchie, for many years the editor of the ancient *Richmond Enquirer*, was elected printer to both houses of Congress. Father Ritchie's election seems to have given offense to some of the political magnates of the period, and Garrett Davis, of Kentucky, who was then a member of the House of Representatives, and a Whig in politics, took advantage of the dissatisfaction among the Democrats, and, with the aid of the Whigs and the dissatisfied members of Mr. Ritchie's party, secured the passage of a resolution which overthrew the organ system of executing the public printing, and provided that the work should thereafter be done by the lowest bidder.

The joint resolution of August 3, 1846, is as follows:

JOINT RESOLUTION OF AUGUST 3, 1846.

"*Resolved, etc.*, That the Secretary of the Senate and the Clerk of the House of Representatives be, and they are hereby, authorized and required, at the beginning of the final session of every Congress, to advertise for four weeks successively, in all the newspapers published in the city of Washington, for sealed proposals for supplying the Senate and House of Representatives respectively, of the next ensuing Congress, with the necessary printing for each; which advertisement shall describe the kind of printing and the quality of paper required, as near as may be, in the execution of the work; and said advertisement shall divide and classify the printing of the respective houses as follows: One of bills and resolutions; one of reports of committees; one of journals; one of executive documents; and one for every other description of printing; each class to be a separate job, and to be provided for by separate contract. The said advertisement shall contain a designation of the place in the said city of Washington where such sealed proposals shall be received, and the day and time at which said Secretary and Clerk will cease to receive any further proposals. And the Secretary and Clerk aforesaid shall provide suitable samples of the printing required, and of the paper on which the same is to be executed, to be kept, at the place so designated as aforesaid, at least twenty days successively before the time of receiving proposals shall expire, open to the inspection of all persons desiring to make proposals for the printing aforesaid, intelligence whereof shall be contained in said advertisement. Immediately on the expiration of the time for receiving said proposals, they shall be opened by the Secretary and Clerk aforesaid, in the presence of the Vice-President, or President of the Senate, and the Speaker of the House of Representatives, and of such persons making proposals as may wish to be present. And the Secretary of the Senate, under the supervision of the Vice-President, and the Clerk of the House, under the supervision of the Speaker, shall thereupon let each class of said printing to the lowest bidder, who shall furnish satisfactory evidence of his practical skill and his ability to do the work, and who shall offer good and sufficient security for the faithful execution of the jobs and contracts undertaken by him. And thereupon the Vice-President, or President of the Senate, and its Secretary, and the Speaker of the House and its Clerk, shall proceed to take bonds with good and sufficient security for the due and faithful performance of the work ; and the officers aforesaid shall immediately thereafter report to their respective houses all such lettings of printing, and the contracts relating to the same : *Provided*, That the said proposals shall remain sealed until the time appointed for examining the same.

" SEC. 2. That a committee, consisting of three members of the Senate and three members of the House of Representatives, shall be chosen by the respective houses, which shall constitute a Committee on Printing, which shall have power to adopt such measures as may be deemed necessary to remedy any neglect or delay on the part of the contractor to execute the work ordered by Congress, and to make a pro-rata reduction in the compensation allowed, or to refuse the work altogether should it be inferior to the standard ; and in all cases the contractor and his securities shall be responsible for any increased expenditure consequent upon the non-performance of the contract. The committee shall audit and pass upon all accounts for printing ; but no bill shall be acted upon for work that is not actually executed and delivered, and which they may require to be properly authenticated."

*　　*　　*　　*　　*　　*　　*　　*

Section 3 provides that motions for the printing of extra copies of all documents shall be referred to the Committee on Printing of the respective houses; and directs the payments for printing to be made from the contingent fund of each house.

Section 4 repeals conflicting laws.

This system, which proved the most expensive of any tried up to this time, and perhaps the most unsatisfactory—being a repetition of the abuses, only on a larger scale, sought to be corrected by the act of 1819—remained in operation until 1852. Under this law the first contractors were Cornelius Wendell and Chas. Van Benthuysen. The testimony taken before a committee of the House, and of the Senate also, when this matter was investigated in 1852, shows that this firm took the work at such low rates that sufficient profits were not given them, and the contractors, although they filled their contract, were greatly out of pocket at the end.

The next printer under the contract system was Father Ritchie. He performed the work up to the expiration of his contract; but at the next session of Congress claimed damages, for loss, which were accorded him in the sum of $50,000.

Mr. Boyd Hamilton became the next contractor. He executed the printing down to 1852, when he failed, and gave up the contract.

The printing for the first six years under this law cost the Government $3,462,655.12, or almost as much as the printing under the act of 1819 cost during the many years it was in force.

THE LAW OF 1852.

The next general law on the subject, and which involved a radical change in the system, prices, and mode of executing the printing, was passed on the 26th day of August, 1852. It embodies a great many features of the present law under which the office is operated, and, although quite lengthy, I deem it worthy of a place here, *in extenso*.

ACT OF AUGUST 26, 1852.

"*Be it enacted*, etc., That the joint resolution entitled "Joint resolution directing the manner of procuring the printing for each house of Congress," approved August 3, 1846, be, and the same is hereby, repealed.

"SEC. 2. That there shall be a Superintendent of the Public Printing, who shall hold his office for the term of two years, who shall receive for his services a salary of $2,500 per annum, and who shall give bond with two sureties to be approved by the Secretary of the Interior, in the penalty of $20,000, for the faithful discharge of his duties under this law. The said Superintendent shall be a practical printer, versed in the various branches of the arts of printing and book-binding, and he shall not be interested, directly or indirectly, in any contract for printing for Congress or for any department or bureau of the Government of the United States. The first Superintendent under this law shall hold his office until the commencement of the Thirty-third Congress, and the Superintendents thereafter appointed shall hold their offices for two years, commencing with the first day of the session of each Congress.

"SEC. 3. That it shall be the duty of said Superintendent to receive from the Secretary of the Senate and Clerk of the House of Representatives all matter ordered by Congress to be printed, and from the several chiefs of departments and heads of bureaus all matter ordered by them, respectively, to be printed at the public expense, and to keep a faithful account of the same, in the order in which the same shall be received, in a book or books to be by him kept for that purpose. He shall deliver said matter to the public printer or printers in the order in which it shall be received, unless otherwise ordered by the Joint

Committee on Printing. He shall inspect the work, when executed by the public printer or printers, and shall record in a book or books, to be by him kept for that purpose, the dates at which the returns of said work are made, and whether the same is executed in a neat and workmanlike manner, upon the paper furnished to the public printers by said Superintendent, and the amount allowed by said Superintendent for said printing. It shall be his duty to supervise the execution of the public printing, to inspect the work when executed, and to see that the same is done with neatness and dispatch; to report every failure or delinquency of duty on the part of the public printer, and from time to time to report the said delinquencies to the Joint Committee of Congress on Printing. He shall issue his certificate for the amount due to the public printer for such work as shall have been faithfully executed, which certificate shall be made payable to the public printer at the Treasury of the United States, and shall not be assignable or transferable by indorsement or delivery to any third party. Said certificate of the Superintendent shall be a sufficient voucher for the Comptroller to pass, and for the Treasurer, upon the order of the Second Comptroller, to pay the same.

"Sec. 4. That it shall be the duty of the said Superintendent of the Public Printing to advertise annually in one or more newspapers of general circulation in the cities of Boston, New York, Philadelphia, Baltimore, Washington, New Orleans, Louisville, and Cincinnati, for the space of sixty days prior to the first of December, for sealed proposals to furnish the Government of the United States all paper which may be necessary for the execution of the public printing, of quality and quantity to be specified in said advertisements, from year to year. He shall open such proposals as may be made, in the presence of the President of the Senate and Speaker of the House of Representatives, on the first Tuesday after the first Monday of December annually, provided a Speaker shall have been elected, or as soon thereafter as a Speaker shall be elected, and shall award the contract for furnishing all of said paper, or such class thereof as may be bid for, to the lowest bidder, whose sample, accompanying his bid, shall most nearly approximate to the quality of paper (size, weight, and texture all considered) advertised for by the said Superintendent. The sample offered, with the bid accepted, shall be preserved by the said Superintendent, and it shall be his duty to compare these with the paper furnished by the public contractor; and he shall not accept any paper from the contractor which does not conform to the sample preserved as aforesaid. It shall be the duty of the Superintendent of the Public Printing to deliver the paper for the printing of the United States, upon the requisitions of the public printer or printers, and to charge him or them therewith; and as the printing is returned and passed by the said Superintendent, he shall credit the public printer with the quantity used in the public service. It shall be the duty of said Superintendent to have the requisitions of the printer and the returns of paper by the printer balanced at least once in each year, and in default thereof to report the same to Congress for such proceedings as Congress may direct. In default of any contractor under this law to comply with his contract in furnishing the paper in proper time and of proper quality, the Superintendent is authorized to advertise for proposals, as hereinbefore provided, and award the contract to the lowest bidder; and for any increase of cost to the Government in procuring a proper supply of paper for the use of the Government, the contractor in default and his securities shall be charged with and held responsible for the same, and shall be prosecuted upon their bond, by the Superintendent, in the name of the United States, in the circuit court of the United States for the District of Columbia.

"SEC. 5. That the public printer shall be required to execute each job of printing intrusted to him within thirty days from the date of its delivery by the Superintendent, except bills, reports, and joint resolutions, which shall be returned as the Clerk of the House or Secretary of the Senate shall require, unless, for good reasons shown, the Superintendent of Printing shall extend the time. And should the printer detain any matter longer than thirty days, a deduction of five per centum shall be made by the Superintendent from the account of the printer for such job, and an additional deduction of five per centum for an additional detention of twenty days. If the public printer shall detain such matter for sixty days, the Superintendent shall withdraw it entirely, and shall employ another printer to execute the same with promptness, upon the terms provided by law, and in such case the public printer shall not be allowed therefor.

"SEC. 6. That the Superintendent of the Public Printing shall not be directly or indirectly interested in the business of the public printing, or in any material to be used by the public printer, or in any contract for furnishing paper to Congress or to any department or bureau of the Government of the United States. For any violation of this provision, the Superintendent of the Public Printing shall forfeit his office, and may be indicted before the district courts for the District of Columbia, and if found guilty, shall be imprisoned in the penitentiary of the District of Columbia for any term not less than one or more than five years, and, in addition thereto, may be fined in any sum from one thousand to ten thousand dollars.

"SEC. 7. That when any document shall be ordered to be printed by both houses of Congress, the entire printing of such document shall be done by the printer of that house which first ordered the same. And whenever the same person or the same firm shall be printers for both houses of Congress, and both houses shall order the same document to be printed within three weeks of the same time, composition shall be charged but once for said document; and no sum shall be paid to said printer for altering the headings from the form in which he printed them first to the form or forms in which such document shall afterwards be printed.

"Sec. 8. That there shall be elected a public printer for each house of Congress, to do the public printing for the Congress for which he or they may be chosen, and such printing for the executive departments and bureaus of the Government of the United States as may be delivered to him or them to be printed by the Superintendent of the Public Printing.

"The following rates of compensation shall be paid from time to time for such printing as may be ordered by Congress:

"First. For bills and joint resolutions: For composition per page, 50 cents; for press-work, folding and stitching, for 580 copies, 32½ cents per page; and at the same rate per page for any greater number, not exceeding 1,000 copies.

"Second. For reports of committees and the journals of both houses, with indexes, and the executive documents of each house, embracing messages from the President, reports from the executive departments, bureaus and offices, and documents and statements communicated therewith, with indexes; resolutions and other documents from State legislatures; memorials, petitions, treaties, and confidential documents for the Senate; for compensation per page, octavo: for small pica plain, $1; for small pica rule, $1.50; for brevier plain, $1.50; for brevier rule, $2; for nonpareil rule, $3.75. For the composition of tables larger than octavo size, per 1000 ems, 70 cents; but the page of octavo size shall contain not less than 1600 ems when printed in small pica; and the body of all plain matter shall be so printed, except extracts, yeas and nays, and addenda, which shall be printed in brevier type. All rule and figure work shall be printed in royal octavo form, with small pica, each page containing not less than 1600 ems, if the matter to be printed can be brought into pages of that size with that kind of type, so as to be read with facility and convenience. If it cannot, it shall be printed with brevier type, each page containing not less than 2800 ems; and if it cannot be brought into a royal octavo page with brevier type, so as to be understood with facility, it shall be printed with nonpareil type, each page containing not less than 4200 ems; and when it cannot be brought into a royal octavo page with nonpareil type, so as to be read with facility, it shall be printed with brevier type in a broadside, showing the whole table at one view, and be so filled that it can be bound in a royal octavo volume. When matter is leaded, the composition shall be counted as if the matter were printed solid, and not leaded. For press-work folding and stitching of royal octavo size: for 1,250 copies, 32½ cents per page, and at the same rate for any greater number not exceeding 1,500 copies. For press-work, folding and stitching of each table larger than royal octavo size, for 1,250 copies, $1.25 per page, and at the same rate for any number not exceeding 1,500 copies. The following deductions on account of folding and stitching copies reserved for binding shall be made : For royal octavo size, per page, for each 100 copies, ¼ of a cent; for each table larger than octavo, ¼ of a cent; and the following additional charges shall be allowed for trimming, folding, and stitching, and inserting each map, chart, diagram, or plate in the copies not reserved for binding: for each 100 copies, 10 cents. There shall be allowed for press-work on treaties, reports, and other documents, when ordered to be printed in confidence for the use of the Senate, at the following rates: For the press-work, folding and stitching of 65 copies, 6 cents per page, when of the royal octavo size, and $1 per page for 65 copies, when the matter cannot be contained in the royal octavo page in any type hereinbefore specified ; and allowance shall be made at the same rates for any greater number of copies than 65, and not exceeding 100.

"Third. For tabular statements of the orders of the day, lists of yeas and nays, circular letters, and miscellaneous printing ordered by Congress, not hereinbefore specified: For composition for plain work, per 1000 ems, 50 cents; for rule and figure work, 50 cents per 1000 ems; for press-work, folding and stitching, 100 copies, per page, for royal octavo, or smaller size, 10 cents; for quarto post, 20 cents; for foolscap and any larger size, 20 cents. But the following deductions shall be made from the press-work, folding and stitching additional numbers to the numbers usually ordered by Congress of matter included in the foregoing specifications, to wit: When the number ordered exceeds 5,000 and does not exceed 10,000, 2 per centum; when the number exceeds 10,000 and does not exceed 20,000, 5 per centum; when the number exceeds 20,000, 40 per centum.

"The press-work, folding and stitching, of all printing not herein provided for, shall be done by the ream; the rates shall be $2 per ream when printed on one side, and $4 per ream when printed on both sides; when any amount less than one ream is ordered, it shall be counted and settled for as one ream.

"Sec. 9. That the regular number of documents ordered by Congress shall be printed in octavo form, on paper weighing not less than 56 pounds for each 480 sheets, and measuring 24 by 38 inches, and the extra numbers shall be printed on paper weighing not less than 45 pounds for every 480 sheets, and measuring 24 by 38 inches. The paper for any other species of printing ordered by Congress, may be of such size and quality as the Superintendent of the Public Printing may deem suitable and proper.

"SEC. 10. That the public printer or printers may be required by the Superintendent to work at night as well as through the day upon the public printing, during the session of Congress, when the exigencies of the public service require it.

"SEC. 11. That the same prices shall be paid for printing for the executive departments that are paid for printing for Congress, except for printing post-bills, which shall be printed on paper not less than 16 by 26 inches, and for printing on parchment. There shall be paid for printing the post-bills at the rate of $1 per 1,000 sheets, and at the rate of $10 per 1,000 for printing parchments; but nothing shall be allowed for altering post-bills when the alteration consists in the mere change of a postmaster's name: and nothing herein contained shall prevent the heads of executive departments from employing printers out of the city of Washington, to execute such printing for any of said departments as may be required for use out of Washington, when the same can be executed elsewhere as cheap as at the rates herein specified, increased by the cost of transporting the printed matter to the State or States where such matter may be required for use in the public service.'

Section 12 provided for the appointment of a Joint Committee on Printing, and section 13 for the repeal of conflicting laws, etc.

Under this law the President appointed John T. Towers, who was at that time a prominent citizen of the District of Columbia, and afterwards Mayor of the city of Washington, Superintendent.

Mr. Towers was a practical printer, having finished his trade in the office of Duff Green when he was printer to the Senate in 1830. He was afterwards foreman in the office of Thomas Allen, when the latter gentleman was printer to the Senate. Mr. T. subsequently established a book and job printing office, which he successfully conducted until his appointment as Superintendent of Public Printing, which office he held until December, 1853, when his term expired by limitation of law. He died in 1857.

A. G. Seaman succeeded Mr. Towers as Superintendent in 1853, and served for two terms—four years—when he was in turn succeeded by George W. Bowman, of Pennsylvania. John Heart became Superintendent in 1859, and remained in office until March 23, 1861.

General Robert Armstrong was elected printer to the House of Representatives on the 27th of August, 1852, and on the following day was also elected printer to the Senate. Among the candidates for election to the office secured by General Armstrong appear the historic names of Horace Greeley, W. P. Brownlow, and H. J. Raymond. General Armstrong was re-elected printer to the House, December 7, 1853; and on the 12th Beverly Tucker, of Virginia, was elected printer to the Senate. General Armstrong died while in office, and was succeeded by A. O. P. Nicholson, of Tennessee.

February 13, 1856, after numerous ballots were taken, Cornelius Wendell, the founder of the Government Printing Office, was elected printer to the Senate.

Among the candidates appear the names of John D. Defrees, the present Public Printer, Francis P. Blair, jr., and Owen Follett, of Columbus, Ohio, who, for many years, was well known in the West by reason of his connection with the publishing firm of Follett, Foster & Co., of Columbus.

December 9, 1857, General J. B. Steadman was elected printer to the House; and December 17, William A. Harris was elected printer to the Senate.

The most protracted struggle in the election of printer occurred during the First Session of the Thirty-sixth Congress. The first ballot was taken on February 13, 1860, and balloting was continued, with numerous short postponements, up to the 2d of March, when Tom Ford, of Ohio, was declared elected. Among the candidates was Mr. Defrees, who, up to the fourteenth ballot, was the leading candidate. Mr. Defrees' name was withdrawn, however, at his request, and on the fifth ballot thereafter Mr. Ford was chosen.

In the Senate, A. O. P. Nicholson was again elected printer, January 31, 1856, and served until the election of General Bowman, January 17, 1860.

Although the act of 1852 was a decided improvement over that of 1846, the printing under it proved very expensive; but the main difficulty was the want of an office with proper facilities for executing the printing promptly and uniformly. The demands of the Government had increased to such an extent that, up to 1856, no single printing office in Washington was capable of handling all the printing required; and the result was that a variety of styles, etc., prevailed in the printed documents, which gave general dissatisfaction, and produced much inconvenience. The erection by Mr. Wendell of the large establishment on H and North Capitol streets, which afterwards became the Government Printing Office, somewhat relieved these troubles; but, as he had to run his chances in getting the work, no certain remedy followed his enterprise.

In 1861, the Government became the owner of what is now known as the Government Printing Office building, under the act of June 23,

1860. The contract for its purchase was consummated on the 1st day of December, 1860, and approved by the Joint Committee on Printing of the two houses of Congress on the 12th of the same month. The law of June 23, 1860, is now embodied, in an abbreviated form, in sections 3756 to 3828 of the Revised Statutes, and will be found almost in its entirety in the appendix to this volume.

Mr. John Heart, of Pennsylvania, served out his term of office under the old law, up to March, 1861, when, on the accession of Mr. Lincoln to the Presidency, John D. Defrees, of Indiana, was appointed the *first* Superintendent of Public Printing, after the purchase of the building and machinery, etc., and assumed charge of the establishment on the 23d of March, 1861.

Upon Mr. Defrees devolved the task of reorganizing the mode of executing the public printing, and devising the many checks and safeguards for its prompt and economical execution. The present complete system of keeping the accounts, and rendering the proper vouchers for work performed, was inaugurated during his first term as Superintendent; and from an office with 300 employés, Mr. Defrees has seen it increase until it now gives work, in its busiest season, to more than six times that number.

Mr. Defrees remained Superintendent until 1866, when he was removed by Andrew Johnson, and Cornelius Wendell appointed. Mr. Wendell, however, did not have long to serve, as Congress at its next session changed the mode of appointment and name of the office, and Mr. Defrees was elected by the Senate, and restored to his old position under the title of Congressional Printer.

A faithful biographical sketch of the present Superintendent of Government Printing would have to include a reference to all the important political events of the past forty or fifty years, in most of which he has played no inconspicuous part. In a work of this character such a sketch, although it would doubtless prove both interesting and instructive, is not expected—indeed, might not be deemed appropriate by many—and the author will therefore confine himself to a statement of facts, with as little elaboration as possible.

JOHN DOUGHERTY DEFREES was born at Sparta, Tennessee, on the 8th day of November, 1810. His father, dissatisfied with a State which permitted and fostered slavery, determined to make his home in Ohio, to which State he removed in 1818, settling in Piqua.

At the age of fourteen young Defrees was apprenticed to learn the printing business, which at that time meant press-work as well as typesetting. After serving three years the office failed, and he started out on a tramp as a journeyman printer. During this tour he worked at Xenia and Cincinnati, Ohio, and on the *Louisville Journal.* The latter paper was edited and published by George D. Prentice, between whom and young Defrees an acquaintance was made which soon grew into a warm friendship, and which continued until the death of this eminent journalist and poet many years afterwards.

Returning to Ohio after a brief absence, we next find the subject of this sketch writing in the clerk's office at Lebanon. He was now in his eighteenth year. The business of the office was not sufficient to employ all his time, and being both industrious and ambitious, he determined to devote his leisure moments to reading law. This he at once commenced, under the guidance and instruction of Messrs. Collet & Corwin, the Mr. Corwin of the firm being the distinguished Thomas Corwin, of that State. From the day he entered the office of these gentlemen he seems to have gained the esteem and confidence especially of the junior member of the firm—a gentleman who was so shortly to gain the name of the most brilliant and gifted orator of his generation. In after years, when the name of the "Wagon Boy" of Ohio was as familiar as a household word, and he was being courted by the great of the land, and revered and almost worshiped by the humbler class of citizens, he seems never to have forgotten his former pupil, but kept up his intimate relations of friendship by visits and an uninterrupted correspondence, which ceased only with the close of his honored life.

In 1831, in company with his brother, Joseph H., Mr. Defrees left Ohio for Indiana, and eventually located at South Bend, St. Joseph County. This county was then occupied by the Pottawatomie Indians. Here he and his brother established a newspaper, which they continued to manage until the year 1833. In this year he was licensed by the Supreme Court of Indiana to practice law, and, selling out his interest in the newspaper, he commenced the practice of his profession at South Bend. He continued in the practice of law for some years, and met with gratifying success. During his residence here he several times represented St. Joseph County in the lower branch of the Legislature, and afterwards the counties of St. Joseph, Marshall, and Fulton in the State Senate.

While a member of the State Senate, in 1845, he purchased the office of the *Indiana State Journal*, a paper published at Indianapolis, and shortly thereafter removed to that city. As the editor of this journal he soon became known throughout his own and in neighboring States as one of the most fearless, caustic, and brilliant political writers in the West. From the time he was able to form opinions of his own he espoused the principles of the Whig party, and until the time of the disintegration of that party he was one of its ablest supporters and most trusted leaders. He was for many years Chairman

Public Printer.

of the Whig State Central Committee of Indiana, and was a Delegate to the Whig and National Republican Conventions of 1848, 1852, and 1856. As a party manager he was regarded as one of the ablest the State ever produced. His acquaintance in the State was perhaps larger than that of any other person resident there prior to 1861. There was not a county, a township, or even a school district in which he had not a number of acquaintances, and with whose feelings, interests, and desires he was not familiar. This extensive acquaintance gave him a great advantage in the many hotly-contested battles which periodically occurred between the Whig and Democratic, and afterwards between the Republican and Democratic parties of his adopted State.

During the Presidential contest of 1848, Mr. Defrees became known to most of the leaders of the Whig party throughout the country. Many years previous he had made the acquaintance of Mr. Clay, to whose cause he had been and still was most devotedly attached, and whose confidence and esteem he had gained and continued to retain up to the time of the death of that great statesman.

Some weeks after the close of the contest which resulted in the election of General Zachary Taylor, he was invited by Mr. Crittenden, then Governor of Kentucky, to visit him at his home for the purpose of meeting the President-elect, who was to stop over with him for a day or two on his way to Washington. It was at this meeting that General Taylor tendered him an important mission abroad, which he declined with thanks; remarking as he did so that there was no position within the gift of the President-elect of sufficient importance to induce him to leave the country even for a brief period.

Henry Ward Beecher, now one of the most distinguished and eloquent preachers of the age, was a resident of Indianapolis when Mr. Defrees took charge of the *Journal.* He soon became an occasional contributor to the paper, and ultimately a regular writer on subjects relating to the farm and garden. As editor of the agricultural department of the *Journal,* he is unquestionably entitled to the honor of being regarded as the pioneer of the agricultural literature of the West. This gentleman, who has since attained such distinction as a divine, no doubt did his first newspaper writing for this journal.

Mr. Wendell, who was Superintendent under President Johnson, was born at Cambridge, near Albany, N. Y., in 1813, and died at Northampton, Mass., October 9, 1870. He was educated in a printing office, where, with remarkable ability and industry, he soon acquired a knowledge of the printer's art. His first connection with the printing for the Government was when he, with Mr. Van Benthuysen, obtained a contract under the Garrett Davis resolution of 1846. His subsequent career in connection with the Government printing is familiar to many of the older printers of the present day. Although connected with that branch of the Government service for many years, as contractor, subcontractor, and Superintendent of Printing, and during some of the most troublesome periods of its history, his character for probity was never called in dispute. His success in executing the printing was in a great degree attributed to the excellent relations which always existed between him and his employés.

Mr. Almon M. Clapp, late editor and manager of the *National Republican* newspaper of Washington City, superseded Mr. Defrees April 15, 1869, having been elected to the office by the Senate. Mr. Clapp is now one of the recognized prominent citizens of Washington. He was born at Killingly, Conn., September 14, 1811, and removed with his father in 1818 to Western New York, then a comparative wilderness. His father purchased and opened a farm, and young Clapp remained with him until his fifteenth year, when he entered a small printing office in the village of Geneseo as an apprentice. In 1828 he went to the then village of Buffalo, where he completed his education as a printer in the office of Day, Follet & Haskins. He afterwards, attended a classical school for a few months. In 1833 he ventured into the mercantile business, which proved disastrous financially ; and in 1835, with the aid of friends, he established a small weekly newspaper, the *Aurora Standard*, which he published and edited successfully for three years.

In the winter of 1837–'38, Mr. Clapp, who held a commission as captain in the New York State Militia, was ordered with his company to Buffalo, in the emergency of a threatened war with Canada. He was in the service three months, when the difficulty was adjusted, and he was relieved, but remained in the city, and in July of that year became connected with the proprietorship of the *Commercial Advertiser*. In 1839 he disposed of his interest in that paper, and embarked in the book and job printing business, and in 1846 established the Buffalo *Express*.

Mr. Clapp has always been an active politician, first as a Whig and then as a Republican. Among the public offices which he has held were Clerk of the Board of Supervisors of Erie County in 1839, Loan Commissioner of the United States Deposit Fund for ten years, member of the Legislative Assembly in 1853, to which office he declined a re-election, and Postmaster at Buffalo from 1861 to 1866, when he was removed by President Johnson. In 1857 he was a candidate for Secretary of State on the Republican ticket, and shared his party's defeat, and was also defeated as the Republican candidate for Congress in 1866.

Soon after his retirement from the office of Public Printer, he became managing editor of the *National Republican,* at Washington, which position he occupied until January, 1881. He still resides in Washington, holding no public position, but much respected by the entire community.

An act approved July 31, 1876, provided "that so much of all laws or parts of laws as provide for the election or appointment of Public Printer be, and the same are hereby, repealed, to take effect from and after the passage of this act; and the President of the United States shall appoint, by and with the advice and consent of the Senate, a suitable person, who must be a practical printer, and versed in the art of book-binding, to take charge of and manage the Government Printing Office, from and after the date aforesaid; he shall be called Public Printer," etc.

Prior to the passage of this act, the officer in charge of the Government Printing Office, as previously stated, was called "Congressional Printer"; but in 1874 a proviso was attached to an appropriation bill which repealed, upon the first vacancy that should occur, the law relating to the election of Congressional Printer, and provided that thereafter the officer should be called Public Printer. Up to July 31, 1876, no vacancy having occurred, the act of that date was passed, providing for the change in the title of the officer.

Under this law Mr. Clapp was appointed Public Printer by President Grant, and remained in office until the present incumbent, Mr. Defrees, was commissioned by President Hayes, on June 1, 1877.

CHAPTER II.

THE GOVERNMENT PRINTING OFFICE.

SUPERINTENDENTS OF PUBLIC PRINTING FROM 1852 to 1881.

NAME.	FROM—	TO—
John T. Towers	Sept. 1, 1852	Dec. 6, 1853
A. G. Seaman	Dec. 7, 1853	Dec. —, 1857
Geo. W. Bowman	Dec. —, 1857	May 12, 1859
John Heart	May 13, 1859	Mar. 4, 1861
John D. Defrees	Mar. 23, 1861	Aug. 31, 1866
Cornelius Wendell	Sept. 1, 1866	Feb. 28, 1867
John D. Defrees	Mar. 1, 1867	April 14, 1869
A. M. Clapp	April 15, 1869	May 30, 1877
John D. Defrees	June 1, 1877	....

CHIEF CLERKS IN THE OFFICE OF SUPERINTENDENT OF PUBLIC PRINTING FROM 1852 TO 1881.

NAME.	FROM—	TO—
William Towers	Sept. 1, 1852	Aug. 31, 1868
Madison Davis	Sept. 1, 1868	April 15, 1869
H. H. Clapp	April 16, 1869	May 31, 1877
Madison Davis	June 1, 1877	June 30, 1877
A. F. Childs	July 1, 1877	....

FOREMEN AND ASSISTANT FOREMEN OF PRINTING FROM 1861 to 1881.

Foremen of Printing.

James English	from 1861 to 1865.
John H. Cunningham	" 1865 to 1867.
Chas. E. Lathrop	" 1867 to 1869.
Harrison G. Otis	" 1869 to 1870.
N. F. Ethell	" 1870 to 1871
Henry T. Brian	" 1871 to 1877.
A. H. S. Davis	" 1877 to ——

(37)

Assistant Foremen of Printing.

John H. Cunningham	from	1861 to 1865.
Richard W. Claxton	"	1865 to 1866.
Madison Davis	"	1866 to 1867.
E. J. Burnham	"	1866 to 1867.
M. R. Woodward	"	1867 to 1869.
D. W. Flynn	"	1869 to 1870.
H. T. Brian	"	1870 to 1871.
R. W. Kerr	"	1871 to 1873.
J. M. A. Spottswood	"	1873 to ——.

FOREMEN AND ASSISTANT FOREMEN OF BINDING FROM 1861 TO 1881.

Foremen of Binding.

George P. Goff	from	1861 to 1866.
John Tretler	"	1866 to 1867.
George P. Goff	"	1867 to 1869.
J. H. Roberts	"	1869 to ——.

Assistant Foremen of Binding.

J. H. Roberts	from	1861 to 1866.
A. Fitzsimmons	"	1866 to 1867.
J. H. Roberts	"	1867 to 1869.
Jas. Mattingly	"	1869 to 1871.
Jas. W. White	"	1871 to ——.

PRESENT ORGANIZATION OF THE OFFICE.

Office of Public Printer.

	Date of appointment.
JOHN D. DEFREES, Public Printer	June 1, 1877.
Albert F. Childs, Chief Clerk	July 1, 1877.
John Larcombe, Disbursing Clerk	April 1, 1861.
H. H. Twombly, Executive Clerk	July 1, 1877.
J. R. Offley, Entry Clerk	July 1, 1877.
W. H. Collins, Estimate Clerk	July 1, 1878.
Chas. B. Hough, Clerk	July 1, 1877.
A. H. Post, Record Clerk	July 1, 1878.
David Nicholson, Telegraph Operator	Feb. 1, 1874.

Foreman of Printing and Assistants.

A. H. S. DAVIS, Foreman of Printing	June 1, 1877.
J. M. A. Spottswood, Assistant Foreman of Printing	Mar. 1, 1873.
R. W. Kerr, Assistant	July 1, 1877.
H. Groshon, Assistant in charge of Job Room	Dec. 8, 1880.
O. H. Reed, Assistant in charge of Press Room	June 1, 1877.
A. J. Donaldson, Assistant	July 1, 1877.
J. D. Eskew, Assistant in charge of Specification Room	June 1, 1877.
E. W. Oyster, Assistant in charge of Record Room	July 1, 1877.
D. W. Beach, Assistant	July 1, 1877.

P. L. Rodier, Assistant in charge of Branch Office..........May 17, 1869.
T. B. Penicks, Superintendent in charge of Folding Room....Mar. 1, 1867.
Geo. Fordham, Assistant...April 1, 1871.
Alex. Elliott, jr., Superintendent in charge of Stereotype Dep't..Sept. 1, 1869.

Foreman of Binding and Assistants.

J. H. ROBERTS, Foreman of Binding......................April 15, 1869.
Jas. W. White, Assistant Foreman of Binding ....May 1, 1871.
A. D. Stidham, Assistant...................................Aug. 1, 1877.

OFFICE OF THE PUBLIC PRINTER.

The office of Superintendent of Public Printing was created by the act of August 26, 1852, which provided that he should be appointed by the President, that the term of office should be two years, the compensation $2,500 per annum, and the bond for the faithful performance of the duties $20,000. The duties of the Superintendent under this law, however, were only those of an auditor, and did not embrace the many and onerous labors devolving upon that officer upon the passage of the law creating the Government Printing Office.

The joint resolution of December 18, 1862, increased the bond of the Superintendent to $40,000, and it was again increased, by the joint resolution of January 15, 1866, to $80,000. The salary of the Superintendent was also raised, during the war, to $4,000.

On the 22d of February, 1867, an act was approved which provided for the election of "some competent person, who shall be a practical printer, to take charge of and manage the Government Printing Office," and providing also "that the person so selected shall be deemed an officer of the Senate, and shall be designated Congressional Printer." This new official was to be governed in the discharge of his duties by the laws then in force in relation to the Superintendent of Public Printing, and the latter office was abolished.

The office of "Public Printer" was created by the act of June 20, 1874, which says: "That so much of the act entitled 'An act providing for the election of a Congressional Printer, * * * as provides for the election of such officer by the Senate * * * shall cease and determine and become of no effect from and after the date of the first vacancy occurring in said office; that the title of said officer shall hereafter be Public Printer, * * * and said office shall be filled by appointment of the President, by and with the advice and consent of the Senate."

Up to July, 1876, no vacancy having occurred, an act was passed on the last day of that month repealing all laws concerning the election or appointment of Public Printer, and providing that the President should appoint, upon the passage of the act, with the advice and consent of the Senate, a "suitable person, who must be a practical printer," etc., to take charge of and manage the Government Printing Office; and providing that he should be called "Public Printer." By the same act the bond of the Public Printer was increased to $100,000.

BRIEF SYNOPSIS OF THE LAWS RELATING TO THE DUTIES OF THE PUBLIC PRINTER.

The Public Printer must be a practical printer, versed in the art of book-binding, and has charge of the property belonging to, and the management of, the Government Printing Office. He receives a salary of $3,600 per annum, and gives bond in the sum of $100,000. He purchases all the materials and machinery necessary for the office; takes charge of all matter to be printed, engraved, lithographed, or bound; keeps an accurate account thereof, in the order in which it is received; and must see that the work is promptly executed, and deliver, to the officer authorized to receive them, all the sheets, or volumes, blanks, etc., which are printed, bound, etc., for the Government.

He is required to appoint a foreman of printing and a foreman of binding, who must be practically and thoroughly acquainted with their respective trades. He is also authorized to appoint four clerks at $1,800 per annum, one at $1,400, and one at $1,200 to keep the accounts of the Congressional Record; and by the act of June 20, 1878, he is also authorized to employ three additional clerks of class three, to make estimates, etc.; and by the act of June 19, 1878, a chief clerk is provided for at an annual salary of $2,000 in lieu of one of the fourth-class clerks.

He may employ, at such rates of wages as he may deem for the interest of the Government and just to the persons employed, such proof-readers, compositors,* pressmen, binders,* laborers, and other hands as may be necessary for the execution of the orders for public printing and binding authorized by law.

The Public Printer, the Foreman of Printing, and the Foreman of Binding, are prohibited from having any interest, direct or indirect, in the publication of any newspaper or periodical, or in any printing, binding, engraving, or lithographing, or in any contract for furnishing supplies of any kind. The Public Printer is required to submit to the Joint Committee on Printing, at the beginning of each session of Congress, estimates of the quantity of paper of all descriptions required for the public printing for the ensuing year; and shall, under

---

* By a late act, the price paid "printers" and "book-binders" is limited to forty cents per hour or fifty cents per thousaud ems for composition.

their direction, advertise for proposals for furnishing the same, as specified in schedules to be furnished applicants. No contract for supplying paper is valid unless approved by proper authority. He may be authorized to make purchases of paper in open market whenever the immediate wants of the office require it.

Plate-work or maps, diagrams, etc., when the cost does not exceed $250, may be procured by the Public Printer in open market; but when exceeding that amount, the contract for furnishing them shall be awarded the lowest bidder. The Joint Committee on Printing, however, can authorize him to make immediate contracts for lithographing or engraving, whenever the exigencies of the service do not justify advertisement for proposals.

No printing or binding not provided for by law can be executed at the Government Printing Office; but Senators and Representatives may, upon the payment of the actual cost thereof, have bound such books, maps, charts, or documents as they may designate; and also may have extracts from the *Congressional Record* printed, upon paying for the same.

The form and style in which the printing of binding ordered by any of the Departments shall be executed, the material and size of type to be used, shall be determined by the Public Printer, having proper regard to economy, workmanship, and the purposes for which the work is needed.

By a late law, passed June 20, 1878, the Public Printer is required to do all binding, except when the same is authorized by law or ordered by Congress, in plain sheep or cloth. Record and account books, and the binding for the Library of Congress, the Library of the Patent Office, and the Library of the State Department, are excepted from this restriction.

The Public Printer is required to deliver to the proper officers of Congress the reports of the Executive Departments and the accompanying documents at the annual meeting of Congress in December, and the other annual documents as soon thereafter as practicable.

He delivers to the Secretary of the Interior all books and documents authorized by law, except such as are printed for the particular use of Congress, or of the President, or of any of the Departments.

He receives advances from the Secretary of the Treasury, not exceeding two-thirds the penalty of his bond, of such sums of money as may be necessary to pay for work and material; and he settles the accounts of his receipts and disbursements in the manner required of other disbursing officers. All moneys received from the sale of extra documents, of paper shavings, and imperfections, are deposited in the Treasury, to the credit of the appropriations for public printing, binding, etc., and the amount so deposited is subject to his requisition in the manner prescribed by law.

CHIEF CLERK'S OFFICE—DUTIES, ETC.

The present working force of this office consists of the Chief Clerk, financial clerk, executive clerk, entry clerk, estimate clerk, clerk in charge of the Record, telegraph operator, and telephone operator. It is the duty of the Chief Clerk to make contracts for lithographing, mapping and engraving, make orders for paper, take charge of all orders for extra documents, besides the general executive work of the office. The financial clerk receives from the different foremen and assistants in charge of the several rooms a statement of the time each person has been employed during the preceding month, and makes up monthly pay-rolls for the amounts earned, and disburses the money to the persons so employed. In addition to this he pays all the accounts of the office of whatsoever character, from the smallest item to the largest amounts for paper, material, etc. All of the large sums appropriated, with the exception of the amounts paid for paper, which are sent direct from the Treasury Department on certification from the Public Printer that the amounts are correct, pass through his hands. The executive clerk takes charge of the requisitions for work from the Executive Departments, makes jackets for the same, noting thereon the number of copies to be printed, amount, size, and weight of paper required, and any instructions to be observed by the many different persons through whose hands it passes before its completion. The estimate clerk makes up from data furnished by the persons working on the various jobs, who note thereon as the jackets pass through their hands, the cost, as near as it can be ascertained, of each and every job. It is the duty of the entry clerk to keep, in books kept for that purpose, the estimated cost of these several jobs, and keep an account with the Executive Departments, to see that they do not exceed the amount allowed them by Congress. In addition to this, he examines the paper as it is received from the contractor, to see that it conforms in all respects to the stipulations contained in the contract.

Connecting the Government Printing Office with the Capitol, Executive Mansion, and different Executive Departments, are three telegraph lines, built and owned by the Government. In addition to this the Atlantic and Pacific and American Union Telegraph Companies have lines running in for the accommodation of the employés. Besides the telegraph, the office is connected with all the Executive Departments, and many commercial houses and private dwellings, by five telephone lines, and these will soon be found inadequate for the requirements of this extensive establishment.

MACHINE AND CARPENTER SHOP.

The Machine and Carpenter Shop is located in the south end, on the ground floor of the addition built in 1879, and its dimensions are 110 feet long by 18 feet wide. There are employed here 1 chief engineer, Mr. M. T. Lincoln, who has been in the service of the office ever since its erection, 1 assistant engineer, 5 machinists, 5 carpenters, 1 plumber, and 1 painter. These employés are engaged the year round in the manufacture of new and the repair of old machinery, desks, cases, shelving, etc., and the care and preservation of the many delicate machines in use in the office. There are 1 ten-horse power engine, 3 engine lathes, 1 hand lathe, 1 planing machine, 1 shaping machine, and 2 drill presses, in constant use in the shop.

STEREOTYPE VAULT.

Only a small proportion of the many thousands of stereotype plates annually cast in the Foundry attached to the Government Printing Office are for preservation. The Agricultural Report, the Abridgment of the Annual Reports of the Executive Departments, and a great majority of all other works on which are printed 15,000 or more copies, are stereotyped as a matter of economy and convenience, and, after the edition is printed, the plates are sent to the Foundry and remelted for the production of other plates. Works of a scientific character, of instruction, and matters of current interest, on which there is a *probability* of additional copies being ordered in the future, are stereotyped, and the plates carefully preserved.

When the office was purchased, of course there were no plates whatever transferred with the property. The large number of plates now in the Stereotype Vault, with the thousands of cuts and diagrams of all conceivable designs and figures, is the result principally of the accumulations of a single decade, although, for want of proper storage facilities, for many years the effort was mainly to reduce the production and the number for preservation to the lowest possible limit. Within the past few years the room devoted to this purpose has been greatly enlarged, and the present capacity of the vault, only a small portion of which, however, is fire-proof, is sufficient to accommodate something more than 220,000 quarto and octavo plates, and 12,000 or 15,000 more could be packed in boxes and stored away in the passages.

There are now stored in the vault 51,176 quarto plates, and 53,760 octavo and the smaller sizes, in addition to which there are about 43,000 plates of the *Congressional Record* alone. These do not include the metal and composition plates of the *Congressional Globe*, recently purchased by the Government.

The value of the metal in these plates—averaging the different sizes—is probably about 25 cents each, or a total of nearly $37,000.

WAREHOUSE FOR PRINTING–PAPERS, ETC.

The warehouse for printing-papers, and all cap, imperial, and other papers used in the manufacture of books, blanks, and blank books, is in the new 1879 wing, on the ground floor, and is as nearly fire-proof as it is possible to make such a compartment. It opens into the Press Room on the north side, and the many tons of paper passing through it in the course of a year are transported to the wetting-room and other parts of the Press Room where it is required, on trucks. It is difficult to give the uninitiated reader an idea of the vast quantities of paper used in such an establishment as the Government Printing Office. A ream of printing-paper, 24 by 38 inches, if spread out in single width, would cover a space 24 inches wide and something over 1,583 feet in length. The daily issues to the Press Room, however, will probably exceed, in the busy season, 250 reams; but if we call it 200 reams daily, it will amount to 62,600 in a year; and if this were spread out in single sheets, it would cover a space 2 feet wide by 99,095,800 feet, or $187\frac{2}{3}$ miles, in length.

But this is only *one* kind of paper. The thousands of reams of paper used for covers, blanks, and blank books, are not included, but, if added to the above, would undoubtedly treble the amount. Papers are received in rolls (for the Bullock Press), in boxes and bundles, by rail and New York and Philadelphia steamers. In a year the quantities arriving would be about as follows: Bank-note and parchment and bond papers, 432,226 sheets; cardboard, postal cards, etc., 655,-420 sheets; 45- and 53-pound book-paper, 53,000 reams; other book-papers, 25.000 reams; besides tons of other papers not enumerated.

The employés consist of one superintendent and assistants. A daily report of the amount and kind, or quality, of every sheet of paper remaining on hand at the close of business, as well as that issued the day previous, is rendered to the chief clerk, so that at all times the business office of the Public Printer has at its command all necessary information concerning the supplies of each kind of paper on hand. All these papers, except the printing-papers, are issued upon jackets, and can only be obtained from the warehouse upon these, or written orders from the requisition clerks in the main office.

BINDERS' WAREHOUSE.

The warehouse for binders' materials is located in the south wing, and is in charge of a clerk, who superintends the receiving and issuing of all material for use in the Bindery. With the exception of binders' boards, for which, on account of their great weight, a warehouse is provided on the ground floor, all binders' materials are stored here. The stock in this room consists of ledger papers, leathers and muslins of various kinds, twines, surplus tools, etc.

THE STABLES, ETC.

The new addition to the building (authorized by the law of March, 1881) is intended to occupy, in part, the ground covered for many years by the stables and Roller House. A new and much more convenient and commodious stable for the accommodation of the live stock belonging to the Government Printing Office is now in course of erection on the rear of a lot adjoining the west end of the building, in which will be provided room for horses, and the wagons, harness, etc.

There are used, in the delivery of printed matter, etc., to Congress and the Departments, from 4 to 6 wagons, and from 8 to 12 horses.

WATCHMEN.

For the protection and preservation of the property and building against fire, theft, etc., a regular corps of watchmen are employed. Every part of the main building, the stables and other outhouses, and the yard, is visited every hour during the night. Those on duty at night number six, and their names are: L. A. Cassard, Captain; William E. Miller, R. W. Simmons, John Tolbert, George Oyster, and Charles D. Bradley. Those on duty during the day-time are: W. H. Murphy, Captain; James A. Patterson and George Gordon.

MINOR ITEMS.

In 1861, and for several years previous, the wages ot printers, pressmen, book-binders, etc., in Washington, were $14 per week; in February, 1863, the compensation was increased to $16; in December, 1863, to $18; in June, 1864, to $21; and in November, 1864, to $24. The wages of the workmen remained at the latter figure until the passage of the act of February 16, 1877, which reduced them to 40 cents per hour for skilled workmen, the rate now paid.

In 1861, before all the binding was done at the main office, a fire destroyed the building on Louisiana Avenue, between Ninth and Tenth streets, occupied by Mr. John Pettibone, the contractor, in which the Government sustained a loss of some $15,000 or $20,000 in printed matter, which had been sent from the main office to the contractor for binding. The works destroyed consisted of 563 copies of the first volume of the Patent Office Report for 1860, and 53,939 copies of the second volume of the same report. This is the only loss by fire the office has sustained in the twenty years it has been the property of the Government.

In January, 1878, three accomplished sneak thieves, who had previously been shadowing the office—as was proved by a subsequent examination into the matter—succeeded in abstracting from the safe, by means of false keys, during the temporary absence from the room of the paymaster, some $9,000; and although the parties were afterwards arrested in New York, and indicted, they were never brought to justice, nor was the money ever recovered. At the second session of the Forty-sixth Congress, after a thorough investigation of the matter by the proper committees of both houses, a bill was passed reimbursing the Public Printer for this loss.

Mr. Larcombe, upon whom this misfortune most directly fell, has been the disbursing officer of the Government Printing Office ever since its establishment ; and a more painstaking and faithful official— or one more capable—is not in the service of the Government to-day. He has disbursed, in sums from one dollar up to thousands, an aggregate of more than $30,000,000, every cent of which has been accounted for to the satisfaction of the accounting officers of the Government.

An order was sent from the office to a New York type-founder in July, 1877, for 60,000 pounds of type. This amount was subsequently increased about 15,000 pounds, making perhaps the largest single order ever given by a printing office, or filled by a type-founder, since the art of printing was discovered. The long primer type in use in the Document Room alone will weigh about 50,000 pounds, the brevier type about 35,000 pounds, and the nonpareil something over 25,000 pounds. Of course, to keep these enormous fonts in the best working order, almost daily requisitions are made upon the founder for "sorts."

One of the largest jobs ever undertaken by the office since it came into the possession of the Government was commenced a few months ago in the Document Room. I refer to the printing of the official records of the war, or perhaps better known by the title "Rebellion Records." Colonel Scott, the officer in charge of this work at the War Department, estimates that these records will make 96 large octavo volumes, of about 800 pages each, or 76,800 pages. As 10,000 copies of each of these volumes are to be printed for Congress, some idea may be formed of the formidable character of the task. It will require nearly 50,000 reams of paper to print these copies, which, at $4 per ream, will amount to $200,000. The composition will probably exceed 250,000,000 ems, and the number of books will be 960,000.

Some of the volumes issued by the Government in the past have been very elaborate and expensive. In looking over the subject, it appears a mystery how so much money could be put into a single volume. Below is a short list of the more expensive publications issued from 1852 to 1861:

Explorations of the Valley of the Amazon—2 vols........$55,865 99
Astronomical Expedition to the Southern Hemisphere—
    2 vols... 83,332 33
Naval Expedition to Japan—vols. 1 and 3............... 140,851 30
Report of the Committee on Troubles in Kansas........ . 25,576 17
Report on Commercial Relations (1857)—2 vols.......... 83,034 03
Report of Mexican Boundary Surveys—2 vols. and maps..157,796 85
Pacific Railroad Surveys—11 vols., completed in 1860....863,513 00
Major Delafield's Report on the War in the Crimea........130,439 38
Explorations for a Railroad from Saint Paul to Puget Sound
    —2 vols...146,168 14
The Covode Investigation—2 vols..................... 64,662 75

All the above books were printed before the establishment of the Government Printing Office. Since the present mode of executing the printing was inaugurated, I find some costly printed matter, but nothing to compare to the lavish outlay of the few years preceding. Subjoined is a list involving the greatest expenditure of money under the present system:

Report on the Conduct of the War—3 vols..............$13,968 38
Diplomatic Correspondence (1865)—4 vols.............. 74,578 52
Report of the Committee on Reconstruction—2 vols...... 53,507 84
Impeachment of Andrew Johnson...................... 20,198 75
Ku-Klux Report, completed in 1872—13 vols............ 54,022 00
Three Volumes of Census Report for 1870...............120,870 70
Compendium of the Ninth Census.................... . 79,279 50
Revised Statutes, 1st edition—2 vols.................. 89,017 84

It is very rare now that the cost of a book reaches $20,000, if the Agricultural Report be excepted; and a careful survey of the whole matter has convinced the writer that the era of expensive printing for the Government is past, and that the cost, if the amount of printing to be done did not increase so rapidly, should yearly decrease, with the better facilities and improved machinery.

Although the annual expenditures now for printing and binding are not any greater than they were just previous to the war, it is believed that the amount of work turned out is nearly twice as great. This is brought about from various causes: first, there is more economy practiced, and no middlemen are paid for doing nothing; second, a better system of supervision of the work has been inaugurated; third, the substitution of labor-saving machinery for hand power; and fourth, the better facilities that are afforded for the prosecution of the work by the Government owning the office.

———

Some volumes of large size, under the pressure of great hurry, have been printed in the Document Room in an almost incredibly short space of time. The engrossed copy of the Revised Statutes is, perhaps, the most notable instance. The Statutes numbered 1038 pages. The copy was received by the Public Printer at 5 p. m. on Wednesday, and a *bound copy* was placed in the hands of Mr. Poland, who had charge of the matter in the House, at 12 o'clock noon on the following Saturday. The printing required the greatest care, as it was being prepared for the signature of the President. The matter was read by the proof-readers *three* separate times.

Another instance: The answer of the Board of Public Works of the District of Columbia to certain inquiries propounded by the Committee on the District of Columbia of the House, and numbering some 500 pages of the most difficult and tedious matter known to printers, was received in the office on Thursday, and the work completed, ready for delivery to the Capitol, before the office closed on Saturday evening. The amount of composition in this document will aggregate more than 4,000,000 ems, and, taking into consideration the difficult class of matter of which it is composed, it was perhaps the most rapid piece of printing ever executed in this country.

A still later instance occurs to me: When (Feb., 1879) the subject of the confirmation of the appointment of collector and surveyor of customs at New York was before the Senate, a confidential communication from the President relating thereto was ordered to be printed. It made 440 pages, the main portion of the matter being in brevier type, with a plentiful sprinkling of nonpareil tabular matter throughout. This was put in type, and printed, and delivered to the Senate, in 36 hours after the work was commenced in the Document Room.

The necessities of Congress for the rapid execution of its printing are yearly increasing. That which, a few years ago, was expected in two weeks or a month, is now looked for, if not demanded, from the Printer in a day or a week.

The hours of labor in the Government Printing Office and its various branches are from 8 a. m. to 5 p. m., with an intermission of one hour—from 1 to 2 p. m.—for dinner.

During the sessions of Congress, however, the employés in the several divisions of the main office are frequently detained until late at night.

———

The surroundings of the office have undergone a great change in the past twenty years. When the establishment came into the possession of the Government in 1861, there were very few residences and not any places of business in its immediate vicinity. The square lying directly north of the office—and bounded by H street on the south and I on the north—was occupied by but a single residence. Now there are not less than one hundred and fifty two and three story brick houses on this one square—the average value of which cannot be less than $3,000. On all that property lying north of H street to K, and extending east to First street northeast, there were, twenty years ago, less than a dozen residences; but within the past ten years more than a hundred two, three, and four story houses have been erected, and are occupied by clerks, professional and business people, and employés of the office. The property lying south and southeast of the office has also been vastly improved, and hundreds of new houses erected. H street both east and west of the office is assuming metropolitan airs, in a business way, and is capable of furnishing man or beast with all the necessaries of life, and many of the luxuries.

———

During the war a regiment of soldiers, consisting of employés of the Government in Washington, was organized, and known as the Interior Department Regiment. Companies F and G of this regiment were made up from persons employed in the Government Printing Office—the latter company comprising employés in the Bindery, and the former those engaged in the printing department of the office.

Further along is presented a roster of these companies. Company F was formed quite early in the war, at a time when Washington was threatened from foes within and without, for the purpose of assisting in guarding the Government property, and to repel any foe in case the city was attacked. The organization of this company was kept up for a year or two, but, as the city became filled with soldiers from all sections of the land, it was permitted to die out. During the time the organization was preserved, it was supplied with arms by the Government; certain hours of the day were allotted to drilling and instruction in the manual of arms; and at night a regular detail for guard duty was made. The employés soon became accomplished "veterans." At this period—1861—the persons employed in the Bindery were quite few in number, and no military organization was effected; but in 1864, when Washington was threatened by the rebel General Early, the old company (F) of printers, pressmen, etc., was promptly reorganized, with H. R. Lahee as Captain, W. A. Ensinmyer as First Lieutenant, and Daniel Harbaugh as Second Lieutenant. The binders then organized Company G. From the best information I can obtain, it appears that Company F, as reorganized, was mustered into the United States service about July 11, 1864, and after having been supplied with all the paraphernalia—including arms and ammunition—belonging to the soldier, the company was marched, on the afternoon of that day, to one of the forts in the vicinity of the Insane Asylum, where it remained on duty until the following day, when the rebels, having been beaten in their fight with the Sixth Army Corps, retreated. The printers, having laid aside their weapons of destruction, resumed their places in the office. The other company was not mustered into the service until the day following, and the delay in the muster prevented the company being dispatched to the field.

I have been unable to obtain any official or other list of Company F as organized in 1864. The list here given is that of the company as it originally existed early in 1861. The roster of the binders' Company G is also unofficial, but is believed to be, in the main, correct.

J. H. Roberts, now the Foreman of Binding, and who appears in the list as a "high private," was elected quartermaster of the Interior Department Regiment; and George P. Goff, who was Captain of Company G, was at that time Foreman of Binding.

The following is as complete a roster of these two companies as I have been able to obtain. Those in *italics* have since died, and those with a star (*) are still employed in the office:

COMPANY F.

COMMISSIONED OFFICERS.

Captain—*James English;* First Lieutenant—*William McLeod;* Second Lieutenant—*Charles F. Lowry.*

NON-COMMISSIONED OFFICERS.

Sergeants—*Daniel Harbaugh,* Norval W. King, *Charles D. Parsons, and John Miller.

Corporals—Richard Cronin, *A. G. Seaman,* *William L. Scott, and Thomas Harper.

PRIVATES.

Appleby, A. J.	*Franklin, Wm.*	Mortimer, H.
Arnold, H. H. B.	*Gillen, R.*	Mackey, S. A.
Allen, C. T.	*Grey, E. N.*	*Malone, T.*
*Burnham, E. T.	*Gordon, A.	Murray, C. W.
*Boss, J. P.	*Graham, John.*	*Mulloy, Thos. J.*
*Bowen, G. W.	*Gordon, George.	Nott, Wm. E.
Brown, J. S.	Hall, G. W.	Pittman, F. C.
Bennett, A. R.	*Hurley, J.*	*Porter, R. A.
*Belt, W. M.	*Hough, Chas. B.	*Parsons, A. M.
*Baum, Wm. R.	Hough, J. M. F.	*Robinson, C. W.*
*Burnside, John.	Hall, F. O.	*Rose, Jesse.*
Cunningham, J. H.	Hinchey, James.	Raser, Thos. M.
Caton, George.	*Iardella, L. A.	*Reed, Oliver H.
*Chedal, J. D.	*Jones, Wm. L.	*Robinson, Wm.
*Claxton, R. W.	*Judge, J. J.	*Rodgers, A.*
Cook, A.	Judge, J. G.	*Spedden, E. M.
Clements, L. F.	Johnson, Joseph.	*Schell, C. W.
Charles, J.	*Jones, J. S.*	*Stitt, F. B.
Christine, H. A.	Jackson, Basil.	*Stitt, F. U.
Crandall, J.	Ketcham, O. C.	Shay, W. C.
Campbell, E.	Kelly, R.	Sheer, C.
Crown, J. H.	Kelly, Wm. B.	*Shoemaker, J. K.*
Cullinan, Lott.	*Larcombe, John.	*Spottswood, J. M. A.
Chew, F.	*Laporte, E.*	Sample, D. S.
*Carrier, A. L.	*Lincoln, M. T.	Smith, C. B.
Davis, Madison.	*McNeir, G. A. R.	Scholfield, John.
Davis, S. A.	Maloney, W. W.	Tomlinson, J. S.
*Davison, H. L.	*McPherson, C. D.	*Taylor, Robert.*
Defrees, Rollin.	McElwee, S.	*Woodward, M. R.
De Vaughn, C. J.	*MacMurray, E.*	*Waters, F. J.
DeCanidry, W. A.	*Melvin, J.*	*Wilkes, Joseph.*
*Donaldson, J. A.	McGonegal, S.	Wadsworth, Geo.
Edmonston, E. H.	*Malone, E.	*Walker, H.
Forbes, G. C.	*Murphy, M.*	*Watkins, N.
Fowler, Wm. D.	*Maher, Thos. F.	Wall, Chas.
Frizzell, Wm. J.	*Metcalf, John.	*Wright, B. C.
Fleming, Wm.	*McKenney, James.*	*Wiber, D.*
*Fechtig, L. R.	McNamara, Thos.	*Whaley, J. C. C.*
Franzoni, J. C.	McNamee, Patrick.	*Whitaker, John.

COMPANY G.

OFFICERS.

Captain—George P. Goff; First Lieutenant—*Chas. Lemon; Second Lieutenant—*John J. Byrnes; First Sergeant—Varden Bishop.

PRIVATES.

Bailey, Wm. H.
* Blakeney, J. T.
Bailey, Jno. E.
Bain, Wm. V.
* Behler, John J.
* Burch, Geo. D.
Baylie, Thos. S.
* Burger, Wm. B.
* Beall, J. W.
Burgess, W. G.
Bell, Emanuel.
* Caldwell, P. J.
Clark, G. W.
* Connell, R. A.
* Crawford, S. T.
Cunningham, F.
Dubant, J. H.
Dowden, C. L.
* Elwood, C. T.
Espey, John.
Eldridge, E.
* Espey, H. C.
Elwood, Jas. H.
* Eckloff, E. T.
* Gordon, M. B.
* Graenacher, C. L.
Hollins, J. H. C.
* Hullett, A. G.
Harmer, J. W.
Hotchkiss, W. D.
* Howlett, William.

* Hartford, R. B.
* Hayes, Wm.
Hill, John.
Hite, H. D.
Hill, Michael.
Ingraham, Jas. J.
* Jacobs, Augustus.
Jennings, H. D.
* Knott, Ig. M.
Lawrence, J. L. D.
* Landvoigt, J. A.
* Landvoigt, D. W.
* Meyer, John W.
Marcellus, R. H.
* Metcalf, F. S.
* McLane, Wm.
* Moran, Wm. H.
* May, Thos. O.
McDonald, Wm.
* McCormick, J. H.
* Miller, Frank.
* McKean, Jas. P.
Mattingly, J. W.
* Meushaw, C. H.
* McNamee, Patrick.
Manning, F. A.
McIntire, Henry.
Owen, C. L.
Perkins, John A.
Peters, Wm. H., Jr.

* Penicks, Thos. B.
* Philpitt, F. C.
Pascoe, R. P.
* Pyemont, J. W.
* Roberts, J. H.
* Ratcliff, J. L.
* Roberts, Richard.
* Rosewag, G.
Ridgway, E.
* Stewart, Thos. F.
* Stewart, James.
* Scott, Wm.
* Seibert, F.
Semple, D. H.
* Smith, Moses.
St. Clair, Jos.
Sommers, Israel.
* Triplett, T. M.
* Toomey, Dennis.
Taylor, Wm. H.
* Tafe, Andrew.
Walmsley, Theo.
* White, Jas. W.
Walton, C.
Williss, W. B. R.
Weaver, C. F.
Walker, C. E.
* Weise, Henry.
Ward, John.
Williams, Lewis.

CHAPTER III.

THE PRINTING FOR CONGRESS.

THE printing ordered by Congress annually absorbs nearly one-half of the whole appropriation made for printing and binding for the Government. Much of it is necessarily done at night, and is, therefore, somewhat more expensive than work performed wholly in daylight. It has been truly said that the value of the printing for Congress depends as much upon the *promptness* with which it is done, as the manner of its execution. The main object is to have laid before Congress and the country the condition and wants of the public service in its various branches, as officially communicated by the several departments of the Government. It is of the first importance to intelligent legislation upon these subjects, that the documents should be promptly printed and delivered; and if they are withheld or delayed until the leading measures of the session are matured, the printing is comparatively worthless. In estimating the cost of the Congressional printing, therefore, its value in the assistance and guide it affords our legislators is an important element in the account. For the printing of the numerous extensive public documents, in time to meet the wants of Congress, a large establishment is absolutely necessary. There occur frequently emergencies when the entire force of the office must be thrown upon a single document, the prompt printing of which is considered of great importance.

In 1846 Mr. Benton showed that the Government lost in a single year $1,000,000 through the neglect of the public printer to print a bill or document required just at the close of a session of Congress.

The printing for Congress is known to the Public Printer under the following heads:

Executive Documents.

Miscellaneous Documents.

Reports of Committees.

Printing ordered by resolution of either house.

Printing ordered by concurrent resolution.

Printing ordered by joint resolution, or by law, which is the same thing.

DOCUMENTS, REPORTS, ETC.

Any communication transmitted to Congress by the President or the head of either of the Executive Departments, through the President of the Senate or Speaker of the House of Representatives, is termed an "Executive Document." In the Forty-sixth Congress, there were five hundred and eighteen of these messages ordered to be printed. Some of them are but a page or two in length, but many of them make hundreds of pages, and are, of course, upon all topics relating to the business or policy of the Government.

A Miscellaneous Document is any communication, letter, petition, address, or other written or printed matter, either of a public, private, or political nature, from any official (other than the President or head of an Executive Department) or citizen, or resolutions of recommendation or instruction from State Legislatures, addresses to the President of the Senate or Speaker of the House, or any member of either the Senate or House. Two hundred and forty-nine of these Miscellaneous communications were printed for the Forty-sixth Congress.

For a great many years after the numbering of documents was begun, no separate designation or nomenclature of communications addressed to Congress was made; but for some reason a change was made by somebody's direction, and the separate numbering of the Executive and Miscellaneous matter became customary, and has been the practice in the House since about 1827 and in the Senate since 1833.

We doubt the expediency or convenience of the practice, and believe that if the experiment were tried of numbering all the documents and reports in a single series, it would be found of such manifest advantage that it would ever after be followed.

Another class of literature produced by Congress is the "Reports of Committees." The rules of the House provide for 57 Standing, Select, Special, and Joint Committees, and of course the House has power to increase the number of all except the Joint Committees indefinitely. The rules also provide that with every subject reported upon, the committee making the report must submit it in writing, and that the report shall be printed. The Senate has 49 committees, with like power to increase the number at its pleasure. These several committees, of both houses, had before them, during the Forty-sixth Congress, more than 9,000 bills and resolutions, upon which 3,164 Senate and House reports were submitted and printed. The majority of these reports, however, are small, but some of them make large volumes; and they numbered 7,969 pages for the Senate and 6,544 pages for the House during the Forty-sixth Congress.

The printing for committees—which is done under resolutions of either house—is a large item in the annual budget of expense. Docu-

PRINTING DEPARTMENT—Main Composing, or Document, Room.

mentary evidence is often submitted to committees of so voluminous a character as to be impracticable of examination unless in printed form; and that the committee may evolve a just decision, the matter is printed for their benefit.

The printing under joint resolutions and by law, embraces a different class of work, viz: Extra copies on documents already printed, the printing of valuable annual reports, etc.

The laws are printed in three different forms: first, in the form of documents, each law in a separate, uncovered pamphlet; in the regular pamphlet (quarto) or "Session" form, at the end of each session; and finally, in the form of the Statutes at Large. The expense of this one item is considerable, for a Congress; but as they constitute the essence of all the business of Congress, probably the expense is trifling, considering their value to the whole people, when compared with certain other matters that are annually ordered by Congress.

DISTRIBUTION OF DOCUMENTS.

The usual number of copies printed of the documents and reports of each house of Congress is 1,900, and of bills and joint resolutions 924. These are distributed as follows:

Where delivered.	Senate documents and reports.	House documents and reports.	Senate bills and joint resolutions.	House bills and joint resolutions.
Document-room of the House..........	411	396	440	440
Office of the Clerk of the House........	20	149	20	308
Sergeant-at-Arms of the Senate.........	243	190	244	134
Office of the Secretary of the Senate.....	6	6	15	8
Folding-room of the Senate............	190	......	170	....
Department of State.................	25	25	10	10
Treasury Department..................	1	1	10	10
War Department	1	1	......	....
Ordnance Bureau, War Department.....	1	1	1	1
Office of the Public Printer............	4	4	4	4
File copies.........................	10	10	10	9
Reserved for binding.................	988	1,117	......	....
Total number printed..............	1,900	1,900	924	924

The reserved documents, *i. e.*, those which are subsequently distributed to the various State and Territorial libraries, are bound in volumes of appropriate size (in sheep and calf), and are distributed as follows:

Where delivered.	Senate documents.	House documents.
Senate document-room...........................	112	112
House document-room...........................	313	411
Senate folding-room............................	43	....
Department of State............................	40	40
Department of the Interior......................	420	470
Library of Congress:....	52	52
Library of the House of Representatives.........	7	30
Library of the Court of Claims..................	....	2
Office of the Public Printer....................	1	....
Total reserve............................	988	1,117

Congress has absolute power to order the printing of anything which is not copyrighted, and for the past few years has indulged in the luxury of numerous publications of vast proportions and great expense. A large number of the books printed are of practical value to scientific people, or for preservation; but many of them are only of momentary value or interest, and it is doubtful if their publication will ever repay the Government for the large sums expended in their production.

FORTHCOMING AND ANNUAL PUBLICATIONS OF CONGRESS AND THE DEPARTMENTS.

The following is a list of the most valuable annual and other reports authorized by law or ordered by resolutions of Congress. Some reports, considered of special value and interest to the general public, now in hand to be printed for the Executive Departments, are also included.

This list is designed to give the reader information concerning *forthcoming* publications.

PUBLICATIONS OF THE GEOLOGICAL SURVEY, J. W. POWELL, DIRECTOR.

Geology and Mining Industry of Leadville, Colorado. By S. F. Emmons.

Geology of Eureka Mining District, Nevada. By Arnold Hague.

The Copper Rocks of Lake Superior, and their Continuation through Minnesota. By Prof. Rowland D. Irving.

History of the Comstock Mines. By Eliot Lord.

The Comstock Lode. By George F. Becker.

Mechanical Appliances used in Mining and Milling on the Comstock Lode. By W. R. Eckart.

Coal of the United States. By Raphael Pumpelly.
Iron in the United States. By Raphael Pumpelly.
The Precious Metals. By Clarence King.
Lesser Metals and General Mineral Resources. By Raphael Pumpelly.
Uinkaret Plateau. By Capt. C. E. Dutton.
Lake Bonneville. By G. K. Gilbert.
Dinocerata. A monograph on an extinct order of Ungulates. By Prof. O. C. Marsh.

PUBLICATIONS OF THE BUREAU OF ETHNOLOGY, J. W. POWELL, DIRECTOR.

Ethnology of North America (all 4tos):

Vol. 2.—Grammar and Dictionary of the Klamath Indians. By A. S. Gatchet.

Vol. 4.—In 3 parts: Part 1. Houses and House-life of the American Aborigines, by Lewis H. Morgan; Part 2. Archæology, by Dr. Rau; Part 3. Language of the Southern Indians, by General Pike.

Vol. 5.—Mortuary Customs of the Indians. By Dr. H. C. Yarrow.

Vol. 6.—Grammar and Dictionary of the Dakota Language. By S. R. Riggs.

Vol. 7.—Grammar and Dictionary of the Ponka Language. By J. O. Dorsey.

Vols. 9 and 10.—(The contents of these volumes have not yet been decided upon.)

Annual Report of the Bureau of Ethnology of the Smithsonian Institution for 1879. 8vo.
—— for 1880. 8vo.
—— for 1881. 8vo.

All the above publications are to be issued under the direction of Maj. J. W. Powell, who has been patiently collecting, for more than twenty years, valuable data respecting the ethnological history of the North American Indians, and the natural and geological history of the great Northwest.

HAYDEN'S GEOLOGICAL SURVEY REPORTS.

Vol. 3.—The Vertebrata of the Mesozoic Formations of the Western Territories. By E. D. Cope. 4to.

Vol. 4.—The Vertebrata of the Tertiary Formations of the Western Territories. By E. D. Cope. 4to.

Vol. 8.—Contributions to the Fossil Flora of the Cretaceous and Tertiary Formations of the Western Territories. 4to.

Vol. 13.—Fossil Insects of the Western Territories. By S. H. Scudder. 4to.

Vol. 14.—Zoology. By Dr. Elliott Coues. 4to.

Twelfth, or final, Annual Report. 1 vol., 8vo.

Bulletin No. 2, Vol. 6. Annotated list of the Birds of Nevada; Osteology of the American Tetraonidæ, and other articles. 8vo.

SURVEYS WEST OF THE 100TH MERIDIAN (UNDER CHARGE OF CAPT. GEO. M. WHEELER).

Vol. 7, and a Supplement to Vol. 3, are in hands of printer. 4tos.

PUBLICATIONS AUTHORIZED BY CONGRESS AND THE DEPARTMENTS.

Congress.

Abridgment: Is simply an abridged edition of the Annual Reports of the Executive Departments. 1 vol., 8vo.

Appropriations, New Offices, etc.: Report of Secretary of the Senate and Clerk of the House (made at the close of each session of Congress), of appropriations made and new offices created. Pamphlet, 8vo.

Atlas of Colorado, Hayden's : A revised and corrected edition has just been ordered by Congress. A very valuable Atlas. Sold by Public Printer at $3.50, delivered at the office; wrapped and registered, $3.75.

Attorney-General, Annual Report of the. 1 vol., 8vo.

———— Digest of Opinions of the : A full and complete digest of volumes 1 to 16 of the Opinions of the Attorneys-General was ordered at the Second Session of the Forty-sixth Congress. 8vo.

———— Opinions of the : Published from time to time, in volumes of about 600 pages. Volumes 15 and 16 have just been issued. 8vo.

Biennial Register, or Blue Book : Containing a complete list, with compensation paid each, of all persons employed under the Government of the United States. Is issued each year that a new Congress assembles. 2 vols. of late years, 4to.

Capitulation of the Turkish Empire : Report of the Secretary of State concerning the. Pamphlet, 8vo.

Coast Survey: Annual Report of the Superintendent. 1 vol., 4to. Reports for 1879 and 1880 not yet printed.

Commerce and Navigation. Part I : Annual Report of the Bureau of Statistics on the Commerce and Navigation of the United States. 1 vol., 8vo.

———— Part 2 : Internal Commerce of the United States. 1 vol., 8vo.

Commercial Relations of the United States: Annual Report of the Secretary of State on the. 1 vol., 8vo. Report for 1880 not yet printed.

Congressional Directory: Contains list of Senators and Representatives in Congress, with brief biographical sketches of each, their residences in the several States, and official residence in Washington; also, the residences, etc., of all the principal officials in Washington. Pamphlet, 8vo. Issued always at the commencement, and generally at the close, of each session of Congress. Usual price by mail about 20 cents.

Continental Congress, Acts of the : Has been authorized by Congress. Is in preparation.

Court of Claims, Opinions of the : Issued every year between July and December. 8vo·

Debates of Congress—The Congressional Record : Published daily during the sessions of Congress, and at the end of the session bound in volumes. Large 4to.

Farr, Hon. E. W.: Memorial Addresses on the life and character of. 1 vol., 4to.

First Comptroller of the Treasury, Decisions of the : The first volume of these decisions in press. Will probably be an annual publication hereafter. 8vo.

Fish and Fisheries, Commissioner of: Annual Report of the. 1 vol., 4to. Reports for 1879 and 1880 not yet printed.

Gold and Silver in the United States : Report of the Director of the Mint on the Annual Production of. 1 vol., 8vo.

Iron, Steel, and other Metals, Report of Board to Test : A very valuable publication for those interested in such matters. 2 vols., 8vo.

Jefferson's Desk : Proceedings in Congress upon its presentation to the United States by J. Randolph Coolidge. A sort of memorial volume. Size and style not yet known.

Land Commission, Report of the : Consists of 4 vols. Vol. 3 is a very interesting history of the original acquisition, etc., of all the public domain.

Laws of the United States : Are issued at the close of each session of Congress, and are known as the Session Laws. At the end of each Congress they are arranged in numerical order and printed, and are then known as the Statutes at Large. 1 vol. in either case.

Medical and Surgical History of the War : This valuable series was first ordered by the joint resolution of March 3, 1869, since which time 4 volumes have been issued. There remain yet to be issued—one volume of which is now in the hands of the printer—2 volumes. At the last session of Congress, resolutions for printing another edition of the first 4 volumes of the series were considered, and it is probable that at no distant day they will be ordered.

National Board of Health : Annual Report of the. 1 vol., 8vo. Reports for 1879 and 1880 not yet printed.

Paris Exposition Reports : The most complete, handsome, and valuable Exposition reports ever printed at the office. In 5 vols., 8vo. A limited number for sale by the Public Printer, at $5 per set.

Revised Statutes, Supplement to : To embrace the laws of a general nature from the publication of the second edition of the Revised Statutes to the close of the Forty-sixth Congress. 1 vol., 4to. In hands of printer.

Smithsonian Institution : Annual Report of the Secretary. 1 vol., 8vo. Report for 1880 not yet printed.

Surgeon-General's Office, Catalogue of the Library of the : This consists of abbreviated titles to all known publications relating to medical science, and is perhaps the most complete of its kind ever attempted. The first volume has just been issued. 4to.

Transportation Routes to the Seaboard : Report of a Committee on. Made in 1874. A reprint. 1 vol., 8vo.

Trichinæ in Swine : Report of the Secretary of the Treasury concerning. 1 vol., 8vo.

War of the Rebellion, Official Records of the : This official history of the late war will consist of about 96 volumes, in three series. The first 5 volumes of Series No. 1, and 2 volumes of Series No. 3, are now in press. 8vo. Price $1 per volume.

Executive Departments.

Agricultural Department :

Annual Report for 1880. 1 vol., 8vo.

Special Report No. 35 : Statistics relating to the culture of the grape, and the production of wine. Pamphlet, 8vo.

———— No. 33 : Diseases of Swine and other Domestic Animals. Pamphlet, 8vo.

Bureau of Education (Interior Department) :

Annual Report of the Commissioner for 1879. 1 vol., 8vo.

———— for 1880. 8vo.

Special Report on Instruction in Drawing and Art Education. Pamphlet.

———— on Industrial Education in the United States. Pamphlet.

Circular of Information No. 6, 1880 : Instruction in Chemistry and Physics. Pamphlet.

———— No. 7, 1880 : Spelling Reform. Pamphlet.

———— No. 1, 1881 : Construction of Library Buildings.

———— No. 2, 1881 : Education in France. Pamphlet.

———— No. 3, 1881 : Historical Sketches of the University of Bonn. Pamphlet.

———— No. 4, 1881 : Proceedings of Department of Superintendents. Pamphlet.

Census Office (Interior Department) : Report of the Superintendent of the. Tenth Census.

Entomological Commission (Interior Department) :

Second Annual Report on the Rocky Mountain Locust and other Injurious Insects. 1 vol., 8vo.

Third Annual Report on the Rocky Mountain Locust and other Injurious Insects, with a Bibliography of Economic Entomology.

Bulletin No. 3 : Report on the Cotton and Boll Worms, with means of counteracting their ravages ; a revised edition. Pamphlet, 8vo. By Chas. V. Riley.

Bulletin No. 6. General Index and Supplement to the Nine Reports on the Insects of Missouri. By Charles V. Riley.

Bulletin No. 7. The Grape-vine Phylloxera, and other Insects Injurious to the Grape-vine. By Charles V. Riley.

Bulletin No. 8. Insects Injurious to Shade and Forest Trees. Pamphlet, 8vo. By Chas. V. Riley.

Patent Office (Interior Department):

Classified Abridgment of Letters Patent. In preparation, and will be for sale by Commissioner of Patents when issued.

Smithsonian Institution (Interior Department):

The Smithsonian Institution will publish, in 1881, the following works:

An index of names used for zoological genera, comprising nearly 70,000 titles. By Prof. Samuel H. Scudder. 8vo.

New edition of rainfall tables, with charts of the precipitation for spring, summer, autumn, winter, and the year. By Chas. A. Schott. 4to.

The Meteorology of Providence, R. I. By Prof. A. Caswell. 4to.

A subject index and a synopsis of the scientific writings of William Herschel. By Prof. E. S. Holden. 8vo.

Discussion of the Barometric Observations of Prof. E. S. Snell. By Prof. F. H. Loud. 8vo.

Index Bibliography of the writings of Prof. S. F. Baird. 8vo.

Tables showing the amount of precipitation of rain and snow for each month and year at upwards of 2,000 stations in the United States. 4to.

Proceedings of the National Museum for 1880. Vol. 3. 8vo.

Nomenclature of North American Birds. By Robert Ridgway. 8vo.

Report of the Smithsonian Institution for the year 1880. 8vo.

Record of the Progress of Science in 1879 and 1880. By Profs. Abbe, Farlow, Barker, Gill, Holden, Mason, and others. 8vo.

Bulletin United States National Museum: Flora of the District of Columbia. By Prof. L. F. Ward. 8vo.

Directions for collecting specimens of natural history, with special reference to deep-sea dredging. By Richard Rathban. 8vo.

Synopsis of the Fishes of North America. By Prof. D. S. Jordan. 8vo.

Bibliography of the Ichthyology of the Pacific Coast of North America. By Theodore Gill. 8vo.

Bulletin United States Fish Commission. Vol. 1. 8vo.

Report of the United States Fish Commission. Part 7. 8vo.

Report on the International Fishery Exhibition at Berlin, 1880, and on the present state of the fisheries of Europe. By G. Brown Goode, Deputy Commissioner. 8vo.

In connection with the Tenth Census, a report on the present condition and past history of the fishing industries of the United States.

Naval Observatory (Navy Department):

Astronomical and Meteorological Observations U. S. Naval Observatory, 1877. This volume will include, besides the regular work of the Observatory, six appendices, many copies of which will be issued separately. The subjects are:

1. Investigation of the Objective and Micrometers of the 26-inch Equatorial.

2. The Multiple Star Σ 748 in Nebula Orionis.

3. Longitude of Princeton, N. J.

4. Longitude of Cincinnati Observatory.

5. Nebula of Orion.

6. Observations of Double Stars.

Astronomical and Meteorological Observations U. S. N. Observatory, 1876. This volume for 1876 is nearly ready for issue in two Parts. Part I contains the usual astronomical and meteorological work. Part II contains:

1. A Subject Index to the Publications of the United States Naval Observatory 1845–1875.
2. Reports on Telescopic Observations of the Transit of Mercury, May 5–6, 1878.
3. Reports on the Total Solar Eclipses of July 29, 1878, and June 11, 1880.

Nautical Almanac Office (Navy Department):
American Ephemeris and Nautical Almanac for the year 1884. Large octavo, 508 pp.
American Nautical Almanac for the year 1885. 8vo, 270 pp.
The Ephemeris is not published for general distribution, but is sold by the Superintendent of the Nautical Almanac Office, Washington, D. C., to the public at cost. The cost is averaged at $1 for the American Ephemeris. A smaller volume, adapted to the meridian of Greenwich, is published and sold by the agents of the Navy Department at 50 cents per copy.
Clock and Zodiacal Stars, a catalogue of 1,098 standards. 4to, about 170 pp.
On Gauss's Method of Computing Secular Perturbations. By G. W. Hill. 4to. Pamphlet.

Secretary's Office (Navy Department):
Navy Register: Gives a complete roster of the officers and vessels of the United States Navy. Is published once each year, about July. 1 vol., 8vo.

Coast Survey Office (Treasury Department):
Tide Tables for the Atlantic and Pacific Coasts. Small 8vo. For sale by regularly authorized agents of the Treasury Department.
A Treatise on Projections. 4to.

Chief Signal Officer (War Department):
Instructions to Observer Sergeants. Pamphlet, 8vo.

Engineer Bureau (War Department):
Professional Papers No. 23. Submarine Mines; Report upon Experiments and Investigations to develop a System of. 1 vol., 4to.
Notes illustrating Military Geography of the United States. 8vo.
Translation of Treatises on River Improvements. 8vo.
Index to Annual Reports of Chief of Engineers from 1866 to 1869. 8vo.

Adjutant-General's Office (War Department):
Army Register: Gives a complete roster of all the officers on the active and retired lists of the United States Army. Small 8vo. Is published about January 1, each year.
Army of the United States, Regulations of the: A new edition of the Revised Army Regulations is now in press. 1 vol., 8vo. Also a pocket edition, 12mo.

ANNUAL REPORTS OF THE EXECUTIVE DEPARTMENTS.

The Annual Reports of the Executive Departments are generally printed between the months of September and April of each year, and consist of the following volumes:

State Department: Generally 2 vols., 8vo, containing the President's annual messages to Congress and correspondence of the Secretary of State through Ministers and Consuls with foreign Governments.

Treasury Department: 1. Annual Report of the Secretary of the Treasury on the State of the Finances, with the reports of the Treasurer, the several Auditors, Registers, Comptrollers, etc., and Bureau officers generally; 2. Report of the Comptroller of the Currency; 3. Report of the Commissioner of Internal Revenue; 4. Report of the Life-Saving Service. All 8vos.

War Department: 1. Report of the Secretary of War, embracing the Reports of the General of the Army and the Generals commanding Military Divisions or Departments all over the United States; 2. Report of the Chief of Engineers, generally consisting of 3 vols.; 3. Report of the Chief of Ordnance; 4. Report of the Chief Signal Officer of the Army. All 8vos.

Navy Department: Annual Report of the Secretary of the Navy, embracing reports of all the Bureau officers. 8vo.

Post-Office Department: Annual Report of the Postmaster-General, embracing the Reports of the First, Second, and Third Assistant Postmasters-General; the Auditor of the Treasury for the Post-Office Department, etc. 1 vol., 8vo.

Interior Department: 1. Report of the Secretary of the Interior, embracing the Reports of the Commissioner of Indian Affairs and Commissioner of the General Land Office; 2. Reports of the Auditor of Railroad Accounts, and of the various Benevolent and Reformatory Institutions under the protection of the Government; 3. Report of the Commissioner of Education. 8vo.

District of Columbia: Annual Report of the Commissioners. 8vo.

It is but quite recently—within the last ten òr fifteen years—that the publications of the Government have attracted special attention. Congress has been very generous in its assistance to all laudable researches of a scientific character, and the production of numerous valuable and interesting monographs and reports has been the result. Unfortunately, however, no proper provision has been made for the dissemination of these costly publications. Congress orders a few thousand copies of these books, and the Senators and Representatives distribute them to their constituents; but the probability is that the farmer, who would be most interested in the Agricultural Report, receives a work on Fossil Insects, or an Indian dictionary; while the scientific man, who could appreciate the real value of the books sent the farmer, is compelled to look for geological data in a treatise on trichinæ in pork. If a system of distribution could be devised whereby books issued from the Government Printing Office could be sent to those, and those only, who are searchers in the special fields of science to which the books relate, the real value and importance of Government publications would be greatly increased.

There is a law on the statute-books, however, which permits any person to subscribe for any Government publication issued under the authority of law. It is as follows:

"If any person desiring extra copies of any document printed at the Government Printing Office by authority of law shall, previous to its being put to press, notify the Congressional Printer of the number of copies wanted, and shall pay to him, in advance, the estimated cost thereof, and ten per centum thereon, the Congressional Printer may, under the direction of the Joint Committee on Public Printing, furnish the same.''—Sec. 3809 Rev. Stats.

A later law specifies copies of ''bills, and reports, and other public documents,'' as coming within the meaning of the above section.

This seems very generous on the part of the Government, in furnishing to its citizens these books at so trifling an advance upon the first cost; but how are those interested in such matters to find out what or when any public document will be put to press? There is no list of forthcoming Government publications in existence, with the exception of the imperfect one here presented, and therefore it is impossible for those wishing to subscribe to do so. In the case of some publications of marked peculiarity or interest, the information may be furnished through the daily press; but probably even this comes too late to enable the would-be purchaser to avail himself of the provisions of the law. This will probably be remedied, as it should be; and when proper provision is made, the Government Printing Office will have entered upon a career of usefulness much in advance of its present importance.

CHAPTER IV.

THE PRINTING OFFICE BUILDING.

HON. JOHN A. GURLEY, a member of the House of Representatives, delivered a speech in the House when the subject of creating a Government Printing Office was under consideration, in which he used the following pertinent language:

"If there is any public service in this country which, in preference to almost any other, should be performed by the immediate and special agents of the Government, it is that of Congressional and executive printing; and this fact will appear the more obvious if we consider that it is necessarily interwoven with the law-making power of each house, and cannot, by any possibility, be separated from it. *It is no exaggeration to say that it is not only a leading but an essential element of national legislation; for the information which it affords must always control, to some extent, the action of those engaged in it. Without it, how can gentlemen intelligently frame their bills, draw up their reports, or even vote understandingly?*

"But it is not only a *positive*, but a *daily* and almost hourly necessity while Congress is in session. It is just as essential to the healthy action of this legislative assembly when here convened, as our ordinary food is to the healthy action of our bodies and minds. There exists about the same necessity for the regular appearance in print of bills, documents, and reports, as for the appearance every morning upon the table of the breakfast.

"It is unlike any other department of Government service. For ships you can wait; for guns you can generally wait; and, ordinarily, you are in no special hurry for the various munitions of war; but you cannot be deprived of your printing for a single day without serious embarrassment and loss of time. *In the sense, therefore, of a leading element of the law-making power, the public printing underlies your armies, it underlies your navies, and every other arm of the national service; and in this important particular, therefore, bears no analogy to the other departments of the Government.*"

By a joint resolution introduced in Congress by Mr. Gurley in relation to the public printing, and subsequently passed by both houses of Congress and approved by the President June 23, 1860, the Superintendent of Public Printing was "authorized and directed to have executed the printing and binding authorized by the Senate and House of Representatives, the Executive and Judicial Departments, and the Court of Claims; and to enable him to carry out the provisions of this act, he is hereby authorized to contract for the erection or purchase of the necessary buildings, machinery and materials for that purpose."

In compliance with this law, negotiations were entered into, which resulted in a contract between John Heart, the Superintendent of Public Printing, on the part of the United States, and T. Crowell, by which the property now occupied by this office, being part of square 624, and containing 46,397 feet, became the property of the United States, at a cost of $135,000. The purchase included the building and all the machinery, type, paper, and, in fact, all the material required for a complete printing office.

The building, etc., is described, in the Annual Report of the Superintendent of Public Printing of January 1, 1861, as follows:

"The public printing establishment is situated at the northeast corner of square 624, at the corner of H street north and North Capitol street. The lot is 264 feet 9 inches on H street, by 175 feet 3 inches on North Capitol street, containing 46,397 feet, and affording ample space for any additions or improvements that may be deemed desirable. The building consists of a printing office and bindery, four stories high, with a breadth of 61½ feet and a depth of 243 feet; a paper warehouse 59 feet 7 inches by 79 feet 2 inches; a machine shop 22 feet 2 inches by 25 feet, for repairing and renewing the presses and machinery; a boiler house 20 feet 7 inches by 26 feet; a coal house 23 by 27 feet; a wagon shed 25 feet 4 inches by 24 feet; and stables 23 feet by 41 feet 2 inches. These buildings are all of brick, built of the best materials and in the most durable manner, and were erected under the supervision of Edward Clark, esq., now the architect of the Interior Department, expressly for the purpose of executing the public printing and binding. * * * They are completely isolated from any contiguous building, being bounded on the north and east by public streets, on the south by a 30-foot alley, and on the west by a vacant lot of 21 feet 9 inches, included in the purchase."

*   *   *   *   *   *   *   *

An estimate of the value of the material, etc., on hand at the time of the purchase is found in the Annual Report of the Superintendent, 1861, and is as follows:

```
26 printing presses.....................................$36,375.00
Type, metal, furniture, etc..............................13,150.00
Steam-engine and appendages..............................12,000.00
Hydraulic presses........................................6,000.00
Drying-room fixtures.....................................3,000.00
Gas fixtures.............................................2,175.00
Standing presses and fixtures in the wetting-room, standing presses,
     machinery, and fixtures in the Bindery and Folding Rooms, machinery
     and fixtures in the Machine Shop, cases, chases, imposing-stones, stands,
     water-pipes, heating-pipes, horses, wagons, etc...19,534.00
                                                        ───────────
                                                        92,234.00
Building and lot........................................54,311.00
                                                        ───────────
                                                        146,545.00
```

The original cost of the above to Mr. Wendell was about $180,000.

The original building was erected and occupied by Cornelius Wendell, and was used also as a private office. At the time it was constructed and fitted up as a printing office, it was considered one of the most complete establishments of the kind then in the country. It embraced all the modern conveniences, and the material and facilities for doing the work were all of the newest and most approved kind.

The Superintendent of Public Printing, in his Annual Report of January 12, 1857, speaks of the office as follows:

"Since the adjournment of the last session of Congress, the printer to the House of Representatives, with a spirit of enterprise worthy of all commendation, erected at a very great expense, and doubtless with much risk as to the future productiveness of the investment of capital, the most complete and extensive printing establishment on this continent. The printing of Congress, during late years, has increased to such an extent that there was no building in the city of Washington which afforded space and suitable architectural arrangements for bringing out the work with desirable expedition and neatness; and the tenure by which the public printer holds his office is so uncertain, that, until now, no one felt disposed to encounter the risk involved in an undertaking of this character. The facilities thus afforded will not only enable this office to furnish the larger orders for printing with greater dispatch, but will also enable it to make still further improvements in the general appearance of the public printing."

At the time the building was erected and fitted up as a printing office, its facilities were considered amply sufficient to not only execute all the work required by both houses of Congress, but also to perform any and all work which might be obtained from private parties as well;

but not many years after its purchase by the Government, the rapid increase of the work rendered an enlargement actually necessary, and in 1865, after repeated and urgent calls upon Congress for money, the first addition to the main building was made.   The new extension, fronting on H street, and extending west from the west end of the old part, was 60 feet, by a depth running south of 76 feet.

Five years later, in 1870, the second addition, extending south on North Capitol street from the east end of the main building 113½ feet, with a general width of 61½ feet, was made.   The second story of this wing is divided into six apartments; one of which is used as the private business office of the Public Printer, two for the accommodation of the clerks in the Public Printer's office, one for a Library, and the other two are used by the proof-readers, copy-preparers, etc.

Again, in 1879, a fire-proof building was added, running south from the west end of the main building 86 feet 6 inches by 53 feet 8 inches —thence east 60 by 60 feet; also two four-story fire-proof hall-ways, 12 feet wide each, connecting the old house with the new wing.

All these extensions, which are very substantial and perfect in their workmanship, are four stories in height, and made to harmonize in style of architecture with the main or old house.   Thus the building— when the new wing just provided for is erected—will occupy, exclusive of the boiler, coal-house, and stables, more than 40,205 square feet, and give a floor space for workmen and material of 160,820 square feet, or nearly 4 acres.

The addition alluded to above as just having been provided for by Congress will connect the east end of the extension of 1879 with that of 1870, and will be 93 by 60 feet, and four stories in height.   It will probably be ready for occupancy during the coming fall.   This addition will give the form of the whole building that of a rectangular quadrangle, with a court in the center.

In 1878, Congress made an appropriation of $3,000 for fire-escapes for the building.   The Public Printer contracted for the building of these escapes at $2,244.   They are of brick and iron, and circular in form, are constructed outside the building, and are very substantial; so that should a fire occur, in spite of every possible precaution, these will afford additional and ample means of escape to the employés. These escapes do not communicate with the second floor, from which sufficient places of exit were already provided, but are for the exclusive use of the third and fourth floors.   As an additional precaution against fire, chemical fire-extinguishers have been provided, and certain employés are instructed in their use.

On the ground floor of the main building are situated the Press and Dry-Press Rooms, Paper Warehouse No. 1, fire-proof Vault for Stereo-

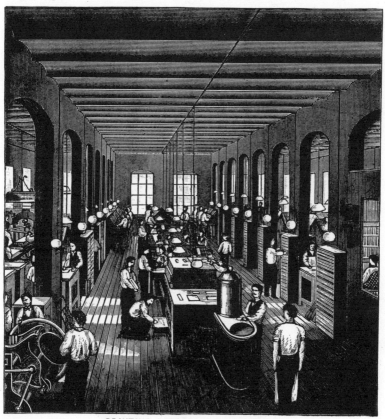

PRINTING DEPARTMENT—Job Room.

type Plates and Cuts, the Machine and Carpenter shops, and in the court the roller, boiler, and coal houses, and until quite recently the stables.

On the second floor are the offices of the Public Printer, the Chief Clerk, the Disbursing Clerk, the Foreman of Printing, the Document Room, the Job Room, the Stereotyping and Electrotyping Departments, the Proof Room, etc.

The third floor is occupied by the Binding Department and Warehouse No. 2 for binders' materials.

On the fourth floor are the Folding Room, the Congressional Record Room, the Patent Office Specification Room, and Warehouse No. 3.

The new addition will be occupied by a general extension of the overcrowded branches of the office, which are sadly in need of additional working room for the more economical and expeditious execution of the work.

Two large elevators transport material and work to the different rooms, and one small box elevator, for hurried work and small jobs, from the ground to the fourth floor.

The office is provided with every requisite known to the craftsmen of the day for the execution of the printing and binding in a neat, expeditious, and workmanlike manner, and undoubtedly uses more material and executes more work than any other printing office in the world. Ever since its organization as a national office, it has had a struggle for existence, as its creation destroyed forever the contract and "organ" systems of executing the public printing in this country.

There are now employed in this immense establishment—which has been truthfully called the "largest printing office in the world"—from 1,500 to 1,800 people, who are divided among the different departments, which are elsewhere more particularly mentioned.

CAPACITY OF THE OFFICE FOR DOING GREAT QUANTITIES OF WORK.

The capacity of the office for doing vast quantities of work is illustrated by the following information, taken from the report of the Public Printer for 1880.

The first table exhibits the amount of work executed for the Executive Departments and Congress during the fiscal year ending June 30, 1878; and the second one the amount for 1879:·

1878.

	Blanks, envelopes, &c.	Pamphlets and documents.		Blank books.	Miscellaneous binding.
		Number of copies.	Number of pages.		
Executive Departments.	69,388,336	949,761	120,797	120,150	31,631
Congress............	5,569,317	17,908,510	114,100	580	12,474
Total..........	74,957,653	18,858,271	234,897	120,730	44,105

1879.

	Blanks, envelopes, &c.	Pamphlets and documents.		Blank books.	Miscellaneous binding.
		Number of copies.	Number of pages.		
Executive Departments.	98,097,933	3,451,086	119,201	246,564	16,289
Congress............	7,714,653	15,250,312	110,749	677	9,987
Total..........	105,812,586	18,701,398	229,950	247,241	26,276

The following table shows the amount of work executed during the fiscal year ending June 30, 1880 :

	Blanks, envelopes, &c.	Pamphlets and documents.		Blank books.	Miscellaneous binding.	Memorandum blocks.
		Number of copies.	Number of pages.			
Executive Departments.	122,713,897	4,331,299	122,888	340,708	27,794	311,744
Congress............	8,553,575	12,802,500	108,722	728	11,344	17,265
Total..........	131,267,472	17,133,799	231,610	341,436	39,138	329,009

As an evidence of the increase of the work in the office, the number of blanks printed during the fiscal year ending June 30, 1879, exceeded those printed during the previous year by 30,854,933, and the blank books by 126,511 ; and the increase of blanks printed during the fiscal year ending June 30, 1880, over those printed during 1879, is 25,454,886, and of blank books 94,195. The increase of the work during the first quarter of the fiscal year 1880–'81, as shown by requisitions from the Executive Departments, exceeds that of the last fiscal year during the same time by twenty-five per cent.

The largest edition, in book form, of any publication issued from the office is that of the Agricultural Report, which for several years past has numbered 300,000 copies. The cost per copy of this volume, which usually is limited for convenience in handling to from 500 to 650 pages, is about forty-five or fifty cents. Of course, in the way of blanks, orders are received for millions of copies at a time. As an example in this particular may be mentioned the money-order blanks. Nearly every person, at some time, has had occasion to fill out a "money-order," or receive one and get it cashed at some post-office. There are printed about one million copies of this form every six weeks, and they are in constant, daily use at every money-order office throughout the country. Also the books required at each of these offices, specially printed, with the names inside and out, and numbered, counted, and paged. These two items are very considerable, and regularly increasing from year to year, with the growth of population and the necessary establishment of new money-order offices.

The Capitol, by its House of Representatives and Senate officers, has had printed at times as high as *four million* envelopes, supposed to be mainly for "campaign purposes."

During the Census years heretofore the number of blanks called for has been enormous—upwards of *twelve* or *fourteen* millions—but during the last year the system has been somewhat changed, and the edition is smaller in actual blanks.

When it is remembered that every Custom House, Land Office, Internal Revenue Office, Pension Agency, Post-Office, Treasury Branch Office, War, Navy, Consular and Diplomatic Office relating to the service of Uncle Sam has its sprinkling of, not only blanks, but expensive books and pamphlets, furnished and bound here, some idea may be formed of the ponderous and perpetual labor involved, and the untold material consumed every day and year.

PRINTING FOR THE EXECUTIVE DEPARTMENTS.

The printing for the Executive Departments was transferred to the Government Printing Office on the 3d of March, 1861. Immediately previous to that time it was done by the printer to the Senate. In July, 1869, under the law of Congress to that effect, the Commissioner of Customs transferred to the office the printing and binding for all the Custom Houses of the United States. This work had been done previously by private printing offices in the several localities where the customs were collected, and the transfer suddenly precipitated a large additional amount of business upon the office. For instance, during the first month after this change, orders were received for 4,416 blank books, printed and plain, of all sizes, from cap to imperial, and for

1,510,300 blanks, of all sizes in use, for the Customs service. About this period also the Post-Office Department concentrated its entire printing and binding in the office, which, with the Customs work, increased the item of blank-book binding alone at least 100 per cent. over any previous period in the history of the office.

CHAPTER V.

THE PRINTING DEPARTMENT.

DOCUMENT ROOM.

THE office of the Foreman of Printing is located in the east end of the Document Room.

The Foreman of Printing has a general supervision, under the law, over all the different branches of the office in which the printing is done, and, upon the verbal or written request of the Assistant Foremen in charge of the different divisions, makes requisitions upon the Public Printer for all material and supplies required in the execution of the work. It is also his duty to make a monthly report to the Public Printer, of the number of hands employed, and the amount and character of the work performed.

In his office are kept, in separate books, under proper headings, all the work (done in the Document Room) received from the Executive Departments, the Courts, and from both houses of Congress. From the office of the Chief Clerk "jackets" are sent to the Foreman of Printing, with the manuscript of each job or volume, the jacket being the voucher upon which the Foreman performs the work. Upon the receipt of the manuscript, the Foreman of Printing places it in the hands of copy-preparers, who, after numbering each sheet in the order in which it is to be put in type, mark the different kinds of type in which it is to be set, indicating also whether the volume is to be in octavo, or quarto, or any of the other numerous sizes in which books are printed in the establishment. The manuscript is then transferred to the Assistant Foreman of Printing, who has immediate charge of the mechanical branch of the work in the Document Room, and by him is parceled out to the compositors.

The current printing for Congress is sent directly to the Foreman of Printing by the Printing Clerks of the Senate and House of Representatives, during the sessions of Congress, the executive and miscellaneous documents being numbered in separate series at the Foreman's Office, and entered in a book kept for that purpose. The reports of committees and the bills and resolutions are numbered by the Printing Clerks at the Capitol.

During the Forty-sixth Congress 518 executive and 294 miscellaneous documents, 3,164 reports of committees, and 597 laws, aggregating 81,348 pages, and over 9,000 bills and resolutions, which would probably number 36,000 pages more, in addition to the unusually large amount of miscellaneous printing for the use of the committees of the two houses of Congress and the Departments, were received and recorded in the Foreman's Office. Jackets for all the Congressional printing, of whatever nature, are here prepared.

The second floor of the main building, including the addition of 1865, is known as the Document Room. It is 303 feet long, 243 feet of which is 60 feet wide, and 60 feet 76 feet wide.

The stands for compositors are arranged on the north and south sides of the room, and the imposing-stones, make-up stands, galley racks, and cabinets, and the many other appurtenances which are necessary in a large office, occupy the center of the floor. Two hundred and fifty to three hundred compositors, which is about the average number employed, can be accommodated here, in addition to the floor-hands, makers-up, and laborers.

When the office was purchased in 1860, this room contained 93 double stands for compositors' cases, 349 pairs of cases, 19 imposing-stones, 108 chases, 41,300 pounds of type of various kinds, and 335 galleys, mostly wooden, and 2 small proof-presses. There are now in constant use 202 double stands, 2,400 pairs of cases, 30 imposing-stones, more than 200,000 pounds of type, besides about 150 fonts of type used for title-pages and headings, 400 chases of all sizes, 6 proof-presses, including three 2½ by 6 feet, and one Washington press, 24 by 38, and about 20 cabinets for extra type and cases.

At the present time (March, 1881), there are employed here, exclusive of the proof-reading corps, which occupies a room immediately adjoining, about three hundred compositors, makers-up, floor-hands, and laborers, including three female compositors and about thirty apprentices.

The composition for all the scientific works published by the Government—which are not only yearly increasing in number, but in the complexity of their preparation—is done in this room. This work embraces all the text-books, or books of instruction, and annual and other reports of the various bureaus of the several Executive Departments, the quarto and annual reports of the geological and geographical surveys of the Territories, all the executive and miscellaneous documents, and the reports of the committees, and the bills and resolutions for both houses of Congress, as well as the thousands of pages of testimony taken by investigating committees, and, with very few exceptions (which are elsewhere stated), all the publications in book form of every branch or bureau or Department of the Government both in and out of Washington.

The composition and proof-reading and general typographical appearance of the Government Printing Office publications—which here have their form and shape and style determined—have attracted the attention of many master-printers and scientific men at home and abroad, and received from them unstinted praise. The "Narrative of the Polaris," and "Hall's Second Arctic Expedition," Clarence King's first volume of the Surveys of the 40th Parallel, and the Paris Exposition Reports, in five volumes, all recent publications, are models of the printer's art in typography, and have been much sought after by scientific and literary people.

The amount of composition performed in the Document Room in the course of a year is simply enormous; the regular monthly average is about 35,000,000 ems, printers' measurement, giving a yearly total of 420,000,000 ems, which, if paid for by the piece, would amount to over $200,000 for composition alone in the Document Room.

PIECE DEPARTMENT.

On the same floor, and forming part of the Document Room, is the Piece Department, in charge of a maker-up, in which are employed some 60 to 80 compositors, engaged principally upon work for the Supreme Court, the Court of Claims, etc. Some of the more expert compositors in the Piece Department earn from $75 to $100 per month. Their constant employment, however, is much more uncertain than that of their more favored brethren in other portions of the office. The Court work is always required at the earliest possible moment, and when the money is exhausted, the force is relegated to private life, and sometimes this enforced idleness lasts for two and three months in the year.

PROOF ROOM.

To the proof-reader more than to any other single individual is the author of a work indebted for the good or bad appreciation of his production. He is unbiased and unprejudiced, and reads the book with an eye only to its perfection. If he is competent and worthy of his calling, he is as unsparing in his silent criticisms as he is nimble with his pencil. He does not stop to criticise it for its statements of facts or fancy—although his constant reading may often enable him to correct the former and ornament the latter—but only for the beauty and symmetry of the language used, and for its correct orthography and grammar. The class of matter passing through a large establishment like the Government Printing Office necessarily embraces treatises upon all the known sciences, and involves a knowledge, for its proper production, of all the modern and dead languages. It is not an uncommon occurrence for the proof-readers in the office to correct the quotations of authors in the ancient and modern languages, and yet I venture to assert that not one in the whole corps has ever had the advantage of a collegiate or classical education. The French, the German, and the Latin tongues are cleverly handled by several of the workmen in the Proof Room, and all their information on these subjects has been acquired while serving at the printing business. "Influence," as the term is understood in Washington, cannot be permitted to exercise its wonted avoirdupois in the Proof Room, where men must be selected solely for their fitness.

There are now in process of printing some highly scientific and typographically difficult works, one dictionary of the Indian language —every word of which is more outrageous to the English tongue than the most outlandish of Russian proper names—and four catalogues of different Government libraries. One of these latter, and the most herculean task of all, is the Index Catalogue of the Library of the Surgeon-General's Office, U. S. A., embracing, as it does, the whole field of medicine and medical literature, by author and subject, from most remote times. A peculiar and truly ingenious system of abbreviation of titles of medical publications has been devised for this work, which it is proposed to extend to all other fields of science, including publications in all the languages. The work upon this catalogue, one volume of which has recently been issued, has received the praise of some of the best scholars for its perfect production, and has excited the admiration of all who have examined its neat and tasteful typographical appearance. To the medical profession it is simply invaluable.

Webster's Dictionary is the standard in the office. The authors of Government publications come from all sections of the country. They are professional and scientific men, highly educated, and their wishes in orthographical matters are, of course, entitled to great weight. Several years ago, when the matter was under consideration by the Public Printer, the decided preference expressed by the great majority of those having business with the office as authors, readers, etc., in favor of Webster's Dictionary, led him to select it as the standard; and thus it became, and still is, the preferred authority in the Government Printing Office in all matters of orthography, definition, etymology, pronunciation, and general information.

The Proof Room is on the second floor, communicating directly with the Document Room and Foreman's Office. In it are employed from ten to twelve proof-readers who read by copy, six to eight silent or second readers, two preparers of copy, three revisers, a copy-holder to each of the first readers, and one messenger, all under the supervision of a chief, himself a proof-reader. Almost every kind of work excepting the *Congressional Record*, the blank work, and the weekly issue of patents, is read in this room.

A record is kept of all work done, of whatever nature, giving the number of pages, the time when read, and by whom, and the final disposition of the proof and copy.

From the commencement of the First Session of the Forty-sixth Congress to the 4th of March, 1881, a period of about two years, there were read and revised in this room of Congressional documents, including the annual reports of the Executive Departments, but excluding the laws, more than 60,000 printed pages of matter for the House of Representatives, and more than 35,000 for the Senate, covering over 350,000 folios of manuscript copy. In the same time the current work for the Departments and the courts was done, and will equal in number of pages and folios of manuscript the Congressional work above cited.

Some of the readers employed here have been engaged in the Government printing for a great number of years; two of them for forty years; one for thirty-four years; three for about twenty-one years, and the others from ten to fourteen years each.

JOB ROOM (EXECUTIVE PRINTING).

The Job Room occupies part of the new fire-proof wing erected in 1879, and is 86 feet 6 inches long by 53 feet 8 inches wide, with a ceiling 13 feet high.

In 1860, the Job Room was quite an insignificant affair as compared with the Job Room of to-day. The only blank work then done for the Government was for the use of the immediate Departments here in Washington. The blank printing for the different branches of the Departments located outside of the Capital City was executed in private printing offices where these branches were located.

The inventory of the office, taken at the time of its transfer to the Government, shows that the material then on hand consisted of about 100 fonts of type, 224 cases, 80 chases of all sizes, 4 imposing-stones, and 25 composing-sticks. These have been increased and replenished from time to time, until there are now in use 448 fonts of type, 781 cases, about 1,200 chases of all sizes, 14 imposing-stones, 240 composing-sticks, 1 Washington hand press, used only for taking proofs, and 1 Degener press for small, hurried work.

The work performed in this department is in part as follows: The composition on blank books, the blank forms, comprising bonds, contracts, pay-rolls, vouchers, schedules, circulars, letter-heads, envelopes, specifications, and, in fact, all species of job printing (excepting that executed at the branch offices at the Treasury, Interior, and Navy Departments), for all the Departments in Washington, the Smithsonian Institution, and for all the post-offices, custom-houses, pension agencies, mints, the railway mail service, signal offices, etc., in all the States and Territories in the United States, and all the blanks, blank books, etc., used by diplomatic and consular officers of the United States, wherever located. The volumes of the Medical and Surgical History of the Rebellion, already printed, and those now in press, as well as the Atlantic and Pacific Coast Pilot, are also done here. These two publications are very elaborate and expensive works, requiring great skill and care in their execution, and have been in course of publication for several years.

The Job Room has on hand, ready for press at any time, without composition, about 18,000 electrotype and stereotype plates of standing forms (forms that are rarely, if ever, changed, except as to dates), of blanks for the Departments.

For the class of work required, it is a most complete and well-managed branch of this great establishment.

A fine corps of workmen is employed in the Job Room. A majority of them have been engaged in the composition of blanks and blank books ever since the organization of the office as a Government institution. Their skill is well known, and will compare favorably with that of any similar class of workmen employed in any office in the country. The work turned out is of the highest order, and has received frequent commendations from competent critics.

PATENT OFFICE SPECIFICATION ROOM.

The total annual receipts of the Patent Office for 1837 were only $33,506.98, but in 1880 they had increased to $749,685.32, and this amount has never been exceeded except in 1866, when they were $757,987.65. The printing for the Patent Office naturally increased with the business of that office. Up to October—I believe the exact date was 13th—1868, the printing of the specifications, etc., was done at a private printing establishment in Washington, under the direction of the Patent Office authorities, and paid for out of the funds of the Patent Office. At that time, however, under the law, it was transferred to the Government Printing Office, and has since continued to be executed there.

The law of January 11, 1871, abolished the publication of the annual mechanical report of the Patent Office, and substituted therefor a weekly report of specifications, with photolithographic illustrations, and in this form copies were printed, photolithographed and bound from the first day of July, 1871. These volumes, which are small quartos, containing from 1,000 to 1,200 pages each, were bound in a strong and expensive manner, and were deposited in the Capital of every State and Territory, in the Clerk's Office of the District Court of each judicial district of the United States—except where such offices are located in State or Territorial Capitals—and in the Library of Congress, that they may be used as evidence in the prosecution and adjudication of patent cases before the United States Courts.

At a little later period, the specifications and illustrations were bound monthly instead of weekly, and this is the custom now pursued, and the system has greatly reduced the expense of binding.

The printing and reprinting of specifications of patents issued prior to November 27, 1866, and reprinting of many of those issued subsequent to that date, has been progressing, and during the past year about 1,000 per month have been executed in the Specification Room, in addition to the regular average issue of 1,200 new specifications monthly, to keep up with the current business of the Patent Office. These old specifications, with the regular issues, represent more than 52,000 pages of large quarto matter turned out of this room in the past year.

In the Specification Room about 70 or 80 of the most rapid type-setters in the office are employed during the greater part of the year, and the average amount of work executed weekly is something in excess of 500 pages quarto, and a monthly volume of specifications of from 1,500 to 2,000 pages, with 350 to 450 pages of photolithographic illustrations. In addition, the Patent Office Gazette, a weekly publication containing the decisions of the Commissioner and the Assistant Commissioner of Patents and of the Courts in patent cases, with the official orders and rulings of the Department, a list of the patents and patentees, etc.—500 copies of which are bound—is also printed in the Specification Room.

The compositors employed in this room are paid for their labor by the piece—which, by the way, I believe to be the only correct system of discharging obligations for the composition of type—and, as a result, there is less jar and dissatisfaction among these compositors than in any other single branch of the establishment. It requires long experience upon the part of both compositors and proof-readers to properly execute this work, owing to the numerous technical and scientific terms used, and the perfection required in the production of the typography of the specifications, as a very slight error frequently necessitates the reprinting. As these specifications are a source of revenue to the Patent Office, the prompt and correct execution of the work is a very great consideration to the Patent Office authorities and to inventors.

The material, etc., in this room consists of about 10,000 pounds of long primer type, 3,000 pounds of nonpareil, and 10 or 12 fonts of types for title-pages, headings, etc., about 100 pairs of cases, 11 imposing-stones, and the usual complement of other auxiliaries that are comprised in the furnishing of a complete printing office.

PRESS ROOM.

Next to the steam-engine, the machine that has contributed most to the world's material progress is the printing press. No other machine can compare with it in contributing to the enlightenment of mankind. From the rude and simple press upon which Dr. Franklin learned his trade, to the marvelous printing presses of the present day, the best talent and most consummate mechanical skill have been diligently employed in bringing the printing machine to its highest perfection. Several years ago it was believed that the very acme of rapidity and completeness had been attained ; but later still, more rapid and more complete printing presses were brought out and placed in operation. Without entering into a history of the progress of printing presses, we may take for comparison the capacities of the Hoe Presses of different eras. The single-cylinder Hoe Press of 1843 printed 1,200 papers, on one side, per hour ; the double-cylinder Hoe Press of 1853 printed 2,500 to 3,000 papers, on one side, per hour ; the four-cylinder Hoe Press of 1858 printed 8,000 to 10,000 papers, on one side, per hour ; the eight-cylinder Hoe Press of 1863 printed 16,000 to 22,000 papers, on one side, per hour ; the Hoe Double-Web Perfecting Press prints, cuts, pastes, and folds 30,000 *papers, on both sides, per hour !*

To the majority of visitors the Press Room is considered the most interesting place in the office. The clank and clatter of sixty ponderous machines, with the whirr and buzz of running wheels, and the hurrying to and fro of an army of workmen and workwomen, give to the Press Room an air of bustle and business which is not perceptible in the other departments of the office. The perfect mechanism necessary in a printing press, and the deliberate and steady way in which all presses "go about their business," is to all people a source of wonder and delight. Here every style of press is seen : from the small Allen Press, upon which are printed the envelopes used by the President of the United States in sending messages to disappointed office-seekers, to the huge Bullock Press, the triumph of mechanism as applied to printing presses, capable of producing 240 impressions every minute.

The Bullock Press. (*Fig. 1.*)—This press is the principal attraction to visitors in the Press Room. It was purchased by the late Cornelius Wendell, in 1866, when Congressional Printer, at a cost of $25,000. It was invented by William Bullock, of Philadelphia ; and the pro-

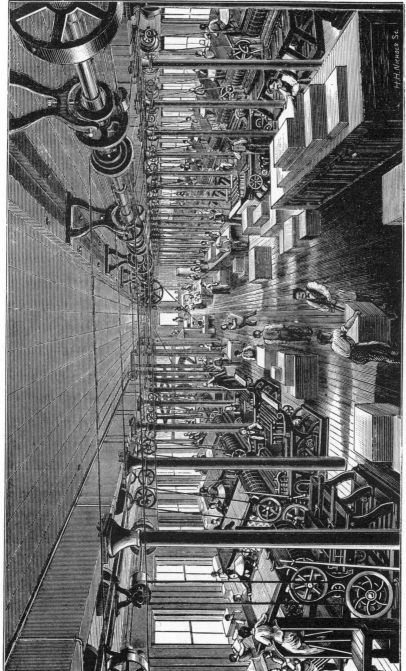

PRINTING DEPARTMENT—Main Press Room.

H. H. NICHOLS Sc.

duction of one of these presses was the direct cause of his death, as it is said that while superintending its construction he met with an accident which terminated fatally. It is of course a self-feeder, and its capacity is twelve thousand per hour ; or, counting both sides, at the rate of twenty-four thousand impressions. From the report of Dr. F. A. P. Barnard, United States Commissioner to the Paris Exposition of 1867, we quote the following concerning this press :

"The most remarkable, however, of all printing presses hitherto invented, is one which was not present in the Exposition, and which was unknown to the reporter until after the preparation of the notices had been completed, and after his return to this country. This is the 'Bullock Press,' so named from the inventor, the late William Bullock, of Philadelphia. Like the Hoe Press, it carries the forms upon the cylinder, but it differs from that press in requiring no attendants to feed it, and in delivering the sheets printed on both sides. It is a great improvement also, realized in this press, that the sheets are delivered silently, the noisy racks of the Hoe Press being wholly dispensed with.

"The substitution of an automatic system of feeding for hand-feeding, which is one of the greatest economical advantages of this press, has been effected by introducing the paper into the machine, after it has been subjected to a moistening operation by passing through a shower of fine spray, in the form of an endless roll. A single roll will contain several thousand sheets, and the printing operation, including the cutting of the paper into proper lengths, will proceed uninterruptedly until the roll is exhausted.''

In the following extract from the *Scientific American* of December 7, 1867, the advantages of this press are more fully set forth :

"The operation is very simple. The roll of paper having been mounted in its place, the machinery is started, unwinds the paper, cuts off the required size, prints it on both sides at one operation, counts the number of sheets, and deposits them on the delivery board, at the rate of eight thousand to fourteen thousand per hour, or, counting both sides, at the rate of sixteen thousand to twenty-eight thousand impressions. The labor is only that of placing the rolls on the press and removing the printed paper, which ordinary hands can do.

"We have seen some most excellent book-printing done on the Bullock machines which are at work in the Government Office in Washington. They are also employed in some of the prominent newspaper offices in Philadelphia and New York. At the *Sun* office in this city (New York) the Bullock Presses have been in use for a long time in turning out the immense daily edition of that paper. Two more presses, the same kind, but of an enlarged and superior pattern, are now being introduced there.''

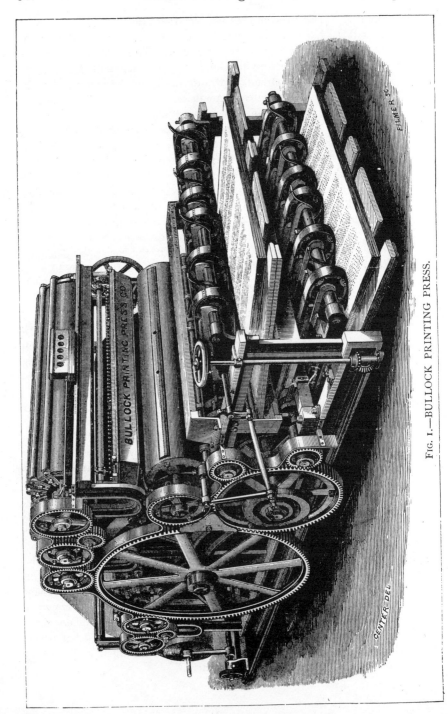

Fig. 1.—BULLOCK PRINTING PRESS.

When the Government bought the office, the Press Room contained four drum cylinder presses and twenty-four Adams Presses, and the work was not sufficient to keep these presses running more than about eight months in the year. The job or Department work was all done on six slow presses. Now the Department work, which consists mainly of blanks for the post-offices, the revenue offices, the custom-houses, etc., requires on an average the constant use of thirty fast presses, running all the year round. The presses now do about the same amount of work in eight hours that presses of the same speed did in ten; the difference being in the improved manner of doing the work, and the system in which it is done. The greatest saving of time is in the improvement of rollers, the old-style roller requiring to be taken from the presses from three to four times each day, at a loss of from twenty to thirty minutes each time, whereas now the improved rollers —costing no more—are not removed from the press more than once in six days.

The Bullock Press runs about nine months in the year, and completes about 500,000 volumes. All publications of 20,000 or over are printed on this press.

Often, even now, with the improved machinery (some doing three times the work of the old-style presses) and the increase in the number of presses, the Press Room is compelled to run two sets of hands, requiring the machinery to be in motion sixteen out of the twenty-four hours, to keep up with the demands made upon the room.

Any one at all familiar with the Government printing for the past twenty or twenty-five years will not only notice the great increase in the quantity, but will be struck with the vast improvement in the quality of the work in every branch. Under the old or contract system, the work in the Press Room was all done by men and boys; but for the past fifteen or twenty years women have taken the place of boys altogether, and they are found to be much more attentive to their work, and give greater satisfaction, and endure the labor with less complaint.

If the printing continues to increase in the same ratio for the next twenty as it has in the past twenty years, it will require a room with double the capacity of the present one to do the press-work for Uncle Sam.

The Press Room occupies 260 feet of the first floor of the main building and contains sixty power-presses, as follows:

1 Bullock Perfecting Press.
1 Allen Patent Envelope Press.
3 Hoe Cap Cylinder Presses.
6 Hoe Super-Royal Cylinder Presses.

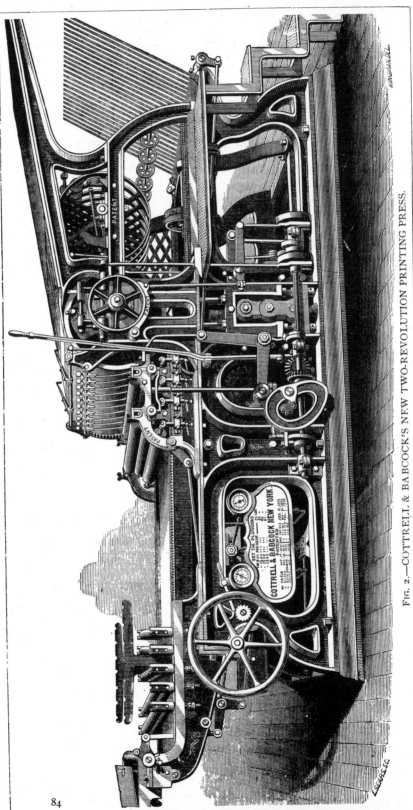

Fig. 2.—COTTRELL & BABCOCK'S NEW TWO-REVOLUTION PRINTING PRESS.

84

19 Hoe Double Medium Cylinder Presses.
12 Adams Double Medium Bed and Platen Presses.
4 Adams Medium Bed and Platen Presses.
3 Cottrell & Babcock Two-Revolution Cylinder Presses.
3 Cottrell & Babcock Cap Cylinder Presses.
1 Cottrell & Babcock Four-Roller Cylinder Press.
7 Cottrell & Babcock Double Medium Cylinder Presses.
1 Low-pressure 150-horse-power Engine.

Outside the Press Room, in the court, are the boilers that supply

FIG. 3.—R. HOE & CO.'S CYLINDER PRINTING PRESS.

the motive power to run the presses and also all the other machinery, and to heat the building in winter. There are two boilers, each of 60-horse-power. During the sessions of Congress, these boilers are never allowed to cool; they are in use from daylight to dark, and from night until morning. The engine of 150-horse-power, low pressure, is located inside the Press Room, on the south side.

The number of hands employed in the Press Room is as follows: 1 Foreman, 1 Assistant, 1 Register, 1 Messenger, 37 pressmen, 5 apprentices, 54 laborers, paper wetters, etc., and 106 lady feeders.

DRY-PRESS ROOM.

The Dry-Press Room, which is on the same floor with the Press Room, and is under the management of a person designated as superintendent, has in use one Gill Calendering Machine, four hydraulic and two standing presses, and gives employment, in the busy season, to about 25 men and sheet boys.

In the Dry-Press Room is located the clerk charged with the delivery of the blanks, envelopes, court records, opinions, and briefs, and the accounting for the same. Job work received from the Press Room is here assorted. That portion requiring ruling is sent to the Bindery, on the third floor; that needing folding, or gathering, or pasting, or counting, to the Folding Room, on the fourth floor; that to be delivered is counted, tied in packages, and forwarded by wagons to the various Departments of the Government, their bureaus and outlying offices. Receipts and bills are here made out, taken and rendered for every job, and filed away at the close of each day's work. There was

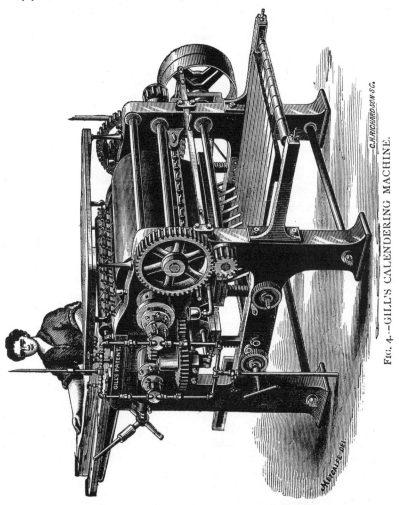

FIG. 4.—GILL'S CALENDERING MACHINE.

an average delivery of about 340,000 blanks, envelopes, etc., *per day*, during the past year, and the number is steadily increasing. Employed upon this general work are two cutters and their cutting machines, four laborers, counting, arranging, and tying up, and the receipt and bill clerk.

MACHINERY.

Fig. 1. *The Bullock Press.*—This press is fully described elsewhere in this chapter.

Fig. 2. *Cottrell & Babcock's New Two-Revolution Cylinder Press.*— Three of these presses are now in use in the Government Printing Office. These presses, which are considered superior to any other press in the office, were manufactured expressly for its use, and were designed especially for printing the *Congressional Record.* They will accommodate 32 pages of ordinary octavo matter, or 16 pages of the *Record*, and are, perhaps, the most useful, durable, and beautiful presses ever built. The great advantage of these machines is the speed and facility with which they can be handled for all kinds of work. The impression among printers, heretofore, has been that a small cylinder was very destructive to type, or at least more so than large drums; but the success that has attended the introduction of Stop Cylinders has completely removed that impression, and has created a demand for Two-Revolution presses that promises in time to drive large drums, above certain sizes, entirely out of the market. In these times of low prices, and consequently small profits, speed combined with good work is an advantage, the value of which cannot be overestimated.

This press, as its name indicates, revolves twice: first, in a raised position to clear the form; the second time, in contact with the form while giving the impression. The largest illustrated forms are printed at a speed of from 1,800 to 2,000 per hour, with perfect safety. Indeed, the speed is limited only by the capacity of the feeder. This press is capable of doing the finest quality of illustrated and color work, in the highest style of the art, and has proved to be the most economical and profitable press yet introduced.

In addition to the above, there are in use in the Government Printing Office three Cap Cylinder, one Four-Roller, and seven Double Medium Cylinder presses, manufactured by Cottrell & Babcock (now C. B. Cottrell & Co.).

Fig. 3 is a small illustration of R. Hoe & Co.'s Cylinder Presses, and represents their super-royal and double medium cylinders—twenty-five of which are in use in the Government Printing Office.

Fig. 4.—*Gill's Hot Rolling or Calendering Machine.*—This is a new machine for the printing office, which will instantaneously dry and press sheets wet from the press, imparting at the same time a fine gloss to the work, thus dispensing with the old system of dry-pressing. It is stated that the claims of this machine have been fully sustained by experience; and that, with the aid of a feeder and a taker-off, from 1,200 to 1,500 sheets, direct from the printing machine, can be dried and hot-rolled in an hour—an advantage not to be at present otherwise obtained. The main features of this machine are a pair of highly-finished chilled metal rollers, and an apparatus for cleaning or taking away the set-off. The rollers are fitted parallel to each other in a frame, and steam is introduced through the axles.

The danger of set-off is obviated by a cleaning apparatus, consisting of a trough under each roller, filled with a solution of alkali, and in which are placed long pads made of strong cloth, containing small pieces of sponge, which press closely to the surface of the roller as it revolves. By these means, ink and other substances calculated to soil the paper are effectually removed. Behind the pads is fitted a rubber scraper, which cleans off any moisture left on the rollers, so that when these are in a position to receive the sheet which follows, they are perfectly clean and free from set-off.

The sheets pass between two highly-polished steel cylinders, which are heated by steam introduced through the axles; and when they leave the cylinders, are carried by means of endless tapes underneath to the taking-off board, etc.

FOLDING ROOM.

Up to 1871, the Folding Room occupied 60 by 200 feet of the fourth floor. In the fall of that year, after the completion of the wing fronting on North Capitol street, additional space to the extent of 60 by 113 feet was added; and again, in 1879, 60 by 60 feet more was allotted to its use; but notwithstanding these additions, the increase of work in this department has been so great that it has been found necessary, at times, to use all the available space in the halls and passages of the entire building for the storage and preservation of the work.

The pay-rolls for July, 1871, show the number of persons then employed to have been 190; while for the month of June, 1880, between 300 and 350 were employed, although the introduction of new machinery enabled the office to dispense with the services of about 100 employés in this room in that month.

In attempting to give the reader a view of this room, I shall not enter into any elaborate technical description of the different processes of treating printed matter in this establishment, as understood by the term "folding," any further than is necessary to a proper understanding of its workings; but will endeavor to show, as briefly as possible, more particularly the extent of this part of the business of the Government Printing Office.

The folding of sheets, maps, or illustrations, the pasting, gathering, collating, etc., are all separate and distinct operations, requiring special care and patience, and, in some cases, a great deal of severe labor.

PRINTING DEPARTMENT—Folding Room, H street wing.

The work is transferred by elevators from the Press Room on the first floor to the Folding Room on the fourth floor, upon trucks. Two of these elevators have a capacity of 1,500 pounds each, and one small box elevator, of about 300 pounds. They are each in charge of a man, whose duty it is to place and replace the trucks upon them, and to deliver printed matter to its proper destination in the Folding Room.

Upon the arrival of the work in the room, it is taken to the respective divisions, to be folded, etc. All large volumes, or jobs, are delivered to the regular folders, or to the folding machines, as the nature of the work demands; all bills, reports, documents, the journals of both houses of Congress, and the printing generally pertaining to the current business of Congress, are delivered to divisions specially provided for them; and all other matter, to another division. A brief description of each division will be found further on. After the work is folded, it is examined by competent employés specially designated for that purpose, whose duty it is to see that the work has been properly performed. It is then taken to the pressing machines, and after being pressed, is tied up in bundles of 500 sheets each, and thence removed to the store-room to remain until the volume is completed, when it is again placed upon the trucks and transferred to the gathering tables, where it is gathered and collated, and thence forwarded to the Bindery to be bound. Before the introduction of the Jones Pressing Machines, the work was dry-pressed before being delivered to the Folding Room. Some classes of work, however, are still subjected to pressing in the old style hydraulic presses.

In all printing establishments except the Government Printing Office, the folding constitutes a part of the binding and not the printing division of the business; but an old law (under which the binding was given out by contract) provided that the sheets should be furnished the binder in a certain condition, which involved the folding; and this law, although it invaded a long-standing custom of the trade, was duly respected, and this is still the custom under which this work is divided in this establishment.

Pasting Illustrations, Diagrams, etc.—During the year 1871, the illustrations pasted in the various documents, reports of committees, etc., amounted in round numbers to 12,000,000, and in the year 1879 to about 26,000,000, showing an increase of over 100 per cent.

Job Work.—The job work, under which head may be classed card work, printing for the Supreme Court, Court of Claims, small pamphlets, etc., for the Departments, and the blanks sent to the Folding Room, is also on the increase. In 1871, it was performed by one man and ten girls, with one small hand-power card machine. It now requires twenty-five to thirty female and two male employés, with two of the most improved card-cutting machines, and also one stripper, run by steam.

Sheet Folding.—This constitutes the principal work in this room, and is performed exclusively by girls. It is probably the most laborious of all work found in a printing office.

An average hand-folder will complete in one day about 3,000 sheets. As an Agricultural Report has in it about 11,400,000 sheets, it would require about 3,800 days' work of a single folder to put it in shape for gathering. Formerly there were from 200 to 250 girls employed on this work alone, but since the folding machines have been put in operation the number has been steadily decreasing, and now but little work of this character is done by hand. This work is all paid for by the piece.

Map Folding.—This requires experienced hands, and is performed by girls. Although not so laborious as ordinary folding, the nature of the work, and the various styles in which it must be done, require the constant attention of the operator. This class of work is also largely on the increase; the number of girls employed has in the last few years increased from 12 to 40.

Pasting.—This work, though somewhat tedious, is perhaps less laborious than folding. To be properly done, the operators should not only be experienced in sheet but also in map folding, as it requires judgment to so arrange the illustrations that after they are pasted in the proper places they will not be cut in trimming the edges of the book. This class of work is steadily on the increase.

Gathering.—This branch of the business has kept pace with the increase in the other departments of the Folding Room. A few years ago twelve girls performed all of this work, but now about thirty are engaged in it.

Congressional Work : Documents, Bills, Laws, etc.—In this division are gathered, stitched, and trimmed all executive and miscellaneous documents, reports of committees, the journals of both houses of Congress, etc. In 1870, nine girls and two men were employed at this work, but now it requires thirty-three of the former and five of the latter, and then often a call is made upon the other divisions for assistance.

To properly perform this work none but first-class hands, who are well versed in all the various kind of labor of the Folding Room, are employed. All documents, reports, bills, resolutions, laws, and work required for the immediate use of both houses of Congress while in session (except the Congressional Record), are here folded, pasted, gathered, stitched, trimmed, counted, and delivered according to law.

The following comparative statements for 1870 and 1880 will show the increase in this branch in ten years:

1870.—41ST CONGRESS, 2D SESSION.

		No. of Copies.
1,135	Documents, Reports, etc., 1,600 copies each	1,816,000
2,648	Bills, Resolutions, etc., 750 copies each	1,986,000
459	Laws, 1,750 copies each	803,250
4,242		4,605,250

1880.—46TH CONGRESS, 2D SESSION.

		No. of Copies.
2,967	Documents, Reports, etc., 1,900 copies each	5,637,300
5,983	Bills, Resolutions, etc., 925 copies each	5,534,275
329	Laws, 1,620 copies each	532,980
9,279		11,704,555

Of the above documents, etc., printed for the Second Session of the Forty-first Congress (1870), all were delivered before the adjournment except 1,135,000 copies, which after the close of the session were gathered in volumes of about 1,000 pages each, and, after indexes were supplied, were bound, and are known as the "reserve documents." The volumes for that session numbered 32, making 34,661 books, aggregating about 34,661,000 pages.

Of those printed for the Second Session of the Forty-sixth Congress, there were delivered in pamphlet form to both houses of Congress, during the session, 2,551,620 copies of documents and reports, 5,534,275 copies of bills and resolutions, and 532,980 copies of laws, making a total of 8,618,875 copies, leaving on hand 3,085,680 copies to be gathered and bound as the "reserve documents." During the year 1880 the number of volumes was 60, making 67,626 books, containing not less than 67,626,000 pages. After these volumes are gathered and collated, they are turned over to the Bindery to be bound. The work gotten out during the session, as above described, is passed over to what might properly be called the accounting branch of this division, and is there counted off into ten different lots, properly labeled, etc. File copies of all these documents, bills, etc., are kept, properly numbered, and stored away.

The employés in this division are frequently required to report for duty at 7 a. m. during the sessions of Congress, and continue at work, with scarcely any intermission, until late at night, and, if the work should demand it, all night, and on Sundays also, as the bills, etc., needed by both houses of Congress must be delivered by twelve o'clock each day. The following will show the amount of matter delivered in a single day in this department of the Folding Room:

No. of Copies.

150 Bills, 925 copies each	138,750
75 Documents, Reports, etc., 860 copies each	64,500
Total	203,250

When it is remembered that these bills, documents, etc., run all the way from two to fifteen hundred pages each, it can easily be seen what expedition and system must be observed in the performance of this work.

The Congressional Record.—The printing of the debates or proceedings of Congress was transferred to this office, as elsewhere mentioned, March 4, 1873. The *Record* is published in two styles, the Daily and the Bound or Book Edition. The Public Printer, under the law, is required to furnish each Senator, Member, and Delegate in Congress a certain number of copies, either of the daily or bound edition, and may sell copies to any one, at a certain price; also to cause the same to be sent through the mails; and not only the members of both houses of Congress, but many people throughout the United States and the Canadas, avail themselves of this privilege.

The persons employed in the folding, gathering, collating, and wrapping the daily *Record* report for duty at three o'clock in the morning, as the *Record* must be in the early mails, and on the desks of Senators and Members by twelve o'clock each day, that the lawmakers may see in print the laws that have been enacted. and the speeches made the previous day. To accomplish this, the work must be done with the utmost system and dispatch. The employés here number fourteen girls and three men, and have in use two stitching and four quarto folding machines. During the Second Session of the Forty-sixth Congress, these employés folded, gathered, collated, stitched, and put up in the 550,000 different wrappers, 874,650 copies of the *Record*, containing in all not less than 31,677,800 pages of printed matter.

The bound *Record* is a stereotyped edition made up from the daily, with the addition of an elaborate index. The number of sheets of sixteen pages each in the bound edition for the Second Session of the Forty-sixth Congress, which were required to be folded, pressed, gathered, and collated, is estimated at 2,532,600.

Accounts.—Most of the females employed in the Folding Room are paid for their labor by the piece. To secure accuracy in the accounts, a system of verification is necessary. At 3 p. m. each day a memorandum of the work performed is entered upon day books, and the amount earned by each person is set opposite her name. This memorandum, by eight o'clock the next morning, is posted in con-

PRINTING DEPARTMENT—Folding Room, North Capitol street wing.

spicuous places, so that each can see that her account is properly made out. If any errors occur they are readily detected, and their nature easily ascertained by a reference to the work performed. After being allowed to remain in these places a sufficient time, the accounts are transferred to a regular time-book. At the end of each month these accounts are added up, and, after examination by the superintendent in charge of the room, are turned over to the paymaster and by him paid.

MACHINERY.

Figs. 5 *and* 6.—Until quite recently all the folding in the Government Printing Office was done by hand; but the office has been supplied, during the past eighteen months, with Chambers Brothers' Book

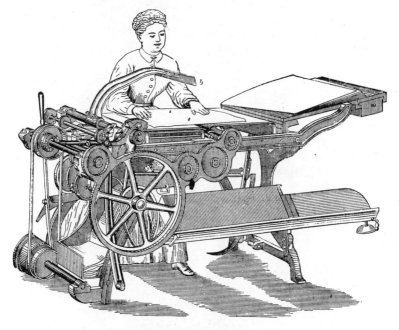

FIG. 5.—CHAMBERS' BOOK FOLDING MACHINE.

Folding Machines. Figs. 5 and 6 give a correct view of these machines. To understand their operation, it must be borne in mind that each sheet of the kind upon which this book is printed is doubled at the middle, that this doubled sheet is next folded through its center, and that this doubly-folded sheet is again doubled together. There are thus three folds to each sheet, and each of these must be exactly in its right place, or the whole book will be irregular in shape. Externally the Folding Machine presents the appearance of a table, the lid divided at the center into two parts. The operator lays the sheet upon the table in such a way that two small pointers pass through two holes in the sheet. These holes were made by two steel pointers in the press when the sheet was printed. These point holes serve as guides in several cases, which we have not thought necessary to enumerate. The elevated knife, which appears in the illustration, now comes down on

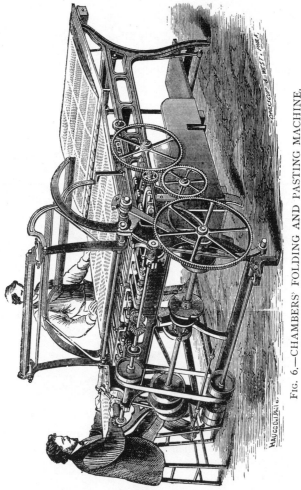

FIG. 6.—CHAMBERS' FOLDING AND PASTING MACHINE.

the sheet over the line of the first fold, and forces it between two rollers, which compress the doubling. This completes the first fold. A second and third knife and pair of rollers, hidden under the cover of the machine, make the second and third folds in the same manner ;

and the triply-folded sheet is dropped into a receptacle at the bottom of the machine. This is the work of the machine for folding an octavo sheet. The folding and pasting machines used in the Government Printing Office on speeches, etc., in addition to folding the sheets as described above, also paste the leaves together at the back, thus saving the expense of stitching, and producing, at one operation and handling of the sheet, a neatly-bound pamphlet ready for trimming and distribution. There are twenty-one octavo and nine quarto machines now in use in the Government Printing Office. When good feeders are engaged at the machines, the capacity of the former is, in eight hours, 10,000 to 11,000 sheets, and of the latter, from 8,000 to 9,000.

Fig. 7. *Jones' Hydraulic Sheet Pressing Machine* is considered one of the most valuable of its kind in the establishment. The machine presses the sheets after they are folded; and instead of the former un-

FIG. 7.—JONES' HYDRAULIC SHEET PRESSING MACHINE.

sightly heaps of loose signatures scattered around the Folding Room, they appear now in neatly tied, compact bundles, of convenient size and shape for handling and storage.

These machines were first introduced in this office during the year 1879. One of the octavo size will press, in eight hours, 50,000 sheets, and one of the quarto machines 40,000. They are also used in pressing books, which, before their introduction in the Government Printing Office, was done on "smashing" machines in the Bindery. Under the old mode of pressing, about half a dozen sheets were placed between fuller boards, and after the press was filled, hydraulic pressure was applied, and allowed to remain for hours. These machines do away with the handling of many millions of sheets alone, and the immense saving of the present mode over the old system is apparent.

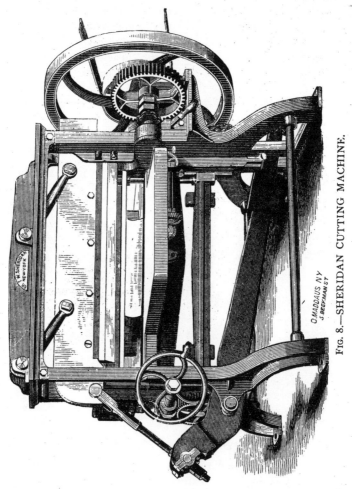

FIG. 8.—SHERIDAN CUTTING MACHINE.

There are in use in the Folding Room six octavo machines, and one quarto machine.

Fig. 8 is a *Sheridan Cutting Machine*. It is a standard machine, and its good qualities are well known to the trade.

Fig. 9. *H. G. Thompson & Son's Pamphlet Stitching Machine.*—This machine stitches with wire pamphlets, catalogues, calendars, flat-back books, etc. The movements of the machine are automatic; it punctures, with needles, the work to be stitched, feeds the wire in the required length, cuts off the same from the staple, drives it into the holes of the book punctured for its reception, and then clinches the same. Its speed is 60 staples per minute, its range of work being from $\frac{1}{16}$ of an inch to $\frac{5}{8}$ of an inch in thickness, and the average pro-

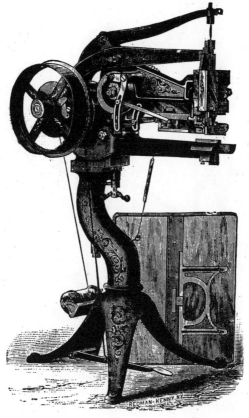

FIG. 9.—THOMPSON'S WIRE BOOK STITCHING MACHINE.

duction being 1,000 books per hour. The machine is manufactured at Milford, Conn.

Fig. 10. This is the *Novelty Pamphlet Stitching Machine*, manufactured by the same parties as Fig. 9. It is especially constructed and adapted for stitching with wire all kinds of thin pamphlets, catalogues, etc. The machine feeds the wire in the required length, cuts the same, forms the staple, is driven through the pamphlet by its own velocity, clinches the staples, the work then being carried by means of rollers. The capacity of the machine is 120 staples per minute, average production 2,000 books per hour; the range of work is from one sheet of paper to $\frac{3}{16}$ of an inch in thickness.

Fig. 11 represents S. Brown's latest improved *Rotary Cutter.* Those in the Government Printing Office have an automatic feeder, which carries the card-strip to the knives, and actuates a counting device which, when a definite number of cards have passed through the

FIG. 10.—NOVELTY WIRE BOOK STITCHING MACHINE.

machine, gives notice by sounding an alarm-bell. The cut cards are delivered from the machine either upon a platform, adjustable boxes, or automatic delivery. The knives are closely fitted on two revolving steel shafts. They come in near contact with each other, and are held firmly in place by a small set-screw.

The feeding of the card-strips to the knives with accuracy is dependent solely upon the automatic feeder, and not upon the skill of the operator. The card-board is first cut into strips by another machine, which has a wider table, and is otherwise specially adapted to this purpose. This machine is called a slitter. The one shown in the illustration is known as a cross-cutter.

The peculiar feature about the work cut on these machines is, that the cut is made on each side of the material towards the center, thus making a clean cut, without leaving a turned or feather edge on the cards.

They run light and noiseless, and will turn out more work with less power consumed than any other form of cutting machine, averaging about 100,000 cards in 8 hours to each machine.

Fig. 12. *Acme Cutting Machine.*—The Acme Paper Cutter shows the great improvement made in that class of machinery during the last decade, and is as much of an improvement over the ordinary cutter as the cylinder press is over the old hand press. It saves both time and

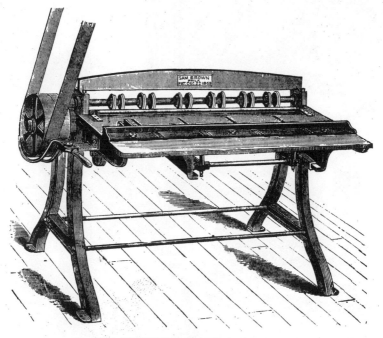

FIG. 11.—BROWN'S ROTARY CARD CUTTER.

labor, and does the work of two ordinary cutters with one operator. The automatic self-clamping is the most distinctive feature, and saves nearly one-half the time and all the hard work required in cutting paper on the old cutters. The new method of moving the gauge by a metallic band is a great improvement—it moves the gauge faster and more accurately, and admits of a correct adjustment of gauge, which is impossible to get on the old crank-and-screw method. The indicator, in connection with metallic band (which is spaced off in inches and fractions), gives the exact distance from knife edge to back gauge, saving the folding and marking of the sheet, and bringing clamp to mark—which also saves much time. The *round* cutting stick, for knife to cut on—in place of the ordinary square ones—gives fifty cutting surfaces instead of eight on square wood. The clamp is made wide, and narrow for small cutting. The machine is finely built and

FIG. 12.—REGULAR ACME CUTTER.

finished, and gives evidence of being a strong and powerful cutter—an ornament to any bindery or printing office—and is without doubt the most improved machine of its class in the world.

THE CONGRESSIONAL RECORD—THE DEBATES OF CONGRESS.

The legislative as well as the executive sessions of the Senate were held with closed doors until the Second Session of the Third Congress, with the single exception of the discussion of a contested election case of a Senator from Pennsylvania, during which the galleries were opened to the public by a special order of the Senate. On the 20th of February, 1794, the Senate adopted a resolution to the effect that after the end of that session of Congress the galleries of the Senate should be permitted to be opened while the Senate should be engaged in its legislative capacity, unless specially ordered otherwise. Of course, during these years—1789 to 1794—the proceedings of this body, preserved and now accessible, are of a very meager character.

The First Session of the First Congress convened on March 4, 1789, but not until April 6 did a quorum appear in the Senate, and in the House not until April 1, 1789.

The debates, or proceedings rather, of the House of Representatives during this period—from 1789 to 1794—were very fully reported by enterprising newspaper men, and appeared in at least two newspapers while the sessions of Congress were held in New York, and one or more while the sessions were held in Philadelphia.

The debates, it seems, however, were very inaccurately reported, or printed, and their appearance in this imperfect form soon gave rise to many complaints and much discussion in the House. In September, 1789, Mr. Burke introduced a resolution on the subject, stating "that the several persons who have published the debates of the House, in the newspapers of the city of New York, have misrepresented the debates in the most glaring manner; often distorting the arguments of the members from the true meaning; imputing to some gentlemen arguments contradictory and foreign to the subject, and which were never advanced; to others, remarks and observations never made; and in a great many instances mutilating, and not unfrequently suppressing, whole arguments upon subjects of the greatest moment, which being done within the House, at the very foot of the Speaker's chair, gave a sanction and authenticity to the publication, that reflects upon the House a ridicule and absurdity highly injurious to its privileges and dignity," and "that to misrepresent the debates of the House, whether it arises from incapacity, inattention, or partiality, has a mischievous tendency to infringe the freedom of debate, and that the House should no longer give sanction to it."

After a lengthy discussion of the resolution, which showed an overwhelming sentiment in favor of permitting a continuation of the publication of the stenographic report of the debates, the resolution was withdrawn. The reporters, however, took offense at the resolution of

Mr. Burke, and withdrew from their seats at the foot of the Speaker's chair, and located themselves in the gallery of the House, with seemingly no intention of again intruding upon the dignity of that body. The proceedings continued to appear as usual, but with many omissions, so much so as to again attract the attention of the House, and at the next session, in January, 1790, the reporters were invited back to their old seats at the Speaker's desk.

In April, 1792, a proposition was submitted to authorize a certain person to take down the debates. A committee was appointed to consider the matter, but the opposition was so strong as to prevent any further action. The House did not want to become responsible for or recognize in any official way the publication of the debates. Several attempts in the same direction were made, up to 1795, but none of them prevailed.

In January, 1796, a committee which had been appointed on the subject reported in favor of having the debates printed by authority of the House, and a proposition involving $4,000 for stenographers—of which amount the proprietors of the *Philadelphia Gazette* offered to pay $1,500—was submitted, but, without further action on the report, the committee early in February following was discharged from the further consideration of the subject.

Various propositions of a similar character were made to the House during the year 1796, but Congress resolutely refused to have anything to do with printing the debates, or involving the Government in any expense in the matter.

In December, 1797, Mr. Thomas Carpenter petitioned Congress, setting forth that he was the editor of the *American Senator*, published during the late session of Congress; that at the commencement of the session he had presented a memorial, praying its support of his work, *i. e.*, publishing the debates; that he had received assurances from numerous individual members of their patronage, etc., but that the enterprise had proved unfavorable to him; and asked for relief in the sum of $2,250.

A committee was appointed to consider the matter, but only two days later reported that they could not recommend relief; and the report was concurred in.

For the next two or three years no reference to the publication of the debates is found in the Annals of Congress; but they continued to appear regularly in a printed form, and the country is indebted for the very full reports now accessible solely to the spirit of individual or private enterprise which animated the printers of that time.

In 1800, November 17, Congress convened in Washington for the first time, and the proceedings of Congress were published in the

PRINTING DEPARTMENT—*Congressional Record Room.*

National Intelligencer, which was established October 31, 1800. The debates were very fully reported and printed in this newspaper, from the first day of the session until its close.

But we find, early in the session, a memorial from Samuel Harrison Smith and Thomas Carpenter, representing that they had undertaken to report the debates of the House, and that, contrary to their expectation, on the suggestion of inconvenience to the members, they had not received permission to occupy a situation within the bar, without which they were unable to state with fidelity the proceedings and debates, and praying the permission of the House to be admitted to the bar. The Speaker, to whom it appears applications had previously been made for seats in the bar of the House for stenographers, stated that he had been compelled to refuse the applicants the permission asked, as it would place the stenographers between the members and the Speaker, and therefore render the preservation of order impossible; that he had informed the applicants, if agreeable to them, he would assign a place in the gallery, which should be set apart for their exclusive use, etc.

After discussion by various members, the matter was referred to a select committee.

On December 9, the committee reported, in substance, "that it is not expedient that the House should take any order on the memorial presented." The discussion of the subject on this day (December 9, 1800) occupies nine columns of the *National Intelligencer*. The vote on adoption of the report of the committee resulted: yeas 45, nays 45, and was carried by the casting vote of the Speaker.

On Monday, January 12, 1801, the stenographer took his place outside the bar of the House—which he had occupied continuously since the prohibition of the Speaker—when he was waited upon by the Sergeant-at-Arms with a verbal message from the Speaker to the effect that the Speaker desired him to withdraw from the area; and the stenographer immediately withdrew, and took a position in the gallery.

On the 15th, the Sergeant-at-Arms again called upon the stenographer, by direction of the Speaker, and desired him to withdraw from the gallery.

The Speaker, Theodore Sedgwick, of Massachusetts, entertained the view that the matters before the House should not be published until after the House had acted upon them; that it was not the business of the public what was before Congress; and that it would best conserve the interests of the public and the members to keep them secret until final action had been taken.

Although the stenographer was virtually expelled from the gallery

BINDING DEPARTMENT—Sewing Room on the left and Ruling Room on the right.

of the House by the decision of the Speaker, the full proceedings of the House appeared in the *National Intelligencer,* as usual.

On the 18th of February, 1801, Mr. Davis, a member of the House, brought the matter of the expulsion of a citizen from the galleries by the Speaker before the House by a resolution, which recited that the Speaker had usurped a power not given him by the rules of the House, and had deprived a citizen of rights which were guaranteed him by the Constitution.

On February 20, the resolution was called up for action. The House, however, refused to adopt the resolution.

The debates and proceedings continued to appear as each session was held in Washington, through the enterprise of the publishers of the newspapers of the capital city, and especially of the *National Intelligencer,* up to 1822, before any other attempt was made to have the Government take charge of the matter.

In that year, however, a committee was appointed and directed to report upon the best mode of giving to the public a "full and correct statement of the debates of the House," and on the 2d of May the committee reported that they had considered the matter, and were of the opinion "that the Government of the United States being a Government which essentially depends upon public opinion, it is a consideration of the first importance that the course pursued by the immediate representatives of the people in Congress should be impartially presented to the public view," and submitted a resolution directing the Speaker to secure, during the approaching recess of Congress, proposals for reporting and publishing, from day to day, a correct account of the debates and other proceedings of the House, and submit the same to the House at the commencement of the next session. This proposition found many advocates, but the opposition—which was principally founded upon the great expense which would attend the enterprise— was too strong for the friends of the measure, and all further action was ended by a motion which prevailed—but which had previously been negatived—to lay the report and resolution upon the table.

In 1824, the publication of the Annals of Congress was commenced under the authority of Congress, and embraced the proceedings and debates of both houses from 1789 to 1824, and comprise some 42 octavo volumes. Under the title of "Register of the Debates of Congress," Gales & Seaton printed 27 additional volumes, bringing the debates down, in book form, to 1837. Subsequently the debates were published in the well-known form of the *Congressional Globe*—large quarto—and comprise 108 volumes, embracing the debates from 1837 to 1873.

Near the close of the last session of the Forty-second Congress

(March 3, 1873), a resolution was passed which provided that "until a contract for publishing the debates of Congress is made, such debates shall be printed by the Congressional Printer, under the direction of the Joint Committee on Printing." Under that authority the publication now known as the *Congressional Record* was first issued.

The Senate was called in Extra Session by the President, and convened on the 3d of March, 1873, and during that session, and on the fifth day of that month, the first number of the *Record* was printed.

Subsequently the Congressional Printer fitted up a complete office for the exclusive use of the *Record*, and the form and style of the publication now so well known to all prominent politicians was determined upon.

Since then the debates of the Forty-third, Forty-fourth, Forty-fifth, and Forty-sixth Congresses have been printed at the Government Printing Office, and for these four Congresses the printed matter aggregates more than 42,000 pages, as follows :

No. of pages in debates of Forty-third Congress	9,018
" " " " " " Forty-fourth "	10,308
" " " " " " Forty-fifth "	10,423
" " " " " " Forty-sixth "	12,500
	42,249

The concurrent resolution agreed to June 4, 1874, provides for the printing of 3,100 copies of the *Congressional Record* for the use of the Senate, and 7,250 copies for the use of the House of Representatives, either daily, as originally published, or in the revised form, as each Senator, Member, or Delegate receiving the same may elect.

During the Second Session of the Forty-sixth Congress, 3,971 copies of the *Record* were delivered to Senators and Members unbound. The number of each volume printed and bound is 6,700, aggregating 40,200 volumes, and these were delivered as follows :

Delivered to Senate folding-room	13,218
Delivered to House folding-room	25,062
Delivered to House library	600
Delivered to Library of Congress	312
Delivered to officers of the House	54
Delivered to Executive Departments, on requisition	72
Delivered to W. A. Smith, on orders from members	12
On hand	870
	40,200

In addition to the above, there are printed and sold to subscribers an average for each session of about 250 to 300 copies.

In 1878, Congress appropriated $100,000 for the purchase from the then owners and proprietors of " 25,000 bound volumes of the *Congressional Globe*, 40,000 unbound volumes of the *Congressional Globe*, 46,000 metal plates for printing the *Congressional Globe*, 24,000 composition plates for printing the *Congressional Globe*, the two-story fire-proof building situated in the rear of the *Globe* building on Pennsylvania Avenue, and the copyright for the complete work," and the law required that the property so purchased should be placed in the custody of the Public Printer, under the direction of the Joint Committee on Public Printing.

This purchase places in the control of the Government the stereotype plates of the proceedings of Congress from 1837 to 1873, in the old *Globe* form, from which it can, at any time, supply new members of Congress at a moderate expense.

RECORD COMPOSING ROOM.

The *Congressional Record* Room is located on the fourth floor of the south wing of the new extension, and is 85 by 52 feet, with a ceiling 25 feet in height in the center, and is furnished throughout in the best manner. The number of hands employed is 1 Foreman, 1 Assistant Foreman, 7 proof-readers, 3 copy-holders, 2 makers-up, 3 floor-hands, 1 messenger, 3 laborers, and about 60 to 80 compositors. This force, of course, varies somewhat during the sessions of Congress, and, with the exception of the Foreman and one laborer, is dismissed at the close of the session.

BRANCH OFFICE, TREASURY DEPARTMENT.

In June, 1869, under the law which required that all the printing and binding for the Government should thereafter be executed at the Government Printing Office in Washington, the Congressional Printer took charge of the printing material in the Treasury Department, and organized in the basement of the Treasury building a branch office. The material found in the possession of the Treasury Department consisted of four power-presses, one ruling and one cutting machine, and a quantity of type and other material necessary for a very complete printing office. The employés were one assistant foreman in charge, one proof-reader, eight compositors, two pressmen, one apprentice, one cutter and counter, four feeders, one ruler, and one laborer.

The office is under the supervision of the Public Printer, and he furnishes the materials, employs the hands, and settles the accounts of the office. As there is a large amount of printing required by the

Treasury Department of a confidential or secret character, this office was established there to avoid the risk of sending out of the building important confidential papers, and thus lessen the liability of their contents becoming known to the public.

The Branch Office now has 50 male and 23 female employés, 9 printing presses, 3 ruling machines, 1 Sheridan paper cutter, and 1 Sanborn stabbing machine. Here are printed the schedules for the 3.65 District of Columbia bonds, the 4, 4½, 5, and 6 per cent. United States registered bonds, which aggregate 4,360 large quarto pages, embracing the names of every holder of a registered bond in the world ; and this work has been supplemented recently by an elaborate index, increasing the number of pages to about 5,000. These pages are kept in type, the changes, or corrections, being made (as the holders of bonds transfer their property) previous to the dates on which interest is to be paid.

The office is very complete in all its details, and is of great convenience to the Treasury Department officials. All classes of work are executed at the Branch Office—from the smallest blank to the largest volume—and the workmanship, as shown by the products of the establishment, is first-class in every particular.

BRANCH OFFICE, INTERIOR DEPARTMENT.

The Patent Office or Interior Department branch of the Government Printing Office was established in July, 1871, when the Patent Office was under the commissionership of General M. D. Leggett, as an adjunct of the office, for the purpose of printing the headings for patent drawings, which, previous to that time, had no uniformity of size or appearance. Its outfit consisted of a single hand-press and several small fonts of type ; and the working force comprised one man and a boy. In 1873, a Gordon Press and several more fonts of type were added, and the working force increased to four employés. In 1874, an additional Gordon Press was added, and the force of employes increased by the addition of another employé. In 1875, the Congressional Printer assumed charge of the office, and it has been since continued as a branch of the Government Printing Office. It at present contains 3 Gordon, 1 Universal, and 1 Washington hand-press, and employs a force of 9 men, one of whom is a book-binder.

In addition to the above, there is also a small branch office at the Navy Department, which is also under the supervision of the Public Printer.

CHAPTER VI.

THE STEREOTYPING AND ELECTROTYPING DEPARTMENT.

THE earliest attempt, so far as known, to produce stereotypes, was made by Jacob Van der Mey, a Dutch printer, in 1698, who soldered the backs of pages of type, making the whole into a solid plate. In this way the plates of books were produced, among them the entire Bible, the metal plates of which were in use until 1711 ; but the immense expense attending this process prohibited its general introduction, and it is not known that any further use was made of the invention.

THE PLASTER PROCESS OF STEREOTYPING.

In 1725, William Ged, of Edinburgh, succeeded in casting plates in plaster molds, and he obtained from the University of Cambridge authority to print the Bible and the Book of Common Prayer ; but, owing to the opposition of the workmen, the plates produced were so full of errors that the editions were suppressed, and the plates seized and melted up by direction of the Government. In 1738, aided by his son, Ged stereotyped an edition of Sallust. The type was set at night, after the other workmen had left, and an edition was printed secretly. This was the first book printed from stereotype plates, cast in molds. The first edition bears the date of 1739, and a Latin inscription on the title-page may be translated as follows: "Not executed by movable types, but by tablets of fused metal." Ged died October 19, 1749, in indigent circumstances. His son endeavored to continue the business, but, failing to obtain needed assistance, abandoned the project, and emigrated to Jamaica, where he died. The process, which had been kept secret, was lost, and no further attempt seems to have been made to revive it until about 1780, when Alexander Tilloch, of Glasgow, assisted by a Mr. Foulis, printer to the University of Glasgow, rediscovered the art, and several books were stereotyped and printed, when again the business was discontinued, partly through financial embarrassments, and partly through the jealousy of the printing trade.

In America, as early as 1743, Benjamin Franklin, assisted by his nephew, Benjamin Mecom, cast several pages of the New Testament. Franklin obtained his knowledge of the invention from Dr. Cadwallader Colden, who probably had learned something of Ged's experiments in England.

Finally, towards the close of the eighteenth century, Earl Stanhope, who had done much towards the advancement of the art of printing, purchased of Messrs. Tilloch & Foulis the secret of their method of stereotyping; and with improvements in the methods of casting and finishing the plates, the invention grew rapidly in public favor, foundries multiplied, and it was conceded that this invention, which had encountered only opposition for seventy-five years, would make it

FIG. 13.—DYNAMO-ELECTRIC MACHINE.

possible to supply the growing demand for books and periodicals, which the more general diffusion of education created.

The first foundry in the United States was established in New York in 1812, by ———— Watts, and in June, 1813, the first book, the Larger Catechism of the Westminster Assembly, was published, printed from plates made by him.

In 1812, David Bruce, of New York, visited London for the purpose of learning the new art, but was only partially successful. Upon his return to this country he opened his foundry, and introduced a machine of his own invention for shaving the plates, so simple and

ELECTROTYPE AND STEREOTYPE ROOM.

perfect in its operation that it has not since been materially improved. To this machine is due much of the superiority of American over foreign stereotype plates. Although the steam shaving machine is

FIG. 14.—STEREOTYPE SHAVING MACHINE.

generally employed for reducing the rough plates, the Bruce machine is still used in all foundries to complete the uniform thickness of the plates.

THE CLAY PROCESS OF STEREOTYPING.

In 1854, Mr. Alexander Elliott, jr., of Washington, D. C., and Willard Cowles, of Boston, Mass., succeeded in producing metallic plates from clay molds. The discovery never attained to that perfection necessary to rènder it useful in the art of printing until 1859, when Mr. Elliott, aided financially by the late William Blanchard, esq., of

Washington City, after the expenditure of much time, patience, and money, succeeded in reducing the discovery to a highly useful invention. It is this process which is now so successfully employed in the rapid and economical stereotyping of this office.

The papier-maché process is also used to a limited extent. By this process a number of casts can be taken from the same mold, which commends its use when duplicate plates are required. A new paper process has recently been perfected by Mr. W. S. Whitmore, an em-

FIG. 15.—ELECTROTYPER'S SAW TABLE.

ployé in the Foundry of the Government Printing Office, wherein paper pulp is substituted for the tissue paper in common use, resulting in a very manifest improvement of the work as compared with that obtained from the tissue mold.

ELECTROTYPING.

In 1839–'40, Mr. J. A. Adams, of New York, made the first step in this valuable discovery, which has since become so useful in the art of printing. The many annoyances formerly attending electrotyping have of late years been almost entirely overcome by the introduction of improved machinery and a more thorough knowledge of the principles and elements incident thereto. The substitution of dynamo-electric machines in place of the chemical batteries is one of the most important of recent discoveries in connection with the business. Two of the Hochhausen dynamo-electric machines are in daily use in this Foundry, and have resulted in great economy of time and money and accomplish the purpose for which they are designed in an entirely satisfactory manner.

FIG. 16.—ELECTROTYPER'S TRIMMING MACHINE.

The Government Printing Office, previous to September 15, 1869, depended entirely upon individual enterprise for its stereotyping, which amounted to something like $10,000 per annum, with a tendency to constant increase. Among the materials transferred from the Treas-

ury Department when the Congressional Printer organized the Branch
Office there, was a quantity of stereotype implements and machinery,
together with electrotyping apparatus.   After a careful examination of
the matter, the Congressional Printer determined to organize a stereotype foundry in connection with and under control of the Government
Printing Office.   On September 15, 1869, the material taken from the
Treasury Department, with some additional purchases, was placed in
an apartment and organized for business, with Mr. Alex. Elliott, jr.,
as Superintendent, and four employés.   This was a "happy thought"
on the part of the Congressional Printer, as the subsequent history of
the Stereotype Foundry abundantly proves.   The first year the work
executed amounted to $18,718.25, at an expense to the Government
of only $9,525.20.   The demands upon the Foundry very rapidly in-
creased, and five years later the value of the work produced was $44,-
860.48; and it is estimated that the present year the work will aggregate more than $60,000.

The Foundry occupies a room fifty feet square, on the same floor
with, and immediately adjoining, the Job Room.   The average number
ber of hands employed throughout the year is about twenty-eight.
The machinery consists of—

3 Stereotype mold presses.
2 Stereotype furnaces.
2 Circular saws.
2 Hand shaving machines.
2 Steam planing machines.
1 Hand machine for thicknessing blocking **wood.**
1 Jig saw and drill.
1 Squaring-up and trimming machine.
1 Plate-beveling machine.
1 Routing machine.
1 Medium proof press.
1 Hydraulic electrotype mold press.
2 Toggle-joint electrotype mold presses.
1 Black-leading machine.
2 No. 2 Hochhausen dynamo-electric machines.
1 Electrotype furnace.
1 Furnace for casting leads, slugs, furniture, etc.
1 Brass rule sawing machine.

The average amount of work executed in the Foundry per day, embracing every variety of blank and job work for the several Departments,
pamphlets, books, etc., is equivalent to about three hundred octavo
pages, in addition to which the Foundry casts all the leads, slugs, and

metal furniture used in all the different departments and branches of the Government Printing Office. The amount of stereotype and electrotype metal cast in the various forms incident to the work will aggregate not less than 180,000 pounds per annum.

FIG. 17.—ELECTROTYPE AND STEREOTYPE PLANING MACHINE.

MACHINERY.

Fig. 13 is a *Dynamo-Electric Machine*, or battery, and is now used by electrotypers generally, in the larger foundries, as a substitute for the chemical battery. It is one of the most valuable additions to the electrotyper's outfit ever invented. The machine is manufactured by Arnoux & Hochhausen, of New York City.

Fig. 14. *Stereotype Shaving Machine.*—This machine consists of a table, on which the plates are planed—reducing the plates to a uniform thickness.   It is a hand-power machine.

Fig. 15. *Electrotyper's Saw Table.*—A machine of general utility, but chiefly used in sawing out and separating surplus metal from plates.

Fig. 16. *Electrotyper's Trimming Machine.*—This simple but valuable machine is adapted to many purposes, but is mostly used in trimming and squaring electrotype plates mounted on solid bodies.   It is manufactured by Huke & Spencer, Chicago, Ill.

Fig. 17. *Electrotype and Stereotype Planing Machine.*—Used in planing off the backs of plates, in the process of their reduction to uniformity in thickness.

CHAPTER VII.

THE BINDING DEPARTMENT.

BOOK-BINDING, as a means of preserving records, laws, and literature, and of perpetuating the events of history, though in a rude state,
has been practiced for about two thousand years. As learning increased
and the intellectual wants of mankind passed from the mere verbal per-
petuation of religion, laws, history, and literature, when tradition was
the only teacher, and when the itinerant poet and singer was the only
historian, they put in writing what before had been transmitted ver-
bally from man to man, and so over all the broad lands. Having
written, they sought some means of preserving the records of transpir-
ing events—something which, if not beautiful, was yet enduring ; something which might keep together their precious labor, and to which
they might refer with certainty and rely upon for durability. Doubtless the first attempt to put passing events in a shape of perfection, as
was then thought, where all who understood the characters might
resort, consult and become learned, were tablets of stone, wood, or
metal. These were uncouth and unwieldy, but they made certain
whatever was written, and were a step in the direction which has cul-
minated in the beautiful and tasteful specimens of book-binding which
adorn the libraries of to-day. The ten commandments were written
on tablets of stone, and so have come down to the present time without
material change of words. For recording contracts, preserving wills,
and legal forms generally, the ancients had recourse to thin sheets of
wood, metal, or perhaps palm leaves ; these were covered with a film of
wax, into which were traced the requisite words by means of a pointed
instrument called a stylus. A book of lead composed of six thin leaves
was purchased at Rome in the year 1699, which measured four inches
long and three inches wide; the leaves were held together by hinges
of lead, and the covers were of the same material. / A peculiarly adhe-
sive mixture, a sort of glue, was invented by Phallarius, an Athenian,
for attaching leaves together. He was honored for it by having a
statue erected to his memory. The University of Gottingen, which
was founded by King George II, has a Bible of palm leaves containing
5,376 leaves. The usual wooden, stone, and metal tablets were, in
form, square or oblong ; but when a more pliant material was discovered, as papyrus or parchment, a very great change in form readily
suggested itself, and the transition from the bulky tablets to the more

(117)

elegant and portable roll was only what the increasing intelligence demanded. The leaves, or rather sheets, were sewed together, making a continuous piece long enough to contain the subject written about, with thongs of the same material, and attached to a roll or cylinder of wood or metal, sometimes of silver or gold, having a knob at each end highly ornamented, and often set with precious stones. The reader could by placing the roll in front of him gradually unroll it and bring the lines of reading successively beneath the eye, and so read or study much more easily than was possible with separate plates or even sheets. The title was displayed in red or other colored ink on fine parchment, and attached to the outside of the roll. A collection of books was found among the Calmuck Tartars, long and narrow, the leaves made of thick bark covered with varnish, and the writing done with white ink on a black ground. The religious houses were the only places where learning existed and where books were made, and the monks, assisted often by slaves, were the book-makers and book-binders; the same person being often the author, illuminator, and binder. The then rude and little-practiced art was not without some attempt at display and fine workmanship on the coverings of books; and though characterized generally by ostentation, untrammeled by taste and judgment, yet many elegant, tasteful specimens of exterior adornment remain in such a state of preservation as to attest that correct judgment, good taste, and purity of design were gradually emerging from the darkness, and only needed the stimulation of demand to advance rapidly. Diamonds and pearls of rare value were bestowed upon book-covers, regardless of their contents, without design or purpose other than to dazzle the eyes of beholders and to parade the wealth of the owners. Ornaments of the precious metals were wrought in fanciful designs; the rarest work was executed with the rudest tools, which would excite the wonder and emulation of lovers of books of the present time. When the city of Buda, in Hungary, was taken in the year 1526, the Turkish soldiers destroyed almost the entire library of 30,000 volumes, mostly manuscripts, stripping off their covers merely for the sake of the valuable ornaments.

Book-binding, as an art in which cultivated taste, combined with neatness and stability of workmanship, became conspicuous about the time of Henry VII or Henry VIII. Many fine bindings executed at that time are yet in existence. During the reign of Henry VIII an edition of the Bible was published, and in three years it reached the seventh edition. This alone gave an impetus to the business, placed it upon a footing of great respectability, and created a lucrative occupation for those who practiced it. During the reign of the last-mentioned monarch was introduced the use of heated stamping-tools which left an impression in gold or in black upon the leather or other mate-

rial with which the book was covered; and the same means remain in use now, although very much improved in style and finish, as well as in variety and design. Queen Elizabeth, for amusement, just as women embroider now, worked patterns on colored silks and velvets, with threads of gold and silver, covers for Bibles and other devotional books, which the book-binders fitted to such volumes as were sent to them. Many famous amateur book-binders have arisen, the most conspicuous being Jean Grolier, a French nobleman and enthusiastic lover of books and of book-binding, which he followed with great devotion. He was the first to introduce the lettering of the title upon the backs of books. He made his own designs, as well as stamps, and they were frequently worked in combination with various colored leathers, being inlaid with great care and precision. Marble paper, now much in use for half-bound books, was first introduced into England from Holland, wrapped around Dutch toys; it was carefully smoothed out and sold to book-binders at a high price, and became at once very popular as a lining for books. But the modern workman has succeeded in making a great variety of marble paper, very much improved over those scraps which found their way into the art in the above surreptitious manner.

In olden times, in churches, all devotional books were chained fast to the desks, and were bound in wood; that is, the sides were of heavy oak, with metallic corners. They were chained in this way in order that they might be at the disposal of the faithful, and at the same time be beyond the cupidity of the irreligious, and also to assure the owners that they were safe.

The University of Leyden, in the seventeenth century, had a long room in which were placed rows of book-shelves, just as the pews are now built upon the floor of a church, and having much the same appearance; these were filled with books, and each volume had its separate chain and lock, and could not be removed without permission of the proper custodian.

When in 1299 a tax was imposed upon the inhabitants of Paris to meet the extravagance of the King, the whole number of book-binders was only seventeen, all dependent on the University of Paris for support.

Tritheimius, Abbot of Spanheim, near the end of the fifteenth century, made a classification of his monks, who were book-binders, in the following way: "Let that one," says he, "fasten the leaves together and bind the books with boards; you prepare those boards; you dress the leather; you the metal plates, which are to adorn the binding."

Atticus had some slaves who were skillful book-binders, *ligatores librorum*, and Cicero in his correspondence with him asks that two of them might be sent to him. One would suppose that a person in order to practice the craft of book-binding ought to be acquainted with the insides of books as well as to be able to bind them, but the appointment of a book-binder to the *Chambre des Comptes* depended upon his entire ignorance, for, before he could be employed he was obliged to swear *that he could neither read nor write.*

The Crusades doubtless had much influence on book-binding, as the Arabs had been for a long time acquainted with the art of preparing skines, and also of coloring, stamping, and gilding them for book covers.

After Henry III had instituted his order of " Penitents," he originated a lugubrious style of binding, calculated more to depress the spirit than to light it up with the truths of religion. It consisted in putting on the sides of books the death's-head and cross-bones, tears, crosses, and other insignia, worked in gilt on black leather, bearing the following device: *Spes mea Deus* — God is my hope.

I have been unable to find that any general law upon the subject of the public binding was in existence prior to the passage of the act creating the Government Printing Office. From time to time certain joint and concurrent resolutions, providing for some specific or special binding, were enacted, but no general regulations have been found. Previous to 1852, I believe it formed one of the duties of the Secretary of the Senate and the Clerk of the House of Representatives, and the accounts were probably paid from the contingent fund of the respective houses. Later, the binding of the extra copies of documents, etc., viz, those in cloth, was given to persons selected by, or who had concluded contracts with, the Joint Committee on Printing; but the copies bound in sheep and leather, known as reserve documents, continued to be done under the supervision of the Secretary and the Clerk, under contract.

The subjects of Government printing and binding, however, are so closely connected as to be somewhat difficult of separation; and it is probable that the laws relating to the former guided the execution of the latter. The reader is therefore referred, for a more extended notice of matters connected with the Government binding, to the "Short History of Public Printing, 1789–'81," found elsewhere in this book.

The Bindery is divided into four departments: 1. The Ruling Room; 2. The Sewing Room; 3. The Forwarding Room; and 4. The Finishing Room.

The impression which prevails in some localities that the work done in this establishment is only of the plain kinds or varieties, viz, in plain cloth or sheep, and that no really handsome or ornamental binding is executed, is entirely erroneous. The law permits certain public officials, and most of the public libraries, to have binding done at the Government Bindery; and these officials and institutions can select the variety qr style of binding desired. Under the operation of this privilege, the class of work executed is as great in variety as that done at any well-regulated private bindery in the country.

Including all classes of binding, of course the quantity turned out in a year is very large, and probably exceeds more than threefold that done in any other binding establishment in the United States.

The growth of this branch of the Government Printing Office has been very great in the past twenty years, as will be seen by the annual

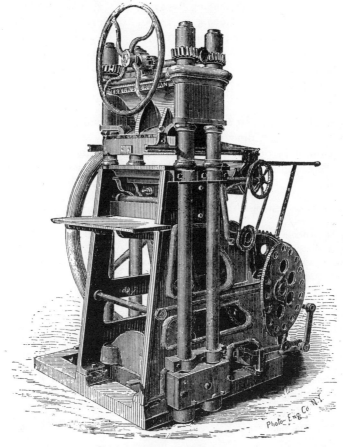

FIG. 20.— EMBOSSING PRESS.

expenditures and the machinery, etc., then and now required in its prosecution. At a certain period of the war, an unnatural increase, like that in the printing, occasioned in a great measure by the large advance in the cost of all kinds of material, etc., took place in the expenditures on account of the public binding, and especially in the ruling department, where millions of muster-rolls for the troops were completed. The following table exhibits the annual expense of the Bindery from 1862 to 1880, and includes the cost of material, labor, etc. :

1862	$106,652.57	1872	$541,663.16
1863	223,945.80	1873	604,249.05
1864	302,947.19	1874	549,078.20
1865	387,288.09	1875	478,071.60
1866	445,009.57	1876	402,069.72
1867	386,203.98	1877	312,780.78
1868	346,723.82	1878	405,752.55
1869	385,219.41	1879	422,242.24
1870	477,603.74	1880	455,593.39
1871	508,442.53		

When the Government assumed control of the building in 1860, the entire force in the Bindery numbered but forty-six persons. The table below gives the number of persons employed in 1860 and 1880, respectively, and also the number and kind of machines then and now required :

	1860.	1880.
Persons employed (male and female)	46	551
	—	—
Ruling Machines in operation	2	21
Cutting Machines running	2	10
Standing Presses in use	4	36
Board Cutters	1	5
Wire Sewing Machines	—	13
Numbering and Paging Machines	—	17
Perforating Machines	—	3
Stamping Presses	—	5
Smashing Machine	—	1
Sawing Machines	—	2
Cloth Cutting Machine	—	1
Knife Grinding Machine	—	1
Backing Machines	—	7
Plows and Presses	—	53
Total Machines	9	175

The Bindery is located in the third story of the Government Printing Office building, and occupies the entire floor, including the east and west wings, or a floor space equal to nearly one acre.

All documents for the use of Congress, the Library of Congress, the several Departments, and the various courts, are bound, and all blank books, of every description, for the use of all the different

FIG. 21.—EMBOSSING PRESS.

FIG. 22.—PLOW AND PRESS.

branches of the Government, are made, at the Government Bindery in this city.

The employés, 240 of whom are females, are divided as follows: forwarders, 140; finishers, 59; rulers, 21; sewers, feeders, and laborers, 297.

The machinery in use is of the latest kind, and illustrations of the more interesting machines, with short descriptions, are included in this volume. The arrangements for executing vast quantities of work, in an expeditious and economical manner, and in the most modern style of the art, are as nearly perfect as human ingenuity has devised. Every convenience and requisite in the way of tools and opportunities are afforded the large corps of operators for the performance of their labor.

RULING ROOM.

The Ruling Room is located in the east wing, fronting on North Capitol street, being a part of the new addition erected in 1870, and is 113 feet long by 60 wide, one-half of which is devoted to the ruling machines.

In this branch all the blanks and blank books used by the Government in the prosecution of its business from one end of the country to the other, as well as for the Departments in Washington, are ruled. Forty hands are employed, and twenty-one ruling machines are in constant use. Some of the ruling required is very complicated, and involves a great deal of patient labor. This intricate ruling is slow work, and instances have been known which required the constant labor of one ruler for eight days to complete a single book.

The history of the Ruling Machine, although comparatively a new invention, seems shrouded in mystery. It has been stated that the first one in existence, which combined the principles involved in the modern ruling machine, was invented by a Frenchman, about the year 1800, who took his invention to England shortly afterwards, and subsequently brought it to this country and patented it here. The attention of inventors has been directed to ruling machines more than to any other class of machinery used in book-binderies. More than fifty different patents have been issued by the United States Patent Office since the first machine was constructed; among the most important of which are the strikers and pen lifters, brought out a few years ago. By the aid of these improvements, a single machine is capable of performing five times as much work, in the same length of time, as formerly.

Ringwalt's Encyclopædia gives the following description of a Ruling Machine:

"The principle of the Ruling Machine is very simple: At each end of a frame a wooden roller is affixed, one of which is turned by a handle. Round these rollers revolves a broad, endless band of canvas or cloth, sufficiently smooth and elastic, and also a series of small cords, so arranged that the paper may be kept in its proper position while it is being ruled. At one end of the machine is a table to which a gauge is attached in such a manner that accurate feeding of the paper can be insured; and after the paper traverses a short distance on the endless band it comes in contact with the ruling pens. They are firmly held in a broad clasp formed of two pieces of wood, united by

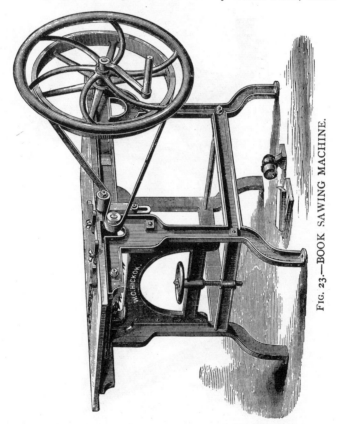

FIG. 23.—BOOK SAWING MACHINE.

screws; and in the improved modern machines this clasp is so completely under the control of the operator that it may be readily moved either to the right hand or left, or slightly varied from its true rectangular position, so as to make the ruling correspond with the irregularities of imperfect paper, or with any description of ruling that may be required. The pens are formed of a peculiar quality of brass, and are simple channels, to convey the ink from its reservoir to the paper. The pens are arranged in sets at various distances from one another, so that rulings of every desirable width can readily be made; and ingenious contrivances facilitate the ruling of lines in which several colors are very closely combined. The ink reservoirs are pieces of flannel lying on the upper end of the pens, and kept thoroughly saturated by means of a small brush. The ink is made of pigments of various colors and materials, and when used it is a thin liquid, flowing freely.

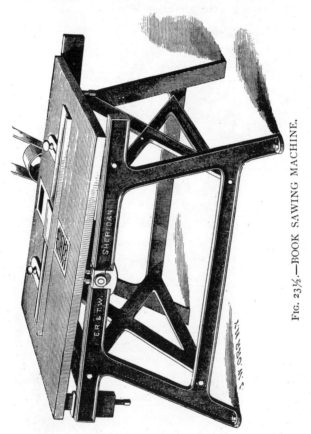

FIG. 23½.—BOOK SAWING MACHINE.

When a sheet is to be ruled it is fed accurately, by the aid of the gauge, and as it passes under the pens it is held firmly by the ends in its proper position on the endless bands. As it passes underneath the pens it receives from them all the rulings in one direction which are deemed necessary, several colors being sometimes simultaneously ruled.''

The machines in use in the Government Bindery have the latest improved strikers and pen-lifters, steam attachments, and ink fountains, and, by a simple mechanical operation, can be changed from strikers to faint-line machines.

The machines are used for ruling note and cap papers, blank books, blank forms, note and letter heads, and in fact any and all classes of

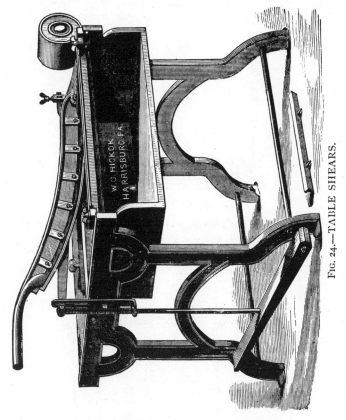

FIG. 24.—TABLE SHEARS.

printed or plain matter requiring perpendicular or horizontal lines, and can be done in plain or fancy colors, as the character of the work may demand.

Without the improvements which have been made from time to time in the ruling machines, the work required in this department could not be performed with less than forty machines. Two persons are employed at each machine: an attendant, generally a man, and a feeder, usually a female.

SEWING ROOM.

The Sewing department is located in the east wing.

The "sewing" of a book is the first operation it undergoes, in this establishment, after it reaches the Bindery. This is the work of females almost exclusively, and evidently has been their occupation ever since the art of modern book-binding was invented. The work is somewhat difficult to describe, and a description here would occupy more space than is at command; besides, we doubt whether any one

FIG. 25.—SEWING BENCH.

not versed in the binder's terms would comprehend the allusions to the *bands*, the *sewing bench*, the *kettle-stitch*, *two sheets on*, *all along*, etc., without seeing the operator in the actual performance of the work. The result, however, is the sewing of the proper number of sheets or

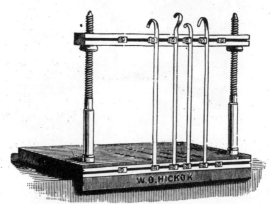

FIG. 26.—BLANK BOOK SEWING BENCH.

signatures together in the order in which they are to appear in the volume, and is altogether different in operation from the ordinary stitching of pamphlets.

There are now engaged in the Sewing Room about 240 employés, nearly all of whom are females, and 13 Wire Book Sewing Machines. All books containing plates, maps, etc., are sewed by hand, as are also the books for the various Government libraries.

In this room are also the Numbering and Paging Machines, of which there are 17, of the most approved make. An ordinary paging machine is about the size of a sewing machine, and is used for "printing consecutive numbers, with great rapidity, on sheets of paper,

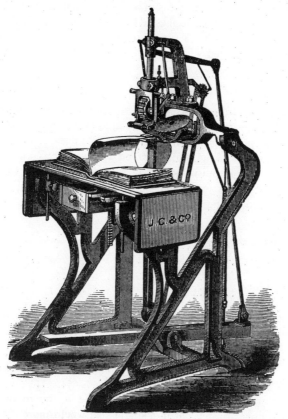

Fig. 27.—SUTCLIFF NUMBERING AND PAGING MACHINE.

check-books, cards, etc. The numbers are usually fixed on the circumference of a revolving cylinder, which is brought down to the paper by some mechanical appliance, by hand or treadle motion; and after the impression has been effected, a section or sections of the cylinder revolve, and another number is ready to be printed. Paging machines usually ink themselves, and are made to print double, treble," etc. The work performed on these machines in the Government Bindery consists, in part, of post-office money orders, both domestic and international, the paging of blank books for the several Departments of the Government and Congress, and the numbering of checks, bonds, etc. But the money-order business, which is so rapidly increasing from year to year, is the principal occupation of these machines. Hundreds of new offices are established every year, and for these, as well as for all those established since the inauguration of the money-order system, millions of blanks are required to be printed annually; and it has been prophesied that if the increase in this service continues in the same ratio a few years more, it will require one-half the space now occupied by the whole Bindery to execute this single class of work for the Government.

FORWARDING ROOM.

The term "forwarding," as applied to book-binding, indicates that branch which takes the books after they are sewed, and advances them until they are put in leather, ready for the finisher; and a person working at this part of the trade is called a forwarder.

The Forwarding Room is located in the main building, fronting on H street. There are employed here about 175 persons, nearly all males, and the following machinery is in use :

Cutting Machines	10
Stamping Machines	5
Board Cutters	5
Smashing Machine	1
Sawing Machines	2
Backing Machines	7
Cloth Cutting Machine	1
Knife Grinding Machine	1
Standing Presses	36
Total	68

All the binding for the Government is done in this room, and the number of volumes turned out in a single year would more than fill the Congressional Library, the largest library in America. Blank books of all conceivable sizes and styles, from the small pass-book, 2½ by 3 inches, to the ponderous double-entry ledger, 21 by 32 inches, and printed volumes, from the smallest size to the largest folio, are bound in this room.

The stamping and marbling are also done here.

The process of marbling is always an interesting one to visitors. It

BINDING DEPARTMENT—Forwarding Room.

is one of the many ways of ornamenting books, and is used alike on the covers, linings, and edges. The process is very simple, when understood, but appears difficult to the uninitiated. The following description of this beautiful art is copied from *Harper's Magazine:*

"There is a favorite style of half-leather binding which involves a

FIG. 28.—ACME AUTOMATIC AND FOOT CLAMPING CUTTER.

process so beautiful, as fairly to entitle it to a separate paragraph. This is where the back is of leather, and the sides of 'marbled' paper. A shallow tank is filled with water in which gum has been dissolved. The different colors are simply ground in water. The marbler dips a brush into a pot, and with a peculiar flirt sprinkles the color into the tank. The color spreads upon the surface in irregular oval forms, just as a drop of oil spreads upon water. He then in like manner sprinkles other colors. These colors will not mix; a drop of one falling upon another merely crowds a space for itself, altering the shape of the first color. A third color does the same thing to both, and so on. Sometimes only one color is used, sometimes half a score. Every color presents a series of forms bounded by curved lines. Thus, if the first color was red and the second blue, if a drop of the latter falls upon the center of a drop of the former, there will be a blue center sur-

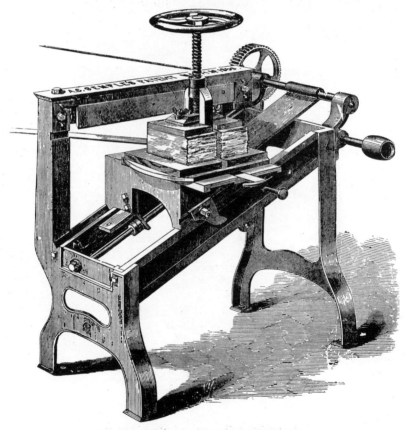

FIG. 29.—SEMPLE CUTTING MACHINE.

rounded with a red ring; if a blue drop falls upon the edge of a red one, there will be a blue cutting into the circumference of a red one; and so on through the whole range of colors, no one of which in any case intermixes with another. The pattern is frequently varied by drawing a long comb through the colors at any stage of the process.

The teeth of the comb pull out the colors into a series of ovals, or rather parabolas.   If the comb, instead of being drawn straight through, has also a motion from side to side, an altogether different pattern is produced ; if drawn twice, lengthwise and crosswise, still another ; and so on, *ad infinitum.*   When the marbler has produced the pattern that suits him for the time, he lays a sheet of paper upon the tank.   This takes up all the colors, just as they lie upon the surface of the gum-water.   A little color will be left around the edges of the tank ; this is struck off by a flat rule, and the process is renewed. This operation, which it has taken so long to describe, is performed

FIG. 30.—KNIFE GRINDING MACHINE.

very rapidly, varying in time with the number of colors and combings. Two minutes for a sheet of paper of the size of sixteen pages of the Magazine is a fair average.   If the edges of a book are to be marbled, the process is the same.   The tank is prepared as before, and the marbler takes as many volumes as he can conveniently hold—the cover not having been put on—and dips the ends and side successively. The sheets are so firmly pressed together that the color only touches the edges, without penetrating between the leaves.   The wonder of the whole process is that while the patterns may be infinitely varied, the operator can by this apparently chance operation produce any number of the same kind. He will, if he wishes, make a thousand successive sheets all apparently alike, though in reality no one is exactly like another. Abroad this process is kept as a great secret. Mr. J. G. Kohl, the famous German traveler, who had visited almost all the great manufacturing establishments in Europe, was never able to see it until it

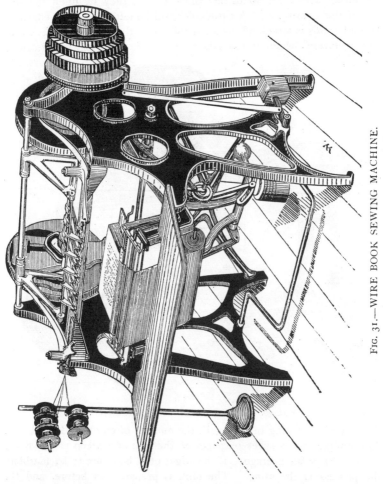

FIG. 31.—WIRE BOOK SEWING MACHINE.

was shown to him in this establishment. The sheets when marbled are rough, and the colors are indistinct. To bring out the full beauty of the tints, and their endlessly-varied combinations, the sheet is burnished. This must be done by rubbing, for no amount of pressure would give it a polish. To effect this, an agate burnisher is fastened to the end of a long perpendicular lever, fixed at one end, and moved back and forward by the steam-engine over a bed having a curve answering to the radius of the circle which would be described by the lever. The sheet is placed upon the bed, which is pressed up by a treadle, and each part brought successively under the burnisher. Nothing less hard than a flint or agate will serve for a burnisher. The

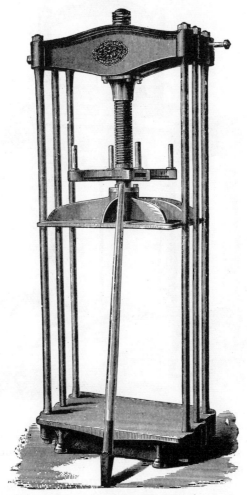

FIG. 32.—STANDING PRESS.

hardest steel would become scratched in a few hours. The hard agate, indeed, requires polishing every few weeks."

The perforating, *i. e.*, making rows of perforations in sheets of order-books, check-books, blanks, etc., is also done in this room. The machine has a couple of cylinders revolving together, the upper one being provided with punches, and the lower one with counterpart holes. As the sheet is passed between them, the holes are made, and the little disks of paper fall into the hollow lower roller. The machine

FIG. 33.—STABBING MACHINE.

FINISHING ROOM.

in use here is susceptible of being adjusted to work of almost any character or size.

FINISHING ROOM.

The "finishing" of a book consists in adding the ornamentation which may have previously been determined upon. The style of ornamentation depends solely upon the taste, skill, and judgment of the master-binder. It may be, as he determines, very simple, or very expensive and tedious; and practically there is no limit to the styles or forms that may be adopted. The work here, however, being mostly of a substantial character, and for preservation more than for the decoration of libraries, is generally done in the plainest styles, or with but little ornamentation.

The finishers are located in the new wing of the 1879 addition, and number 59 persons, all males. No machinery is required in the finishing department, as, from its character, it must be done with the hand, and demands not only skill, but a high degree of art. All the leatherbound books are finished here. In no other establishment, we believe,

FIG. 34.—BACKING MACHINE.

is there so much lettering done on the backs of books. Some of them, when finished, have the appearance of a table of contents. This large amount of lettering becomes necessary, however, from the fact that half a dozen or more books are often bound in one volume. The work requires great skill and intelligence, as the books are of all languages, and are, of course, lettered in the language in which the text is printed.

MACHINERY.

Figs. 18 and 19. *Ruling Machines.*—The former is a single and the latter a double Ruling Machine, and those in use in this office were manufactured by W. O. Hickok, of Harrisburg, Pa. The principle of the Ruling Machine is described elsewhere in this chapter.

Figs. 20 and 21. *Embossing Presses.*—These presses are used for ornamenting the backs or sides of books bound in leather or cloth. They are manufactured by E. R. and T. W. Sheridan, 25 Centre street, New York.

Fig. 22. *Plow and Press.*—This is an implement for trimming off the edges of books, etc. Knight's Mechanical Dictionary describes it

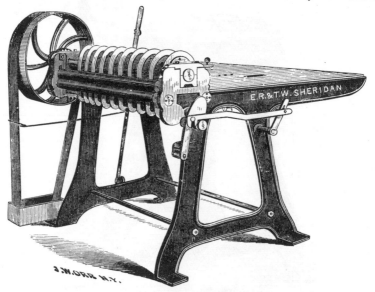

FIG. 35.—BINDERS' ROTARY BOARD CUTTER.

as consisting of two cheeks connected together by two guides, and a screw passing through both cheeks. In one of the cheeks is fixed a cutting blade. The book to be plowed is inserted between two boards in the press, the edges of the sheets projecting sufficiently, and one of the cheeks placed in a groove in the press, which serves to guide its motion. The plow is moved back and forth, and the cheek carrying the cutter advanced toward the other by turning the screw, cutting a longitudinal strip from the edge of the book at each forward motion until its whole surface has been planed off.

Figs. 23 and 23½ are *Book Sawing Machines*, and are used for sawing a groove in the backs of books to admit twine bands on which the books are sewed.

Fig. 24. *Table Shears.*—Are used for cutting binders' boards for covers, etc.

Figs. 25 and 26.—The former is a sewing bench for sewing ordinary books or pamphlets that are to be bound ; and the latter is for heavy blank books.

Fig. 27. *Sutcliff Numbering and Paging Machine.*—These machines, of which there are 17 in operation in this office, combine some specially new features, which render them the most valuable and economical machines now in use. One special feature is that the paper, while being numbered, can drop between the table and the frame ; and the figure heads are so constructed that, in addition to being by far the simplest in use, the wear and tear is so much less that one head will outwear two of other machines. The machines are easily taken care of, and readily changed and adjusted. They are manufactured by John Campbell & Co., 164 William street, New York.

Fig. 28 (see also Fig. 12). *Acme Automatic and Foot Clamping Cutter.*—This is C. C. Child's lately improved Automatic Foot Clamping Cutting Machine. This is one of the most valuable improvements ever put on a cutting machine. It enables the operator to bring the clamp down to a mark, while his hands may be occupied with the work ; or with it he can hold unstable piles until they are fairly clamped by the self-clamping part. It is moved very quickly and easily, and can be used to instantly add to the pressure of the self-clamping part. It leaves the self-clamping part entirely free to clamp the work, relieving the operator of all the hard work, and thereby increasing the speed by which work can be cut. The engraving also shows the new style of band wheel for moving the back gauge. Either of these improvements can be added to any style or size of the Acme Cutter. These machines are used in the Bindery, in the Folding Room, and in the Press Room, for the purpose of cutting blanks and blank books.

Fig. 29. *Semple Cutting Machine.*—This machine is used exclusively for trimming the edges of printed books and pamphlets, and for the purpose it has no superior in the market. Mrs. Mary E. Semple, Lowell, Mass., manufacturer.

Fig. 30. *Knife Grinding Machine.*—This is an illustration of a machine in use in the Bindery for grinding large knives for cutting paper. It grinds them with remarkable accuracy and speed, and is what has long been needed by large establishments. Manufactured by Hickok, Harrisburg, Pa.

Fig. 31. The *Wire Book Sewing Machines* in use in the Government Printing Office were invented by Messrs. Brehmer Bros., of Philadelphia, Pa. Some 200 machines are at the present time in operation in the larger establishments of America and Europe ; and the fact that all

those firms who have tried them, and who have work enough, are con
tinually adding more, gives the best proof that they answer their purpose, and that it pays well to use them.   The special features and
advantages claimed by the manufacturers of these machines are: 1.
That the book sections are secured to the binding tapes or crash with
superior tinned iron wire, instead of thread, thereby insuring an almost
invaluable increase of strength.   2. That any kind of work, whether
school books, literary books, music books, or pamphlets, as also account
books, from the smallest 32mo to the largest bank ledger of Imperial
or even Colombier size, can be bound with equal facility and perfection.   3. That, owing to the fact that the sewing is done through the
fold of each section independently, it makes no difference whether the
number of sections be few or many, one or a hundred, thick or thin
paper.   4. That they occupy but very little space (about as much as
two hand-sewers).   5. That, in point of time, from four to ten fold
more work can be done by the machines than by the former process.
6. That the material used generally does not exceed in cost that which is
required for hand-sewing.   7. That they require very little power (6–10
machines per horse-power).   8. That they are not often subject to re-
pairs, an occasional sharpening of the wire-cutting apparatus being all
that is needed to keep them in good running order.   9. That books
bound by them open flat, and receive a more regular and durable form
than can possibly be acquired by any other process.   The right of sale
of these machines for the United States is in the hands of the Wire
Book Sewing Machine Company, South Seventh street, Philadelphia, Pa.

Fig. 32. *Standing Press.*—Immediately after books are bound, they
are put in presses, such as shown in our illustration, and submitted to
powerful pressure, to prevent them from warping.   The longer they
can remain in these presses, with the power applied, the better it is for
the appearance of the bound book.   There are 36 of these presses in use
in the office.   The illustration represents W. O. Hickok's No. 5 Press.

Fig. 33. *Stabbing Machine.*—This machine is used for puncturing
holes in a pile of folded signatures to enable the thread to be inserted
in sewing the several sheets together, and is used as a cheap substitute
for sewing together folded signatures.   After the holes have been made
in the signatures, they are passed to a sewer, who inserts the thread by
means of a large needle, and securely fastens the two ends together.

Fig. 34 is a *Backing Machine.*

Fig. 35. *Binders' Rotary Board Cutter.*—Is used for cutting binders'
boards for book covers.   The boards are laid upon a table and pushed
up against the gauge, which has previously been set for the width of
the pieces to be cut.   The machine is run by steam power, and does
the work very rapidly.

APPENDIX.

LIST OF EMPLOYES.

Foreman of Printing, A. H. S. DAVIS.

DOCUMENT ROOM.

Assistant Foremen, J. M. A. SPOTTSWOOD, R. W. KERR.

Ackerman, G. H.	Byington, S. McL.	Dunbar, John T.
Adams, Sydney.	Callahan, Geo. A.	Dunlap, O. F.
Alexander, C. J.	Cavis, A. T.	Etchberger, C. E.
Alexander, Oscar.	Chase, W. E.	Evans, W. T.
Baker, F. B.	Chedal, J. D.	Eve, C. W.
Baltzell, John.	Chew, W. P.	Eynon, E. B.
Bangs, D. C.	Clark, J. B.	Fallon, Edw. J.
Barnum, Wm.	Claxton, Rich'd W.	Farrington, C. E.
Barrett, M. F.	Coheane, John C.	Ferguson, John T.
Barrows, B. F.	Cole, W. H.	Ferrier, Sam'l.
Bawn, James.	Connolly, John F.	Fields, Thos. M.
Baxter, Frank A.	Corning, A. E.	Fleury, J. F.
Beall, Seward.	Cowie, A. T.	Flinn, Wm.
Beatty, Alex. P.	Cox, Geo. W.	Flynn, Herbert S.
Berry, Geo.	Craig, J. M.	Foresman, H. All.
Bixler, J. M.	Crooker, W. L.	Franklin, Benj.
Boernstein, H. N.	Crowley, M. L.	Fuller, I.
Boner, John H.	Crutchet, J. E.	Furlong, John.
Boss, John P.	Danenhower, Chas.	Furmage, W. A.
Bowen, And. J.	Davis, C. H.	Gilmore, C. F.
Boyd, Wm. M.	Davis, S. M.	Grant, J. F.
Brewer, Wallace.	Davison, H. L.	Gray, Geo. R.
Brock, W. H.	Deloe, W. W.	Gray, H. W.
Brosnahan, M.	Denison, E. W.	Green, Geo. H.
Brown, C. P.	Denny, H. B.	Gregory, Geo.
Bryant, Miss Louise.	Depue, Chas. F.	Griggs, A. S.
Buckman, John.	Dodge, F. M.	Hall, C. E.
Burges, W. G.	Drew, Benjamin.	Hall, J. N.
Burklin, Geo.	Duling, W. H.	Hammar, G. F.
Burnside, J. S.	Dummer, Geo. E.	Hanleiter, C. R.

Harding, C. T.	Major, Harry B.	Rhoderick, F. A.
Harper, J. H.	Malone, Edward.	Riddle, A. E.
Heffelfinger, Wil.	Maloney, J. M.	Ridgaway, J. M.
Henry, W. C.	Maxwell, B. F.	Robinson, C. M.
Henshaw, C. W.	McDermott, Jno. F.	Robinson, J. K.
Herman, S. H.	McDowell, J. G.	Rodrick, W. F.
Heron, J. J.	McElfresh, H.	Ross, Zidon E.
Higgins, Jno. J.	McFadden, Wm. H.	Sardo, Joe.
Hill, F. M.	McFarlane, W.	Scaggs, E. C.
Holden, Aug. R.	McKean, H. B.	Scaggs, James F.
Hoover, E. C.	McLean, A.	Schell, C. W.
Hosman, Miss A.	McMahon, T.	Schmalhoff, W. L.
Howard, Geo. W.	McNeir, Geo. A. R.	Schoepf, J. H.
Howard, T. W.	McPherson, C. D.	Scott, J. A.
Hughes, Thomas.	Minor, C. L.	Sefton, Wm. C.
Ingalls, Albert E.	Mullan, Samuel E.	Sewall, J. Franklin.
Irving, Amos.	Mundheim, Albert K.	Shaw, O.
Irwin, Miss M. A.	Murray, Jos. V.	Sherman, J. W.
Jamison, I. J.	Myers, D. G.	Shomo, H. L.
Johnson, C. T.	Nelson, J. B.	Shomo, O. V.
Kahlert, J. H.	Nicholson, J. T.	Silvey, R. H.
Kearney, James.	Norton, Wm. H.	Slentz, J. L.
Kearney, Thos.	Nothnagel, H. A.	Slentz, T. S.
Keefer, H. A.	Nott, E.	Smith, E. C.
Kemon, F. C.	Oberley, P. C.	Smith, P. H.
Kendig, M. H.	O'Connell, Jeremiah.	Smith, W. O.
Kerr, R. W., jr.	O'Rourke, J. W.	Snyder, Harry L.
Keyser, H. F.	Otis, Chas. W.	Snyder, J. W.
Kibble, J. M.	Park, Frank E.	Spedden, Ed. M.
King, W. A.	Parran, C. S.	Spencer, Chas.
King, W. Marden.	Patterson, E. H.	Stevens, M. V. B.
Langston, R. E.	Patterson, L. H.	Stewart, Frank I.
Lathrop, F. B.	Pearson, Aven.	Stitt, F. B.
Laurenzi, Geo.	Petrie, L.	Stitt, F. U.
Lefranc, Rémy.	Phillips, S. J.	St. John, F. M.
Lewis, C. M.	Pierce, W. L.	Swan, Benj. A.
Liggett, W. P.	Platt, Hamilton.	Sweeney, W. H.
Livermore, W. H.	Poler, John S.	Taylor, A. H.
Lowdermilk, U. S.	Quantrille, A. R.	Tebbetts, A. W.
Lustig, Chas.	Quein, J. C.	Thomas, E. H.
Maguire, F. Z.	Randolph, A. F.	Thompson, Chas. O.
Mahan, Jas. B.	Randolph, W. F.	Thompson, W. E.
Mahoney, J. A.	Redfield, Edw.	Thomson, A.

Thomson, C. P.
Towers, D. I.
Towers, William.
Towers, W. H.
Travis, F. W.
Turner, J. A. D.
Wall, S. R.
Walton, D. S.
Warren, Edward.
Waterman, C. A.

Watson, W. H.
Webb, Geo. J.
Weber, John.
Wehrly, Sam'l.
West, F. S.
Wheat, E. M.
White, Theo. P.
Whittington, G. T.
Wiler, E. S.

Wilson, C. H.
Wilson, R. B.
Wilson, R. J.
Wilver, John P.
Woodward, L.
Woodward, M. R.
Wright, B. C.
Wright, John.
Young, W.

PIECE DEPARTMENT.

WILLIAM H. NORTON, in charge.

Alexander, C. O.
Allen, O. S.
Atwell, W. R.
Bailey, Geo. W. Y.
Bass, Louis.
Beach, S. S.
Bohn, W. A.
Boyce, I. D.
Bray, R. T.
Brodie, C. C.
Brown, F. W.
Burnside, R. W.
Campbell, J. B.
Chisholm, R. F.
Clarke, B. F.
Cook, A. G.
Cook, W. J.
Crow, J. A.
Curtis, J. L.
Davison, E. W.
Dennesson, W. H.
De Vaughn, C. J.
Dutrow, Jas. Q.
Ellegood, J. E.
Estill, C. L.

Farden, Wm. H.
Fealy, Thomas.
Feehan, Patrick.
Fisher, Edw. Y.
Flagg, Ed., jr.
Garner, J. P.
Goodloe, K. S.
Gorman, Jas. O.
Gosorn, T. H.
Graham, H. A.
Greenwood, R. M.
Griswold, W. A.
Harvie, L. A.
Henderson, W.
Hodges, G. W.
Judge, J. J.
Kirby, Samuel G.
Kirkland, Wm.
Klopfer, N. W.
Lanning, O. N.
Laporte, F. F.
Larcombe, T. D.
Lewis, Frank.
Linton, W. A.
Martin, Herman.

McArdle, H. F.
McIntire, J. A.
Melson, John.
Miller, Chas. R.
Moss, W. H.
Myers, Ellis G.
Patterson, L. H.
Perley, Samuel.
Risdon, J. R.
Rogers, Joseph.
Sandy, T. D.
Schwrar, C. K.
Serra, H. A.
Shiel, Thos. W.
Simms, R. F.
Smoot, E. D.
Stanford, W. W.
Taylor, J. T.
Towers, S. A.
Tuohy, A. G.
Walker, Henry.
Waters, R. M.
Welty, Jas. L.
Williamson, Jas. B.

PRESS ROOM.

O. H. REED, Assistant Foreman in charge.

A. J. DONALDSON, Assistant.

Males.

Barrett, Morris.
Bede, Jas. W.
Bell, Wm.
Benjamin, W. T.
Bennett, Thos. D.
Blair, F. P.
Bradley, Chas. D.
Brown, Jefferson.
Brown, S. T.
Burnside, John.
Bush, John.
Cameron, Wm. S.
Carr, W. H.
Cassard, L. A.
Clarkson, John F.
Coakley, Benj.
Cole, Geo. W.
Cole, Ira E.
Cross, R. T.
Cushley, John A.
Denham, D. H.
Dial, Frank.
Donaldson, Wm.
Dorsey, Samuel.
Dorster, John N.
Dougherty, Michael.
Douglas, Alex.
Duff, Edward.
Dunne, W. G.
Ellsworth, N. T.
Erdman, Geo. T.
Evans, Henry.
Farrington, Wm.
Fitnam, T. H.
Fletcher, Chas.
Fletcher, W. H.
Foskey, Geo. H.
Foskey, Moses.

Fraser, Frank.
Friery, Michael.
Furbershaw, J. H.
Glick, Geo. C.
Gordon, G.
Graham, A. W.
Gray, Andrew.
Gray, James.
Gray, R. A.
Green, J. S.
Griffin, Harry C.
Guillot, Adolphe.
Haddock, C. C.
Hall, Columbus.
Harris, Jas. R.
Holmes, Benj.
Horning, J. E.
Houck, Rob't J.
Hurley, Sam'l.
Hutchison, Wm.
Hyatt, Thos. B.
Iardella, L. A.
Jackson, J. C.
Jones, A. H.
Jones, Jno. W.
Jordan, Sylvester.
Keck, Julius N.
Kelsey, Alanson.
Kreamer, Geo. W.
Lamb, Wm. L.
Lang, Wm.
Louis, M. A. W.
Lydick, J. D.
Maher, Ed. C.
Maher, Thos. T.
Martin, W. P.
Metcalf, John.
Miller, Will E.
Mulloy, G. W.

Murphy, Wm. H.
Noel, John A.
Owings, Thos. H.
Oyster, Geo.
Parsons, C. D.
Patterson, Jas. A.
Pitchlynn, Thos.
Porter, R. A.
Preall, A. J.
Price, Geo. R.
Pursell, J. T. B.
Randolph, John.
Reed, O. H.
Reeves, D. C.
Reynolds, Wm.
Riley, Wm. C.
Roberts, John.
Robinson, F. J.
Robinson, Manson.
Robinson, Sam'l.
Russell, Lewis.
Sardo, A. E.
Sardo, A. E., jr.
Saunders, Wm. E.
Seymour, Wm. S.
Simmonds, R. W.
Smith, J. E.
Soules, E. C.
Stebbins, W. H.
Swift, G. W.
Talbert, John.
Thomas, Lewis.
Thompson, Geo. H.
Whitaker, J. T.
Willard, G. T.
Williams, H. T.
Williams, Robt.
Winne, E. L.

Females.

Allison, Martha.
Antrim, S. M.
Baldwin, Sallie.
Barnes, Ellen.
Bartlett, Bettie.
Baylie, Jennie.
Benter, Maria.
Bickford, B. C.
Blush, Mary.
Bosley, Adelaide.
Boynton, Unetta.
Braunlien, Carrie.
Burke, Catharine.
Callaghan, Mary.
Carlisle, Josephine.
Carpenter, Annie.
Chaney, M. I.
Clark, Victoria.
Clarke, Effie.
Clements, Cecilia.
Cox, Emma.
Cremen, Delia.
Cromelien, Amelia E.
Crupper, Lucy R.
Cunningham, Mary.
Curtis, Maggie.
Cushley, M. T.
Dement, Elizabeth.
Dew, Etta.
Duffy, Maggie.
Flahavhan, Libbie A.
Garthwait, Mollie.
Gaughran, Annie.
Gormley, Margaret.
Goss, A. D.

Hayes, Mary.
Heatley, Annie.
Heatley, Charlotte.
Hickey, Johanna.
Higby, Celinda.
Hill, Mary.
Hopper, Nellie.
Hunter, Mollie.
Hurdle, Mary A.
Hutton, Lola C.
Ingersall, A.
Johnson, Virgie.
Johnston, Ada H.
Johnston, Lizzie.
Keenan, M. V.
Krohr, L.
Langley, Ann D.
Lee, Fannie.
Lisher, Rebecca.
Long, Bettie.
Marcey, Jennie.
McCarty, Ellen.
McCauley, Bettie.
McCormick, M. A.
McGraw, Ella.
McGraw, Nellie.
McKie, Maggie.
McKinzie, Liltie L.
McNamara, Bridget.
McNamara, Mary A.
Miller, Kate.
Mills, Mary.
Mitchell, Annie.
Moore, Cecelia A.
Moore, Sallie.
Nally, Mary.

Nestor, Maggie.
Norfleet, Minnie.
Ober, C. R.
O'Brien, Mary.
O'Brien, Mary.
O'Neal, Alice.
Ourand, Laura V.
Place, Ella.
Pitts, Jennie L.
Pope, A. E.
Potter, A. W.
Proctor, E. M.
Ragan, Mary E.
Reese, Emma.
Reilly, M.
Ricksecker, E. E.
Rizer, Lucy P.
Schermerhorn, C.
Scriver, Addie.
Sinon, Susie V.
Sisson, S. E.
Slagle, Mary L.
Slentz, Anna M.
Sullivan, Maggie.
Swain, Emma.
Sweeney, Margaret.
Tenley, Hattie V.
Tompkins, Henrietta.
Travers, H. A.
Trunnel, Mary.
Turner, H. A.
Van Arsdale, Ida.
Warner, M. E.
Watson, Susan C.
Wheeler, M. V.
Wise, Mary H.

MACHINE AND CARPENTER SHOP.

M. T. LINCOLN, Chief Engineer in charge.

Boteler, L. I.
Boulter, Fred.
Bundy, A. A.
Carrier, A. L.

Gayle, Robt. E.
Hughes, Ellis.
Hughes, Jas. W.
Jewett, Lewis T.

Lincoln, Chas. A.
Robinson, Wm.
Simonds, R. C.

JOB OR EXECUTIVE PRINTING ROOM.

H. GROSHON, Assistant Foreman in charge.

Alleger, Thos. J.	Donaldson, W. B.	McClintock, Jas D.
Atkinson, G. B.	Doughty, O. W.	Mellis, J. C.
Baker, W. S.	Dunnington, Geo. A.	Mickle, J. R.
Bates, Sidney T.	Ells, W. H.	Miles, C. J.
Baum, W. R.	Fleet, B. D.	Nagle, Levi.
Becker, P. M.	Fletcher, J. H.	O'Neill, F. C.
Boulden, Robert.	Fugitt, Benj.	Pritchard, Frank.
Bowen, G. W.	Gawler, Jos. C.	Proctor, Geo. H.
Bowman, S. S.	Goodrick, John.	Sample, A. R.
Bright, J. E.	Greenwood, James.	Shomo, W. H.
Bruce, D. W.	Harries, Geo. H.	Silvey, A. O.
Burnside, F. E.	Haslam Geo. T.	Smith, Jeff.
Cady, L. M.	Hatch, L. D.	Spurgeon, T. C.
Clarke, W. Y.	Howland, G. W.	Summers, Chas. W.
Coburn, E.	Howle, C. A.	Tyrrell, John P.
Covey, D. M.	Hutchinson, W. H.	Underwood, H. C.
Davies, Frank,	Johnson, L. C.	White, Robt. H.
Deneane, Jos. W.	Keefe, J. E.	Work, Jno. W.
Depue, Geo. M.	Marsh, F. A.	Wright, B. F.
Dewar, W. C.		

SPECIFICATION ROOM.

JOHN D. ESKEW, Assistant Foreman in charge.

Arnold, H. H.	Dodge, W. A.	Jones, A. M.
Austin, James.	Eberbach, Edward.	Jullien, L. H.
Baker, C. W.	Fechtig, L. R.	Lackey, J. J.
Barr, M. W.	Fowler, G. W.	Lavalette, W. A.
Boss, C. P.	Garrett, Johnson.	Lewis, Clarence.
Bradley, J. R.	Garrett, J. L.	Lewis, J. T.
Brandon, G. R.	Giusta, Wm.	Mace, T. M.
Burke, L. L.	Gourlay, J. S.	Maloney, F. T.
Burnham, E. J.	Grady, Daniel.	Marriott, E. L.
Bell, S. H.	Grigg, H. B.	Marston, A. P.
Brashears, F. A.	Grumley, E. C.	Martin, C. X.
Briggs, William.	Hall, G. W.	Martin, H. C.
Caton, P. A.	Hamilton, J. P.	Maupin, J. F.
Cox, N. J.	Harford, G.	McAvoy, W. F.
Campbell, J. D.	Heath, T. K.	McCoy, Henry.
Campbell, R. H.	Hunnicutt, G. J. S.	McGowan, T.
Carter, J. W.	Johnson, George S.	McKeever, H. H.
Dodge, J. L.	Johnston, S.	McKnight, A. D.

Miller, W. H.
Mills, J. S.
Montgomery, J. M.
Morse, J. P.
Nelson, W. H.
Palmer, Jos. W.
Perkins, G. W.
Platt, Amos.
Prather, Lloyd.
Pomeroy, J. W.

Priddy, W. T.
Reid, T. P.
Richards, J. M.
Rowell, D. P.
Scott, E. L.
Sinn, J. L.
Smith, C. W.
Snyder, F. P.
Stuart, W. M.

Tarlton, H. C.
Topham, R. B.
Taylor, Samuel.
Torrey, L.
Towers, J. V. R.
Webb, A. W.
Wilkins, F. P.
Wood, T. B.
Young, S. K.

FOLDING ROOM.

THOS. B. PENICKS, Superintendent.

GEO. FORDHAM, Assistant.

Males.

Bailey, John F.
Bain, Jno. J.
Bates, G. W.
Beall, Alpha B.
Berry, Richard.
Bond, Geo. M.
Burgess, I. P.
Burnett, N. P.
Chambers, J. Paul.
Clarke, W. S.
Coombs, Jos. L.
Dutton, J. W.
Eagleston, Alexander.
Flannery, J. A.
Folck, Geo. W.
Foos, Wm. D.
Frank, Luther R.
Gwin, Harry A.
Harford, R. B.
Hayne, Jas. T.
Heck, Wm. C.
Hervey, Rob't.
Hogan, Andrew.
Houghton, A. J.
Keefe, Owen.
Lacey, Jas. T.
Lathrop, N. M. B.
Lee, John.

Moran, H. C.
Moran, W. H.
McCathran, D.
McGivern, Daniel C.
McKenna, Jas.
Ortlip, Chas. J.
Parlin, Edward H.
Pearson, G. L.
Pocher, Simon.
Raub, Geo. M.
Reynolds, Hod.
Rock, A. J.
Sikken, E. A.
Simpson, Josiah.
Steele, Rush C.
Sullivan, T. M.
Tafe, J. A.
Venable, J. L.
Washburn, H. S.
Watson, Henry C.
Webster, W. F.
Weckerly, John.
Wooley, Geo. C.
Females.
Adams, A. S.
Ambrose, M.
Andrews, L. L.
Arnold, G.
Atchison, A.

Bacon, A. W.
Bailey, I. M.
Baker, R. V.
Baker, F.
Ball, Isabella.
Banks, E. E.
Barrett, A.
Barry, J.
Bates, C.
Bauman, S. K.
Bayliss, M. A.
Beatty, Jane.
Belshaw, N. E.
Birth, E. J.
Blair, S. J.
Bowie, A. H.
Bowie, M. E.
Bowie, S. M.
Boyle, M.
Breslin, J.
Brown, Emma.
Brumagim, E. M.
Bryan, Carrie.
Bryan, M.
Bryan, M. L.
Burdette, Edella.
Burgess, Belle.
Burgess, M. A.
Burnett, L. M.

Burwell, O. K.

Burr, J. A.

Burrows, Mollie E.

Butler, A.

Carter, Belle.

Carrico, Emma.

Cary, Julia F.

Chapman, M. C.

Chapman, S. A.

Chase, F.

Chritzman, B. L.

Clancy, M. A.

Clark, E. N.

Clarkson, M.

Collins, A.

Collins, S.

Conover, F. W.

Connell, M.

Connelley, M.

Connor, J.

Cook, M.

Cook, Mattie.

Corbin, M.

Courtney, M.

Cowan, Ann.

Cowing, O. A.

Cronin, K.

Cross, L. M.

Cross, Ada M.

Crow, S. M.

Daily, C.

Daily, H.

Daly, A.

Dame, A. S.

Darby, M.

Dart, L. J.

Davis, L. H

Davis, A. L.

Davis, Maggie B.

Davis, E.

Dickinson, E. A.

Dickson, S.

Diggs, N.

Dinger, Ida.

Doherty, M.

Donnelly, M.

Dorsey, F.

Downing, J. H.

Duffy, B.

Dunne, K.

Dutrow, A.

Dwyer, O.

Edelen, S.

Edelen, I. M.

Edmonston, L. T.

Elliot, J.

Ellis, I. R.

Elwood, M.

Essex, E. J.

Farrell, M.

Faubel, Alice H.

Felix, L. M.

Feltham, S. K.

Fish, Nellie E.

Fisher, A.

Flaherty, M.

Flanagan, M. L.

Flavin, K.

Fleming, M.

Flynn, H. C.

Foley, K. C.

Forbes, J. B.

Fordham, M.

Fowler, C.

Franklin, N. B.

Franklin, V.

Gartrell, M.

Gates, Belle.

Ghant, Annie E.

Giberson, S.

Gibbs, M.

Godey, C.

Godwin, E. W.

Gould, E.

Gould, Annie E.

Graves, M. A.

Griffith, A. I.

Grinnan, J. B.

Hall, M.

Hall, Annie L.

Handebeau, E.

Harbin, M. C.

Harner, Clara A.

Harper, Delia.

Harper, L. V.

Harper, E. J.

Harper, M. A.

Harris, F. V.

Harrison, T.

Hart, Rose A.

Havenner, E.

Hayes, A. A.

Hayes, F. E.

Hays, L.

Hayward, S. E.

Heffell, E.

Henrick, V.

Henry, Mira.

Hess, S.

Higgins, A.

Hill, L.

Hill, Eva.

Hitchcock, F. A.

Hitchcox, J.

Hodge, A.

Hoffman, M. V.

Holbrook, M. A.

Hopkins, M. N.

House, Ellia.

Howard, C.

Howlin, J.

Huber, M. C.

Husted, S.

Hutson, A.

Jack, S.

Jackson, M. V.

Jeffries, H. V.

Johnson, H.

Johnson, M. A.

Jones, M. W.
Jones, E.
Jones, V. A.
Jurix, S.
Keefe, T.
Kennedy, M. A.
Kennedy, T. E.
Kennelly, B.
Kersey, S. E.
Kirsch, M.
Knapp, M. L.
Knott, M.
Korts, R.
La Bille, M.
Lackey, E.
La Covey, Rosa.
Laden, E.
La Fontaine, J.
Landvoigt, Ellen.
Lang, Delia C.
Langworthy, L.
Lansdale, A. E.
Laporte, E.
Lee, A. V.
Long, M. F.
Lord, D.
Lowe, M. E.
Luckett, M. E.
Lusby, C.
Lusby, Florence.
Mac Namee, H.
Maguire Annie.
Mallory, A. R.
Manning, Bertha A.
Mansfield, J. E.
Marche, E.
Mapes, M. A.
Martin, S.
Martin, Alice.
Martin, A.
Maus, C.
May, Sarah J.
McCarthy, M. M.

McCarthy, A.
McChristal, Annie.
McFee, Mattie.
McKenney, L. A.
McLeod, M. A.
McLeod, M. J.
McNamara, M.
McRae, Annie.
McReynolds, Mary J.
Meals, M. G.
Moens, S.
Mooney, Katie.
Morris, Mary C.
Morrow, M. M.
Morse, H. H.
Mulneaux, D. A.
Murphy, H.
Murphy, A.
Murphy, M.
Murray, M. E.
Myers, Helen S.
Nash, A. M.
Naylor, L.
Neale, Mary J.
Nelson, R.
Norbeck, M. B.
O'Connor, M. T.
O'Connor, Mary E.
O'Neill, Mary A.
Orme, Mary A.
Owner, M. E.
Page. M.
Palmer, C.
Parham, J. T.
Parrott, J. E.
Partridge, S.
Phillips, E. C.
Phillips, N. E.
Piggott, A.
Plant, J. E.
Pleasants, A.
Pocock, C. R.
Pope, C.

Porter, Sarah E. J.
Pórter, A. J.
Proctor, E. J.
Pumphrey, Emma.
Purdy, M. V.
Rabbitt, I. E.
Reapsomer, K.
Reese, Kate C.
Reid, M.
Reilly, D.
Richards, E. R.
Ritchie, R. S.
Robinson, Julia.
Rogers, A.
Rogier, L.
Russell, L.
Ryan, M. A.
Sayres, M. A.
Schreiner, H.
Selvey, L.
Sharkey, E. F.
Shepherd, L.
Shepherd, M. J.
Sherwood, M. E.
Sibley, M. A.
Silvers, L.
Sinclair, Lula J.
Smith, M. J.
Spalding, M. T.
Speisser, M E.
Stelle, M. A.
Stevens, K.
Suit, Laura F.
Sullivan, E. C.
Sullivan, A.
Sullivan, M.
Sydnor, E. J.
Taylor, A.
Thomas, E.
Thompson, M. A.
Toole, D. C.
Towers, Florence B.
Tucker, L.

Tyrrell, A. E.
Vannattar, Mollie.
Waidley, Clara L.
Walker, Ida.
Walker, E. V.
Walling, R.
Walls, A. S.
Walsh, M.
Ward, M.
Watson, R. A.

Watson, J. E.
Webster, H.
Webster, G.
Webster, E. I.
Wells, E.
Willard, Nettie E.
Wilson, J.
Wilson, Fannie.
Wingate, N. M.

Withers, F. M.
Woodend, M.
Woolsey, Emma.
Wootton, K.
Wright, C.
Yates, J. I.
Young, C. L.
Young, E. M.
Zell, K.

BRANCH OFFICE, INTERIOR DEPARTMENT.

JOHN T. HECK, in charge.

Bass, Wm. M.
Brewster, John T.
Hall, C. E.

Harrigan, John L.
Hoffman, Frank F.
Hutchinson, C. T.

Nealy, O. H.
Whitford, Geo. A.

STEREOTYPING AND ELECTROTYPING DEPARTMENT.

ALEX. ELLIOTT, JR., Superintendent in charge.

Boyd, Wm. J.
Brown, Perry.
Byrd, Thomas.
Chase, H. W.
Coburn, Frank.
Cowell, H. C.
Daly, W. B.
Detweiler, W. T.
Etchison, L. E.

Gayle, George.
Kelly, W. B.
King, Geo. S.
Laporte, W. M.
Leonard, David.
Livingston, Paul.
Matthews, Edward T.
Parker, John E.
Perrie, George S.

Quinlan, Timothy.
Record, George.
Russell, Charles.
Russell, J. C.
Rowzee, S. L.
Shomo, T. W.
Smith, J. S.
Waters, Byron.
Whitmore, W. S.

BRANCH OFFICE, TREASURY DEPARTMENT.

P. LOUIS RODIER, Assistant Foreman in charge.

Allison, W.
Anderson, Jno. G.
Ashton, E. M.
Belt, Edward C.
Belt, Wm. M.
Boone, Geo. R.
Borland, Alex. T.
Busey, I. W.
Callahan, A.
Carr, John A.
Clark, T. W.

Coakley, G.
Collum, James W.
Cooke, Sallie J.
Corridon, Joanna.
Darby, S. C.
Detweiler, F. F.
Drummond, Walter.
Duvall, Geo. W.
English, Isabel.
Falconer, M. R.
Foley, M. A.

Frazier, G. C.
Gibbons, C. C.
Gordon, A.
Graham, Florence J.
Griffith, Geo. W.
Halleck, J. T.
Holton, A. H.
Hopkins, C. A.
Howell, Carrie C.
Huseman, Ardella B.
Hunt, M.

Hunter, D. H.
Jones, Wm. L.
Joyce, Mary.
Klopfer, E. J.
Laskey, Lulie.
Lehmann, Henry.
Lemmon, Vincent.
Lewis, F. M.
Lowrey, J. H.
McCollum, W. W.
McDermot, Frank.
McGuiggan, A. J.
Meacham, Annie M.
Massey, Florence.
Morcoe, Wm. E.

Nabers, W. F.
Nicholson, John T.
Nyce, Cephas.
Pleasants, Edw. G
Pumphrey, Bettie.
Pumphrey, C. A.
Riley, R. R.
Robinson, A.
Rodier, Henry T.
Rodier, J. E. L.
Rogers, Lou.
Rowan, J. W.
Schlegel, Kate L.
Selby, Wm. H.
Settle, M. V.

Siggers, Geo.
Simons, H. O.
Smith, Chas. A.
Smith, Jesse.
Sprightley, P. S.
Stuart, F. M.
Swain, M. E.
Tulton, Edith E.
Toner, E. T.
Ward, F. J.
Watkins, C. D.
Watkins, N.
Williams, Chas. A.
Wise, Sam'l G.

CONGRESSIONAL RECORD.

E. W. OYSTER, Assistant Foreman in charge.

D. W. BEACH, Assistant.

Bates, Sidney F.
Benerman, S. N.
Boss, James G.
Brooks, W. S.
Caldwell, Stephen.
Campbell, J. F.
Chipley, W. R.
Conrad, J. Warren.
Cottle, Al.
Cyphers, C. M.
Depue, Chas. F.
Dexter, W. H.
Dickinson, Wm. L.
Dickman, John B.
Dinsmore, S. N.
Donn, T. M.
Doyle, D. R.
Eggleston, J. M.
Ellis, H. G.
Etter, A. L.
Fenton, Daniel V.
Forney, J. G.
Frost, Jos. E.
Glass, P. P.

Graham, G. Wilmer.
Hemingway, Chas. B.
Kearns, S. M.
Law, John.
Lewis, Chas. H.
Lewis, F. M.
Light, N. M.
Mann, B. F.
Mattingly, O. F.
Mattingly, Thos. J.
McCarthy, J. A.
McDonald, H. A.
McGill, Frank A.
McNelly, A.
Mendenhall, E.
Miles, C. J.
Mills, B.
Montgomery, J. B.
Morgan, Ed.
Myers, C. S.
Myers, W. H.
Neill, G. W.
Noyes, Melvin.
Painter, Heber.

Ramsey, W. R.
Rogers, James B.
Russell, E. J.
Sanderson, Chas. M.
Sherk, M. J.
Shissler, A. A.
Simpson, Thos. C.
Spencer, Geo.
Stradley, L. P.
Swiggard, John F.
Talley, W. C.
Thomas, John W.
Wallace, F. B.
Walker, Chas. W.
Walsmith, W. F.
Warren, Charles N.
Watson, H. L.
Webster, Geo. A.
Weiss, W. J.
West, F. A.
Winans, W. V.
Winston, Wm. E.
Work, H. L.

BINDERY.

J. H. Roberts, Foreman of Binding.

J. W. White, A. D. Stidham, Assistants.

Males.

Adams, John.
Anderson, Harry.
Alexander, Walter.
Alexander, Douglas B.
Baily, Jas. K.
Barnes, G. O.
Beall, J. W.
Bentzler, Jno. L.
Biehl, Reinhard.
Bishop, Varden.
Blakeney, Jas. T.
Bodensick, George H.
Bogia, Ferd F.
Bradley, W. E.
Britt, G. S.
Britt, Geo. R. P.
Bronaugh, Frank H.
Brunor, J. J.
Buehler, A. J.
Buehler, J. Fr.
Burch, Geo. D.
Burger, W. B.
Byrne, Peter.
Byrnes, John J.
Caldwell, P. J.
Carroll, Michael.
Casey, Jos. E.
Cassard, L. A.
Caton, John P. D.
Chaffee, F. H.
Chase, Henry.
Chedal, Wm.
Clarkson, W. F.
Clinton, James.
Cobb, J. C.
Cole, John.
Coleman, George.
Colignon, Joseph.
Colné, C. C.

Connell, Robt. A.
Conner, Jas. D.
Corlies, Geo.
Cornwell, T. D.
Craerin, James R.
Crawford, S. T.
Cruso, William.
Cunningham, D. J.
Cunningham, F. R.
Cunningham, Robt. E.
Davidson, A. S.
Dawson, W.
Delevigne, Arthur C.
Denham, C.
Denham, L. W.
Dillan, Noah.
Dobbs, H. C.
Doherty, John.
Donn, Frank.
Dowden, W. P.
Dubois, M. A.
Dutcher, T. W.
Duvall, James E.
Eckart, H. T.
Eckloff, C. R.
Eckloff, Edwd. T.
Elwood, C. Thos.
Espey, H. C.
Espey, J. A. B.
Fallon, D. F.
Fields, Chas. O.
Fish, H. C.
Fisher, George W.
Fitz-Simons, A.
Fox, J. W.
Franz, C.
Frisbee, Arthur H.
Fuller, J. F.
Gaisberg, Wm.
Gally, Jos. E.

Gillon, P. C.
Gleeson, John A.
Glover, Wm. M.
Gordon, M. B.
Graenacher, C. L.
Graham, J. H.
Gray, J. W.
Griffith, George.
Griggs, W. L.
Grinnan, R. L.
Hammond, H.
Hammond, Jno. E.
Harrison, J. W.
Handley, Joseph A.
Hardester, T. J.
Harris, Wm. J.
Harvey, Wilson.
Hayes, Wm.
Helff, John C.
Hefferman, Chas.
Henry, A. A.
Hess, G. H.
Holl, E. A.
Hobbs, H. W.
Hodges, John C.
Holtzman, E.
Howlett, Wm.
Hullett, A. G.
Jacobs, Aug.
Jones, J. J.
Jordan, William.
Joy, H. C.
Johnson, Hiram.
Johnston, W. T.
Kane, J.
Keech, L. P.
Keegan, Thomas.
Kehr, Henry J.
Keleher, J. B.
Kelly, T. J.

Kelly, W. T.
Kerr, John.
Kimmell, Frank P.
King, Gustave.
Knight, John E.
Knockey, C. A.
Knott, C. M.
Knott, Igns. M.
Köehler, C. H.
Koockogey, Samuel.
Koon, H. R.
Koontz, Thos. L.
Krener, Chas. H.
Kuhner, Augustus.
Lafferty, E. S.
Landvoigt, Jno. A.
Landvoigt, W. D.
Leach, D. P.
Lee, James.
Lloyd, A. H.
Logan, Robert.
Lybrand, H. C.
Lucas, Burr.
Leitch, John I.
Lemon, Chas.
Lewis, S. W.
Linker, H. S.
Lowey, R. G.
Luhrs, Albert W.
Lyon, G. A.
Maddren, Joseph.
Maddren, J. S.
Maine, John H.
Maloney, William.
Marshall, Wm.
Martin, H.
Mathews, John.
Maurer, George H.
May, Thos. A.
McAllister, Alex.
McCarty, J. R.
McDevitt, C.
Miller, Will E.

Montgomery, J. B.
Moss, J. S.
McCormick, J. H.
McCormick, Martin.
McDonald, J. T., jr.
McGivern, Henry.
McKean, J. P.
McLane, Wm.
McNamee, Chas. A.
McNamee, Patrick.
McPherson, R. A.
Meehan, J.
Melville, Andrew.
Metcalf, F. S.
Meushaw, Thos.
Miller, Frank.
Miner, John.
Morgan, Henry.
Moore, R. W.
Morris, John.
Motherhead, J. C.
Murphy, Daniel.
Murphy, D. A.
Murphy, Wm. H.
Nalley, W. W.
Nally, James.
Nash, E.
Nicholson, Wm. N.
O'Reilly, John.
Orem, George W.
Pancost, T. M.
Paterson, John H.
Peissner, Joseph E.
Pendel, T. F.
Philpitt, F. C.
Pumphrey, Ed. P.
Pyemont, J. W.
Quantrill, Jos. G.
Ratcliff, J. L.
Rathvon, R. H.
Ready, Geo. L.
Reilly, Wm. B.
Reybert, A.

Richardson, W. H.
Ringgold, D. C.
Ritchie, D. E.
Roberts, Richard.
Robinson, Jacob.
Robinson, Jas. S.
Rogier, Chas. G.
Rosewag, G.
Rutherford, Jas. A.
Ryan, Jas. A.
Sage, H.
Sanford, O. S.
Scott, William.
Sherwood, C. R.
Sholes, H. C.
Sheaff, W. S.
Shettle, C. P.
Siebert, Frank.
Siggers, Geo.
Slater, W. P.
Smith, A. A.
Smith, Jas. B.
Smith, Moses.
Songster, Thomas.
Spear, Hiram.
Stewart, Jas.
Stewart, Thos. F.
Stockman, Jas. A.
Strachan, S. S.
Stratton, S. E.
Summers, Arthur.
Snapp, J. H.
Sweetman, Richard.
Swift, Peter.
Taff, Andrew.
Thomas, Alfred.
Thompson, David A.
Thomson, James.
Tilley, Wm. A.
Toomey, Dennis.
Tracy, Geo. L.
Tretler, Chas. E.
Triplett, T. M.

Trout, F. B.
Upshur, Jas. Andrew.
Vessie, A. A.
Wade, R. W.
Walde, John.
Wakeling, E.
Walker, Chas. H.
Walmsley, Edwin.
Walsh, John E.
Waters, Edwin R.
Wells, Chas. W.
Wells, H. L.
Welsh, C. H.
White, Geo. K.
Whitford, Geo. A.
Wiese, H.
Williams, Chas. A.
Williams, George.
Willis, Chas. S.
Willis, H. C.
Wilver, Edward J.
Wood, A. L.
Wright, W. E.
Wroe, Chas. P. P.
Wustenfeld, Chr.
Yokum, J. J.

Females.

Adams, Agnes.
Adams, F. W.
Alexander, Alice.
Andrews, M. L.
Ashton, O. M.
Atchison, M.
Atwell, M. H.
Bailey, Mary E.
Barker, M. E.
Barnes, B. F.
Barron, Mary A.
Barry, Mary E.
Bartlett, C. A.
Bennett, Josephine E.
Bishop, E. A.
Blankman, Eugenie.
Booth, Carrie A.

Bowler, Mary V.
Boyd, M. R. A.
Brannan, Ann.
Brannan, Mary A.
Brown, Emma.
Brown, Mary E.
Burkholder, M. J.
Burse, L. J.
Bushee, R.
Buteler, Kate.
Byrnes, Maria.
Callahan, A.
Calvo, M. E.
Cammack, Virginia.
Campbell, Blanche.
Cantine, Kate.
Carpenter, Mary.
Carroll, Ida.
Carter, F. E.
Cassell, Annie.
Caulk, L. A.
Chamberlain, E. N.
Chapman, Annie.
Christian, S. E.
Clagett, M. B.
Clark, Annie L.
Cleary, M. G.
Coke, Emily F.
Colbert, Maggie.
Colclesser, A. A.
Coleman, Mary E.
Collison, Annie V.
Cowling, Annie.
Crider, J.
Cronin, Margaret.
Cronin, S. E.
Crooks, C.
Crow, Mollie.
Crupper, F. F.
Cushing, S. C.
Cushman, S. C.
Darby, Julia.
Darby, S. C.
Daley, Mary T.

Davis, E. D.
Davis, Ida E.
Devlin, Maggie.
Dickins, A.
Dobbins, Sallie.
Dodge, Ida.
Dodson, M. A.
Dove, Mary F.
Dowden, Kate.
Dowell, F.
Dow, M. E.
Durham, C.
Elms, L. A.
English, Isabel.
Estabrooks, L. C.
Evans, Ida E.
Falconer, M.
Farrar, M. E. M.
Farrell, Mary.
Ferguson, Ella M.
Fithran, M. A.
Fitzpatrick, Mary H.
Ford, Mary A.
Fox, Kate.
Francis, A. C.
Friend, D. B.
Gallagher, Ella.
Gambrill, H. A.
Gates, Jennie.
Gaughran, L.
Gleason, Sadie.
Glover, Ada R.
Goddard, O. V.
Goldsborough, J.
Gordon, Mary S.
Goss, Jennie.
Graves, Frances.
Guerin, Susan.
Haffner, B.
Haines, E. N.
Handley, Regina.
Haswell, Bunnie.
Hearne, E. T.
Hempler, Johanna.

Hendley, M. R.
Henning, S. O.
Henry, Lida.
Hill, Mary E.
Hoffman, Florence.
Holohan, E. J.
Honan, Mary.
Hooper, E. J.
Holt, M. A.
Houck, Susan.
Huntress, Elizabeth.
Hyde, L. A.
Hyde, Maggie B.
Hyson, Lulu.
Jacobson, F. M.
Jenkins, J. F.
Johnston, Alice.
Johnston, E. E.
Johnston, Ella A.
Johnston, Isabella.
Keanan, E.
Kearney, Annie.
Keleher, M. E.
Kelly, Kate.
Kennedy, Sarah C.
Kleiber, Rose.
Knott, B.
Krafft, Nellie.
Lamb, Emma H.
Leach, B. F.
Lemmon, Susan.
Lenman, M. E.
Leonard, E. A.
Lewis, Lizzie.
Lindsley, Annie H.
Locke, Kate H.
Lovell, M. J.
Luce, E. G.
Lynch, Ellen.
Lynch, Mary.
Lyons, Ida E.
Lyons, Johanna.
Lyons, Kate.
Mack, Lizzie.

Macomber, A. L.
Mangan, Elizabeth.
Manning, Mary C.
Marcellus, K. G.
Markham, M.
McCafferty, L.
McCarthy, E.
McCollam, M. J.
McElfresh, Eliza J.
McGoldrack, Mary.
McGraw, M. A.
McGregor, M. A.
McKenney, M. J.
McKnight, Carrie B.
McNamara, Kate.
Meacham, A. M.
Meloy, Anna I.
Metcalf, Mattie.
Michael, Sallie.
Minor, Jane E.
Mitchell, Margaret.
Mitchell, Rittie.
Moreno, Amelia.
Mortimer, D. A.
Morris, L. T.
Morrison, C. F.
Murray, Mary A.
Murphy, Katie A.
Munroe, Jennie L.
Nolan, Mary.
Osborne, Minnie.
Payne, Martha K.
Piggott, L.
Prather, Beatrice.
Pruette, Sadie.
Pumphrey, Cora A.
Rainey, M. F.
Randolph, Annie L.
Reilly, Annie.
Reily, M. Louise.
Riley, Ella.
Ridgely, Ella M.
Robinson, Josie W.
Rogers, Lou.

Rutherford, Jennie.
Ryan, H. E.
Sanderson, E. V.
Schaeffer, Loula.
Settle, M. V.
Shepherd, L. A.
Shields, Margaret.
Shugrue, Mary.
Soper, E. L.
Sorrell, Sarah.
Spriggs, Maggie E.
Stanley, M. J.
Stansbury, S. V.
Stanton, C.
Staples, Kate F.
Steele, Dora.
Stevens, Blanche.
Stevens, L. R.
Stinson, Nellie C.
Stoll, Rosie W.
Straub, Frances.
Sullivan, Ellen.
Sullivan, F.
Sullivan, J. M.
Sullivan, Rosa.
Sweeney, Victoria.
Taylor, Maggie H.
Tenly, E. J.
Thompson, M. J.
Tolson, Rebecca.
Topham, Mary J.
Twitchell, S. E.
Van Alstine, Maria.
Walker, Eva.
Walmsley, M. E.
Walters, Annie.
Washington, A. M.
Wells, Louisa.
Whitemore, Fannie.
Whitney, K. M.
Wilkins, Martha.
Wirt, C. S.
Wren, B. L.
Yerger, E. M.

LAWS RELATING TO THE PUBLIC PRINTING AND BINDING.

[NOTE.—The chapter of the Revised Statutes relating to the subject of the Public Printing and Binding embraces sections 3756 to 3828. In the following compilation the numerical order of the sections is preserved, and any legislation affecting them, passed subsequent to their approval, June 22, 1874, is inserted immediately after that section to which it most nearly relates. Some sections of the Revised Statutes of a general character are also included in the compilation.]

JOINT COMMITTEE ON PRINTING.

How appointed.—SECTION 3756. There shall be a Joint Committee on Public Printing, consisting of three members of the Senate, appointed by the President of the Senate, and three members of the House of Representatives, appointed by the Speaker of the House, who shall have the powers hereinafter stated.

Duties.—SEC. 3757. The Joint Committee on Public Printing shall have power to adopt such measures as may be deemed necessary to remedy any neglect or delay in the execution of the public printing; but no arrangement entered into by them shall take effect until it has been approved by that House of Congress to which the printing belongs, or by both Houses when the printing delayed relates to the business of both.

CONGRESSIONAL PRINTER.

To be elected.—SEC. 3758. The Senate shall elect a person, who must be a practical printer, and versed in the art of book-binding, to take charge of and manage the Government Printing Office. He shall be deemed an officer of the Senate, and shall be called the "Congressional Printer."

Amendments.—*Provided*, That so much of the act entitled "An act providing for the election of a Congressional Printer," approved February 22, 1867, as provides for the election of such officer by the Senate, and provides that such officer shall be deemed an officer of the Senate, shall cease and determine and become of no effect from and after the date of the first vacancy occurring in said office; that the title of said officer shall hereafter be Public Printer, and he shall be deemed an officer of the United States, and said office shall be filled by appointment by the President by and with the advice and consent of the Senate.—20 June, 1874.

That so much of all laws or parts of laws as provide for the election or appointment of Public Printer be, and the same are hereby, repealed, to take effect from and after the passage of this act; and the President of the United States shall appoint, by and with the advice and consent of the Senate, a suitable person, who must be a practical printer, and versed in the art of book-binding, to take charge of and manage the Government Printing Office from and after the date aforesaid: he shall be called the "Public Printer," and shall be vested with all the powers and subject to all the restrictions pertaining to the officer now known as the Public Printer; he shall give bond in the sum of $100,000 for the faithful performance of the duties of his office, said bond to be approved by the Secretary of the Interior. —31 July, 1876.

Provided, That the term "Public Printer" as employed in that part of the act making appropriations for sundry civil expenses of the Government for the current fiscal year which repeals all laws providing for the election or appointment of Public Printer, shall be construed as embracing that officer whether known as Congressional Printer or Public Printer.—15 Aug., 1876.

Salary.—SEC. 3759. The Congressional Printer shall receive a salary at the rate of four thousand dollars a year, and shall give bond, for the faithful discharge of his duties, in the penal sum of eighty thousand dollars, with two sureties to be approved by the Secretary of the Interior.

By the act of August 15, 1876, the salary of the Congressional Printer was reduced to $3,600 per annum; and the act of July 31, 1876, increased the bond to $100,000.

Duties.—SEC. 3760. It shall be the duty of the Congressional Printer to purchase all materials and machinery which may be necessary for the Government Printing Office; to take charge of all matter which is to be printed, engraved, lithographed, or bound; to keep an account thereof in the order in which it is received, and to cause the work to be promptly executed; to superintend all printing and binding done at the Government Printing Office, and to see that the sheets or volumes are promptly delivered to the officer who is authorized to receive them. The receipt of such officer shall be a sufficient voucher of their delivery.

(See also sections 3813, 3814, 3815, 3816, 3817, 3818, 3820, 3821, 3822, Revised Statutes; also pages 175 and 176.)

And whenever it becomes necessary for the Public Printer to make purchases of materials not already due under contracts, he shall prepare a schedule of the articles required, showing the description, quantity, and quality of each article, and shall invite proposals for furnishing the same, either by advertisement or circular, as the Joint Committee on Public Printing may direct, and shall make contracts for the same with the lowest responsible bidder, making a return of the same to the Joint Committee on Public Printing, showing the number of bidders, the amounts of each bid, and the awards of the contracts.—31 July, 1876.

Be it enacted, That the Joint Committee on Public Printing be, and hereby is, authorized to give permission to the Public Printer to purchase material in open market whenever, in their opinion, it would not promote the public interest to advertise for proposals and to make contracts for the same: *Provided, however,* That the purchases authorized by this act shall not in any term of six months exceed the sum of $50 for any particular article required.—1 Feb., 1878.

FOREMEN.

SEC. 3761. There shall be a Foreman of Printing and a Foreman of Binding, who must be practically and thoroughly acquainted with their respective trades. They shall be appointed by the Congressional Printer, and shall each receive a salary at the rate of two thousand one hundred dollars a year.

CLERKS.

SEC. 3762. The Congressional Printer may employ four clerks, at an annual salary of eighteen hundred dollars each; and one clerk, at an annual salary of fourteen hundred dollars, to have charge of the accounts with the departments and public offices.

> By the act of June 23, 1874, the Congressional Printer is allowed an additional clerk of class one, to keep the accounts of the *Congressional Record.*

> By the act of June 19, 1878, a chief clerk is authorized, at a compensation of $2,000 per annum, in lieu of one of the four fourth-class clerks.

> By the act of June 20, 1878, the Public Printer is authorized to employ three additional clerks of class three, to make estimates, etc.

EMPLOYÉS.

SEC. 3763. The Congressional Printer may employ, at such rates of wages as he may deem for the interest of the Government and just to the persons employed, such proof-readers, compositors, pressmen, binders, laborers, and other hands as may be necessary for the execution of the orders for public printing and binding authorized by law; but he shall not, at any time, employ in the office more hands than the absolute necessities of the public work may require.

> *Skilled workmen.—Provided,* That from and after the passage of this act it shall be the duty of the Public Printer to employ no workmen not thoroughly skilled in their respective branches of industry, as shown by a trial of their skill under his direction.—31 July, 1876.

> *Pay.—Provided further,* That from and after the close of the present session of Congress the Public Printer shall pay no greater price for composition than 50 cents per thousand ems and 40 cents per hour for time work to printers and bookbinders.—16 Feb., 1877.

WORK AT NIGHT.

SEC. 3764. The Congressional Printer shall cause work to be done on the public printing in the Government Printing Office at night as well as through the day, during the session of Congress, when the exigencies of the public service require it.

INTEREST IN PRINTING, ETC., PROHIBITED.

SEC. 3765. Neither the Congressional Printer, nor the Foreman of Printing, nor the Foreman of Binding, shall, during his continuance in office, have any interest, direct or indirect, in the publication of any newspaper or periodical, or in any printing, binding, engraving, or lithographing of any kind, or in any contract for furnishing paper or other material connected with the public printing, binding, lithographing, or engraving; and for every violation of this section the party offending shall, on conviction before any court of competent jurisdiction, be imprisoned in the penitentiary for a term of not less than one nor more than five years, and shall be fined in the sum of five hundred dollars.

ESTIMATES FOR PAPER.

Sec. 3766. The Congressional Printer shall, at the beginning of each session of Congress, submit to the Joint Committee on Public Printing estimates of the quantity of paper of all descriptions which will be required for the public printing during the ensuing year.

Advertisements.—Sec. 3767. The Joint Committee on Public Printing shall fix upon standards of paper for the different descriptions of public printing, and the Congressional Printer shall, under their direction, advertise in two newspapers, published in each of the cities of Boston, New York, Philadelphia, Baltimore, Washington, and Cincinnati, for sealed proposals to furnish the Government with paper as specified in the schedule to be furnished to applicants by the Congressional Printer, setting forth in detail the quality and quantity required for the public printing.

> *Standards for printing paper.*—That section 3767 of the Revised Statutes of the United States be, and the same is hereby, amended so that it will read: "The Joint Committee on Public Printing shall fix upon standards of paper for the different descriptions of public printing, and the Congressional Printer shall, under their direction, advertise in two newspapers, published in each of the cities of Boston, New York, Philadelphia, Baltimore, Washington, and Cincinnati, for sealed proposals to furnish the Government with paper as specified in the schedule to be furnished to applicants by the Congressional Printer, setting forth in detail the quality and quantities required for the public printing." And all acts and parts of acts inconsistent with this act are hereby repealed.—25 Jan., 1876.

Specifications of advertisements.—Sec. 3768. The advertisement shall specify the minimum portion of each quality of paper required for either three months, six months, or one year, as the Joint Committee on Public Printing may determine; but when the minimum portion so specified exceeds, in any case, one thousand reams, it shall state that proposals will be received for one thousand reams or more.

Samples.—Sec. 3769. The Congressional Printer shall furnish samples of the standard paper to applicants therefor.

Awarding contract.—Sec. 3770. The sealed proposals to furnish paper shall be opened in presence of the Joint Committee on Public Printing, and the contracts shall be awarded by them to the lowest and best bidder for the interest of the Government; but they shall not consider any proposal which is not accompanied by satisfactory evidence that the person making it is a manufacturer of or dealer in the description of paper which he proposes to furnish.

Time for performing contracts.—Sec. 3771. The award of each contract for furnishing paper shall designate a reasonable time for filling it.

Approval of contract.—Sec. 3772. No contract for furnishing paper shall be valid until it has been approved by the joint committee, if made under their direction, or by the Secretary of the Interior if made under his direction, according to the provisions of section thirty-seven hundred and seventy-five.

Comparison of paper with standard.—Sec. 3773. The Congressional Printer shall compare every lot of paper delivered by any contractor with the standard of quality, and shall not accept any paper which does not conform to it, or is not of the stipulated weight.

Disputes as to quality.—Sec. 3774. In case of difference of opinion between the Congressional Printer and any contractor for paper respecting its quality, the matter of difference shall be determined by the Joint Committee on Public Printing.

Default of contractor.—Sec. 3775. If any contractor shall fail to comply with his contract, either as to time of delivery or as to quantity, quality, or weight of paper, the Congressional Printer shall report such default to the Joint Committee on Public Printing when Congress is in session, or to the Secretary of the Interior when Congress is not in session ; and he shall, under the direction of the committee or of the Secretary of the Interior, as the case may be, enter into a new contract with the lowest and best bidder, for the interest of the Government, among those whose proposals were rejected at the last opening of bids ; or he shall advertise for new proposals, under the regulations hereinbefore stated ; and, during the interval which may thus occur, he shall, under the direction of the Joint Committee on Public Printing, or of the Secretary of the Interior, as above provided, purchase in open market, at the lowest market price, all paper necessary for the public printing.

Contractor charged with increased cost.—Sec. 3776. In case of the default of any contractor to furnish paper, he and his securities shall be responsible for any increase of cost to the Government in procuring a supply of such paper which may be consequent upon such default.

Report of default ; suit, etc.—Sec. 3777. The Congressional Printer shall report every such default, with a full statement of all the facts in the case, to the Solicitor of the Treasury, who shall prosecute the defaulting contractor and his securities upon their bond in the circuit court of the United States in the district in which such defaulting contractor resides.

Purchases in open market.—SEC. 3778. The Joint Committee on Public Printing, or, during the recess of Congress, the Secretary of the Interior, may authorize the Congressional Printer to make purchases of paper in open market, whenever they may deem the quantity required so small, or the want so immediate, as not to justify advertisements for proposals.

ENGRAVING.

Engraving for Congress.—SEC. 3779. Whenever any charts, maps, diagrams, views, or other engravings, are required to illustrate any document ordered to be printed by either House of Congress, such engravings shall be procured by the Congressional Printer, under the direction and supervision of the Committee on Printing of the House ordering the same.

When bids to be advertised for.—SEC. 3780. When the probable total cost of the maps or plates accompanying one work or document exceeds two hundred and fifty dollars, the lithographing or engraving thereof shall be awarded to the lowest and best bidder, after advertisement by the Congressional Printer, under direction of the Joint Committee on Public Printing. But the committee may authorize him to make immediate contracts for lithographing or engraving whenever, in their opinion, the exigencies of the public service do not justify advertisement for proposals.

Lithographing for Land Office.—SEC. 3781. The Congressional Printer may contract for the lithographing of the maps of the several States and Territories accompanying the annual report of the Commissioner of the General Land Office, except the connected map of the public lands east and west of the Mississippi River accompanying the annual report of the Commissioner for the year eighteen hundred and sixty-two, with the additions thereto which may be made from time to time.

Execution of contract; payment.—SEC. 3782. The Congressional Printer shall preserve in his office samples of the paper on which any engravings or lithographs are to be furnished by contract; and he shall not receive any engraving or lithograph which is not printed on paper equal to the sample, or which is not executed in the proper manner or in the quantity contracted for, or within the time specified in the contract, unless, for special reasons, he may have extended the time. The contractor shall not be paid except upon the certificate of the Congressional Printer that the requisites have been complied with.

ACCOUNTABILITY FOR MATERIAL.

SEC. 3783. The Congressional Printer shall charge himself with, and be accountable for, all material received for the public use. The

Foremen of Printing and Binding shall make out estimates of the amount and kind of material required for their respective departments, and file written requisitions therefor when it is needed. The Congressional Printer shall furnish the same to them on these requisitions, as it may be required for the public service, and they shall receipt to him and be held accountable for all material so received.

FRAUDS OF CONGRESSIONAL PRINTER.

SEC. 3784. If the Congressional Printer shall, by himself or through others, corruptly collude or have any secret understanding with any person to defraud the United States, or whereby the United States shall be made to sustain a loss contrary to the intent of the provisions of this title, he shall, on conviction thereof before any court of compe-. tent jurisdiction, forfeit his office, and be imprisoned in the penitentiary for a term of not less than three nor more than seven years, and fined in the sum of three thousand dollars.

ONLY PUBLIC PRINTING, ETC., ALLOWED.

SEC. 3785. No printing or binding which is not provided for by law shall be executed at the Government Printing Office.

PRINTING REQUIRED TO BE DONE.

SEC. 3786. All printing, binding, and blank books for the Senate or House of Representatives, and the executive and judicial departments, shall be done at the Government Printing Office, except in cases otherwise provided by law.

BINDING AT TREASURY DEPARTMENT.

SEC. 3787. Registered bonds and written records may be bound at the Treasury Department.

BUREAU REPORTS.

SEC. 3788. No officer in charge of any bureau or office in any department shall cause to be printed, at the public expense, any report he may make to the President or to the head of the department, except as provided for in this title.

ORDERS AND REQUISITIONS FOR PRINTING.

SEC. 3789. No printing or binding shall be done, or blank books furnished, for either House of Congress, except on the written order of the Secretary of the Senate, or of the Clerk of the House of Representatives, respectively; or for any of the executive departments, except on a written requisition by the head of such department, or one of his assistants.

Provided, That hereafter the Congressional Printer shall print, upon the order of the heads of the executive departments, respectively, only such limited number of the annual reports of such departments and necessary accompanying reports of subordinates as may be deemed necessary for the use of Congress: *Provided, however,* That no expensive maps or illustrations shall be printed without the special order of Congress.—23 June, 1874.

Style of work.—SEC. 3790. The forms and style in which the printing or binding ordered by any of the departments shall be executed, the materials and size of type to be used, shall be determined by the Congressional Printer, having proper regard to economy, workmanship, and the purposes for which the work is needed.

BILLS AND RESOLUTIONS.

SEC. 3791. There shall be printed seven hundred and fifty copies of every bill or joint resolution ordered by either House of Congress, or required by any rule thereof to be printed, unless a different number shall be specifically ordered.

Increased by orders to 925.

PUBLIC DOCUMENTS.

Regular number.—SEC. 3792. Fifteen hundred and fifty copies of any document ordered by Congress shall be printed, and that number shall be known as the usual number. No greater number shall be printed unless ordered by either House or as hereinafter provided.

This number has been increased by recent orders to 1,900, which includes those for distribution by the Congressional Library and exchange in foreign countries. (See secs. 3796 and 3799.)

That section forty-eight hundred and thirty-seven of the Revised Statutes of the United States be, and the same is hereby, repealed and re-enacted to read as follows: " The Secretary of the Senate and the Clerk of the House of Representatives shall cause to be sent to the National Home for Disabled Volunteer Soldiers at Dayton, in Ohio, and to the branches at Augusta, in Maine, Milwaukee, in Wisconsin, Hampton, in Virginia, and the Soldiers' Home at Knightstown Springs, near Knightstown, in Indiana, each, one copy of each of the following documents: The journals of each House of Congress at each and every session; all laws of Congress; the annual messages of the President, with accompanying documents; the daily *Congressional Record*, and all other documents or books which may be printed and bound by order of either House of Congress ; and the Public Printer is hereby authorized and directed to furnish to the Secretary of the Senate and the Clerk of the House of Representatives the documents referred to in this section." —8 Feb., 1881.

Extra copies.—SEC. 3793. All motions to print extra copies of any bill, report, or other public document, shall be referred to the Committee on Printing of the House in which such motion is made.

Notice of order to print.—SEC. 3794. The House first ordering a document to be printed shall immediately notify the other House of such order.

Copies costing over $500.—SEC. 3795. All propositions in either .

House of Congress for printing extra copies of documents, the cost of which exceeds five hundred dollars, shall be by concurrent resolution, which shall, upon its transmission from either House, be immediately referred to the Committee on Printing of the House to which it is sent.

Copies for the Library.—SEC. 3796. The Congressional Printer shall, when so directed by the Joint Committee on the Library, print, in addition to the usual number, either fifty or one hundred copies, as he may be directed, of all documents printed by order of either House of Congress, or of any department or bureau of the Government.

Mail contracts.—SEC. 3797. The annual report of the Postmaster-General of offers received and contracts for conveying the mail shall not be printed, unless specially ordered by either House of Congress.

Number of copies of annual reports, etc., to be printed.—SEC. 3798. Of the documents named in this section, there shall be printed and bound, in addition to the usual number for Congress, the following numbers of copies, namely :

First. Of the documents accompanying the annual reports of the executive departments, 1,000 copies for the use of the members of the Senate, and 2,000 copies for the use of the members of the House of Representatives.

Second. Of the President's message, the annual reports of the executive departments, and the abridgment of accompanying documents, unless otherwise ordered by either House, 10,000 copies for the use of the members of the Senate, and 25,000 copies for the use of the members of the House of Representatives.

> SEC. 75. The Joint Committee on Public Printing shall appoint a competent person who shall edit such portion of the documents accompanying the annual reports of the departments as they may deem suitable for popular distribution, and prepare an alphabetical index thereto.—Rev. Stats.

Third. Of papers relating to foreign affairs, accompanying the annual message of the President, 2,000 copies for the use of the members of the Senate, and 4,000 copies for the use of the members of the House of Representatives.

Fourth. Of the "Commercial Relations," annually prepared under the directions of the State Department, 2,000 copies for the use of the members of the Senate, and 3,000 copies for the use of the members of the House of Representatives.

Fifth. Of the annual report on the statistics of commerce and navigation, exports and imports, merchandise in transit, manufactures, and registered and enrolled vessels, prepared by the Chief of the Bureau of Statistics, 2,000 copies for the use of the members of the

Senate, and 6,150 copies for the use of the members of the House of Representatives.

SEC. 263. The Secretary of the Treasury shall cause the annual report on the statistics of commerce and navigation, required from the Chief of the Bureau of Statistics, to be prepared and printed according to law, and to be submitted to Congress at as early a day in each regular session as practicable, and not later than the first Monday in January.—Rev. Stats.

Sixth. Of the public journals of the Senate and of the House of Representatives, 1,550 copies.

Copies for exchange.—SEC. 3799. Of the documents printed by order of either House there shall be printed and bound 50 additional copies for the purpose of exchange in foreign countries.

See note to sec. 3792.

BIENNIAL REGISTER.

SEC. 3800. Of the Biennial Register, compiled under the direction of the Secretary of the Interior, there shall be printed and bound 750 copies.

SEC. 510. As soon as practicable after the last day of September in each year in which a new Congress is to assemble, a Register shall be compiled and printed, under the direction of the Secretary of the Interior, of which 750 copies shall be published. * * * *—Rev. Stats.

SEC. 511. On the first Monday in January, in each year when a new Congress is assembled, there shall be delivered to * * * one copy of the Biennial Regis- ter.—Rev. Stats.

That in lieu of the number of copies of the Biennial Register now authorized by law to be printed, the Secretary of the Interior be, and he is hereby, directed to cause to be printed 2,500 copies of the said work, to be distributed as follows:

To the President of the United States, 4 copies, 1 copy of which shall be for the library of the Executive Mansion. To the Vice-President of the United States, 2 copies. To each Senator, Representative, and Delegate in Congress, 1 copy. To the Secretary of the Senate, 1 copy. To the Clerk of the House, 1 copy. To the Library of the Senate, 50 copies, of which 1 copy shall be supplied to each stand- ing committee of the Senate. To the Library of the House of Representatives, 75 copies, of which 1 copy shall be supplied to each standing committee of the House. To the Library of Congress, 25 copies. To the Department of State, 250 copies. To the Treasury Department, 150 copies. To the War Department, 50 copies. To the Navy Department, 20 copies. To the Department of Justice, 25 copies. To the Post-Office Department, 100 copies. To the Department of the Interior, 250 copies. To the Department of Agriculture, 5 copies. To the Smithsonian Institution, 4 copies. To the State library and State historical society of each State, and to the executive of each Territory, and to the designated depository of public documents in each Congressional district in the United States, 1 copy each, and the remaining copies shall be kept by the Secretary of the Interior as a reserve, from which he may supply newly-created offices; and members of Congress 1 additional copy.

       *   *   *   *   *

SEC. 2. That hereafter the lists directed by sections 198 and 510 of the Revised

Statutes to be furnished by the several departments and officers of the Government for the Biennial Register shall be made up to the last day of June of each year in which a new Congress is to assemble, and shall be filed as soon thereafter as practicable in the Department of the Interior.—15 Dec., 1877.

That section 2 of the act of December 15, 1877, entitled "An act providing for the printing and distribution of the Biennial Register," is hereby so amended as to read "the 1st day of July" instead of "the last day of June," as the day upon which the lists of the Biennial Register shall in future be made up.—16 June, 1880.

CONGRESSIONAL DIRECTORY.

SEC. 3801. The first edition of the Congressional Directory for each session shall be printed and ready for distribution within one week after the commencement thereof.

SEC. 77. A Congressional Directory shall be compiled at each session of Congress, under the direction of the Joint Committee on Public Printing, and the first edition for each session shall be ready for distribution within one week after the commencement thereof.—Rev. Stats.

ACCOUNTS FOR PRINTING WITH DEPARTMENTS.

SEC. 3802. Whenever Congress makes an appropriation for any department or public office, to be expended "for printing and binding to be executed under the direction of the Congressional Printer," the Congressional Printer shall cause an account to be opened with such department or public office, on which he shall charge for all printing and binding ordered by the head thereof at prices established in pursuance of law; and it shall not be lawful for him to cause to be executed any printing or binding the value of which exceeds the amount appropriated for such purpose.

BINDING.

That the Public Printer be authorized to bind at the Government Printing Office any books, maps, charts, or documents, published by authority of Congress, upon application of any member of the Senate or House of Representatives, upon payment of the actual cost of such binding.—10 Dec., 1877.

Style, estimates, additional clerks, etc.—And hereafter no binding shall be done for any department of the Government except in plain sheep or cloth, and no books shall be printed and bound except when the same shall be ordered by Congress or are authorized by law, except record and account books, which may be bound in Russia leather, sheep fleshers, and skivers, when authorized by the head of a department, and this restriction shall not apply to the Congressional Library. And when any department shall require printing to be done, the Public Printer shall furnish to such department an estimate of the cost by the principal items for said printing so called for; and he shall place to the debit of such department the cost of the same, on certification of the head of the department, Supreme Court, Court of Claims, or Library of Congress, that said printing is necessary; and the Public Printer is hereby authorized to employ three additional clerks of the third class to make the estimates.—20 June, 1878.

Resolved, That the Secretary of the Senate be, and he is hereby, authorized to cause to be bound at the Government Printing Office one copy of any public document desired by any Senator for his personal use.—*S. Res.*, 18 Jan., 1878.

Congressional Library.—That the act entitled "An act making appropriations for sundry civil expenses of the Government for the fiscal year ending June 30, 1879, and for other purposes," approved June 20, 1878, be, and the same is hereby, amended by adding to the clause of said act relating to the binding of books for the departments of the Government, after the words "Congressional Library," the following words: "nor to the library of the Surgeon-General's Office."—27 Jan., 1879.

Library of Patent Office and library of State Department.—That the act entitled "An act making appropriations for sundry civil expenses of the Government for the fiscal year ending June 30, 1879, and for other purposes," approved June 20, 1878, be, and the same is hereby, amended by adding to the clause of said act relating to the binding of books for the departments of the Government, after the words "Congressional Library," the following words: "nor to the library of the Patent Office, nor to the library of the Department of State."—26 Feb., 1879.

ACTS AND RESOLUTIONS.

SEC. 3803. The Secretary of State shall furnish the Congressional Printer with a correct copy of every act and joint resolution as soon as possible after its approval by the President of the United States, or after it shall have become a law in accordance with the Constitution without such approval, and also of every treaty between the United States and any foreign Government after it shall have been duly ratified and proclaimed by the President, and of every postal convention made between the Postmaster-General, by and with the advice and consent of the President, on the part of the United States, and equivalent officers of foreign Governments on the part of their respective countries.

NOTE.—Section 210 is almost identical in language with above, and is omitted.

POSTAL CONVENTIONS.

SEC. 3804. The Postmaster-General shall transmit a copy of every postal convention to the Secretary of State for the purpose of being printed, and the printed copy thereof shall be revised by the Post-Office Department instead of by the Secretary of State.

LAWS AND RESOLUTIONS.

SEC. 3805. The Congressional Printer, on receiving from the Secretary of State a copy of any act or joint resolution or treaty, shall immediately cause an accurate printed copy thereof to be executed and sent in duplicate to the Secretary of State for revision. On the return of one of the revised duplicates, he shall at once have the marked corrections made, and cause to be printed, and sent to the Secretary of State, any number of copies which he may order, not exceeding five hundred, and to be printed separately, and sent to the two Houses of Congress, the usual number.

POSTAL CONVENTIONS.

Sec. 3806. The Congressional Printer, on receiving from the Post-master-General a copy of any postal convention between the Postmaster-General, on the part of the United States, and an equivalent officer of any foreign Government, shall immediately cause an accurate printed copy thereof to be executed and sent in duplicate to the Postmaster-General. On the return of one of the revised duplicates, he shall at once have the marked corrections made, and cause to be printed, and sent to the Postmaster-General, any number of copies which he may order, not exceeding five hundred, and to be printed separately, and sent to the two Houses of Congress, the usual number.

LAWS.

Sec. 3807. At the close of each session of Congress, there shall be printed and bound for the use of the Senate three thousand and for the use of the House of Representatives ten thousand copies of all acts and resolutions so furnished, with a complete alphabetical index, prepared under the direction of the Joint Committee on Public Printing.

Sec. 3808.* The Secretary of the Interior shall cause to be published, at the close of every session of Congress, and as soon as practicable, eleven thousand copies of the acts and resolutions passed by Congress, the amendments to the Constitution adopted, and all public treaties and postal conventions made and ratified since the then last publication of the laws.

Statutes of present and future Congresses.—Sec. 5. That he shall, in like manner, cause to be edited, printed, published, and distributed pamphlet copies of the statutes of the present and each future session of Congress to the officers and persons hereinafter provided, and bound copies of the laws of each Congress to the number of 2,000 copies, to be distributed in the manner now provided by law, and uniform with the said edition of the Revised Statutes.

Distribution of pamphlet edition.—Sec. 6. That at the close of every session of Congress the Secretary of State shall cause to be distributed pamphlet copies of the acts and resolves of Congress for that session, edited and printed in the manner aforesaid, as follows: To the President and Vice-President of the United States, 2 copies each. To each Senator, Representative, and Delegate in Congress, 1 copy. To the Librarian of the Senate, for use of Senators, 126 copies. To the librarian of the House, 250 copies, for the use of the Representatives and Delegates. To the Library of Congress, 14 copies. To the Department of State, including those for the use of legations and consulates, 600 copies. To the Treasury Department, 200 copies. To the War Department, including those for the use of officers of the Army, 200 copies. To the Navy Department, including those for the use of officers of the Navy, 100 copies. To the Department of the Interior,

---

* This section is virtually repealed by the act of 3 Mar., 1875, ch. 130, § 9, vol. 18, p. 401.

including those for the use of the surveyors-general and registers and receivers of public land offices, 250 copies. To the Post-Office Department, 50 copies. To the Department of Justice, including those for the use of the Chief and Associate Justices, the judges and the officers of the United States and Territorial courts, 425 copies. To the Department of Agriculture, 10 copies. To the Smithsonian Institution, 5 copies. To the Government Printing Office, 2 copies. To the governors and secretaries of Territories, 1 copy each. To be retained in the custody of the Secretary of State, 1,000 copies. And 10,000 copies shall be distributed to the States and Territories in proportion to the number of Senators, Representatives, and Delegates in Congress to which they are at the time entitled.

Bound volumes.—SEC. 7. That after the close of each Congress the Secretary of State shall have edited, printed, and bound a sufficient number of the volumes containing the Statutes at Large enacted by that Congress to enable him to distribute copies, or as many thereof as may be needed, as follows : To the President of the United States, 4 copies, 1 of which shall be for the library of the Executive Mansion, and 1 copy shall be for the use of the Commissioner of Public Buildings. To the Vice-President of the United States, 1 copy. To each Senator, Representative, and Delegate in Congress, 1 copy. To the librarian of the Senate, for the use of the Senators, 114 copies. To the librarian of the House, for the use of Representatives and Delegates, 410 copies. To the Library of Congress, 14 copies, including 4 copies for the law library. To the Department of State, including those for the use of legations and consulates, 380 copies. To the Treasury Department, including those for the use of officers of customs, 260 copies. To the War Department, including a copy for the Military Academy at West Point, 50 copies. To the Navy Department, including a copy for the library at the Naval Academy at Annapolis, a copy for the library of each navy-yard in the United States, a copy for the library of the Brooklyn Naval Lyceum, and a copy for the library of the Naval Institute at Charlestown, Massachusetts, 65 copies. To the Department of the Interior, including those for the use of the surveyors-general and registers and receivers of public land offices, 250 copies. To the Post-Office Department, 50 copies. To the Department of Justice, including those for the use of the Chief and Associate Justices, the judges and the officers of the United States and Territorial courts, 425 copies. To the Department of Agriculture, 5 copies. To the Smithsonian Institution, 2 copies. To the Government Printing Office, 1 copy. The Secretary of State shall supply deficiencies and offices newly created.

SEC. 8. That the said printed copies of the said acts of each session and of the said bound copies of the acts of each Congress shall be legal evidence of the laws and treaties therein contained, in all the courts of the United States and of the several States therein.

To be stereotyped and sold at cost.—SEC. 9. That the said laws of each session of Congress shall also be stereotyped and printed for sale, as provided in respect to the said Revised Statutes. And the copies of the said Revised Statutes, and of the said laws of each session of Congress, as issued from time to time, shall be respectively sold at the cost of the paper, press-work, and binding, with ten per cent. thereof added thereto, to any person applying for the same. And the proceeds of all sales shall be paid into the Treasury.—20 June, 1874.

SEC. 9. * * * That the Congressional Printer be, and he is hereby, directed, in causing to be printed and bound an edition of the laws at the close of the session for the use of the Senate and House of Representatives, to print the same from the stereotype plates of the edition prepared under the direction of the Department of State, with the index thereof; and so much of the act entitled "An act to expedite and regulate the printing of public documents, and for other purposes," approved June 25, 1864, as requires the preparation of an alphabetical index, under the direction of the Joint Committee on Printing, be, and the same is hereby, repealed.—3 Mar., 1875.

SUPPLEMENT TO REVISED STATUTES.

Resolved, That the Supplement to the Revised Statutes, embracing the statutes general and permanent in their nature passed after the Revised Statutes, with references connecting provisions on the same subject, explanatory notes, citations of judicial decisions, and a general index, prepared by William A. Richardson, be stereotyped at the Government Printing Office; and the index and plates thereof and all right and title therein and thereto shall be in and fully belong to the Government for its exclusive use and benefit.

That 6,357 copies be printed, bound, and distributed as provided for the distribution of the Revised Statutes by the "joint resolution providing for the distribution and sale of the new edition of the Revised Statutes of the United States," passed May 22, 1878, and joint resolution passed December 21, 1878, and such additional copies, on the order of the Secretary of State, as may be necessary, from time to time, to be kept for sale in the same manner and on like terms as the Revised Statutes are required to be kept for sale, and to supply deficiencies and offices newly created; that for preparing and editing said Supplement, including indexing and all clerical work necessary to fully complete said work, including the legislation of the Forty-sixth Congress, there shall be paid to said editor the sum of $5,000; and each Senator and Member of the present Congress who would not receive copies under said joint resolutions, shall receive the same number of copies as other Senators or Members receive under the same. * * *— 7 June, 1880.

Those portions of the acts referred to above, under which the distribution of the Supplement to the Revised Statutes is to be made, are as follows :

Resolved, That the 15,000 copies of the new edition of the first volume of the Revised Statutes of the United States required by the fourth section of the "Act to provide for the preparation and publication of a new edition of the Revised Statutes of the United States," approved March 2, 1877, to be printed and bound, shall be disposed of by the Secretary of State as follows:

To the President of the United States, 4 copies, one of which shall be for the library of the Executive Mansion, and 1 copy for the use of the Commissioner of Public Buildings. To the Vice-President of the United States, 2 copies. To each Senator, Representative, and Delegate in Congress, to the Secretary of the Senate, and to the Clerk of the House of Representatives, 1 copy. To the librarian of the Senate, for the use of Senators, 120 copies. To the librarian of the House, for the use of Representatives and Delegates, 410 copies. To the Senate of the United States, for distribution, 760 copies. To the House of Representatives, for distribution, 2,920 copies. To the Library of Congress, 14 copies, including 4 copies for the law library. To the Department of State, for the use of legations and consulates, 380 copies. To the Treasury Department, including those for the use of officers of customs, 280 copies. To the War Department, including 5 copies for the use of the Military Academy at West Point, 55 copies. To the Navy Department, including 3 copies for the library of the Naval Academy at Annapolis, a copy for the library of each navy-yard in the United States, a copy for the Brooklyn Naval Lyceum, and a copy for the library of the Naval Institute at Charlestown, Massachusetts, 70 copies. To the Department of the Interior, including those for the use of the surveyors-general and registers and receivers of land offices, 255 copies. To the Department of Justice, including those for the use of the Chief and Associate Justices of the Supreme Court, the judges and officers of the United States and Territorial courts, 450 copies. To the Department of Agriculture, 5 copies. To the Smithsonian Institution, 2 copies. To the Government Printing Office, 2 copies. And the Secretary of State shall supply deficiencies and offices newly created. And that the residue of said 15,000 volumes, together with any further number thereafter printed and bound, shall, by the Secretary of State, be sold at the cost of paper, press-work, and binding, with 10 per centum added thereto.—22 May, 1878.

That out of the 15,000 copies of the new edition of the first volume of the Revised Statutes of the United States required by the fourth section of the "Act to provide for the preparation and publication of a new edition of the Revised Statutes of the United States," approved March 2, 1877, to be printed and bound, the Secretary of State shall furnish to the Post-Office Department, upon the requisition of the Postmaster-General, not exceeding 250 copies, for the use of the officers and special agents of the department and of postmasters at offices of free delivery. —21 Dec., 1878.

EXTRA COPIES OF DOCUMENTS, HOW SOLD.

SEC. 3809. If any person desiring extra copies of any document printed at the Government Printing Office by authority of law shall, previous to its being put to press, notify the Congressional Printer of the number of copies wanted, and shall pay to him, in advance, the estimated cost thereof, and ten per centum thereon, the Congressional Printer may, under the direction of the Joint Committee on Public Printing, furnish the same.

Resolved, That the Public Printer be, and he is hereby, directed to furnish to all applicants copies of bills, and reports, and other public documents hereafter printed by order of Congress, distributed from the Document rooms of the Senate and House, on said applicants paying the cost of such printing with 10 per centum added, and giving the notice required by section 3809 of title forty-five of the Revised Statutes.—8 May, 1880.

ANNUAL REPORTS IN MANUSCRIPT.

When to be delivered.—SEC. 3810. The annual reports of the executive departments and the accompanying documents shall be delivered by the printer to the proper officers of each House of Congress at the first meeting thereof; and the President's message, the reports of the executive departments, and the abridgment of accompanying documents, shall be so delivered on or before the third Wednesday in December next after the meeting of Congress, or as soon thereafter as may be practicable.

SEC. 196. The head of each department, except the Department of Justice, shall furnish to the Congressional Printer copies of the documents usually accompanying his annual report on or before the first day of November in each year, and a copy of his annual report on or before the third Monday of November in each year.—Rev. Stats.

Report on national banks.—SEC. 3811. When the annual report of the Comptroller of the Currency upon the national banks and banks under State and Territorial laws is completed, or while it is in process of completion, if thereby the business may be sooner dispatched, the work of printing may be commenced, under the superintendence of the Secretary, and the whole shall be printed and ready for delivery on or before the first day of December next after the close of the year to which the report relates.

Exports and imports.—SEC. 3812. The Secretary of the Treasury shall furnish a condensed statement of the aggregate amount of the exports to and the imports from foreign countries to the Congressional Printer on or before the first day of November of each year.

SEC. 265. The Secretary of the Treasury shall furnish to the Congressional Printer, on or before the first day of November of each year, the manuscript, prepared for printing, of a condensed statement of the aggregate amount of the exports and imports from foreign countries during the preceding fiscal year.—Rev. Stats.

DOCUMENTS.

Where delivered.—SEC. 3813. The Congressional Printer shall deliver to the Secretary of the Interior, at the room in the Interior Department set apart for that purpose, all books and documents directed by law to be printed for the use of the Government, except such as are directed to be printed for the particular use of Congress, or of either House thereof, or of the President, or of any of the departments.

ESTIMATES.

SEC. 3814. The Congressional Printer shall prepare and submit to the Register of the Treasury, annually, in time to have the same embraced in the estimates from that department, detailed estimates of the amount which will be required for salaries, wages, engraving, lithographing, binding, materials, and any other necessary expense of said printing office for the ensuing fiscal year.

QUARTERLY ACCOUNT.

SEC. 3815. The Congressional Printer shall render to the Secretary of the Treasury, quarterly, a full account of all purchases made by him, and of all printing and binding done in the Government Printing Office for each House of Congress and for each of the executive and judicial departments.

ADVANCES TO CONGRESSIONAL PRINTER.

SEC. 3816. There shall be advanced to the Congressional Printer, from time to time, as the public service may require it, and under such rules as the Secretary of the Treasury may prescribe, a sum of money not exceeding, at any time, two-thirds of the penalty of his bond, to enable him to pay for work and material.

By the act of July 31, 1876, the bond was increased to $100,000.

SETTLEMENT OF ACCOUNTS.

SEC. 3817. The Congressional Printer shall settle the account of his receipts and disbursements in the manner required of other disbursing officers.

MONEYS FROM SALES.

SEC. 3818. The moneys received from sales of extra copies of documents, and from sales of paper shavings and imperfections, shall be deposited by the Congressional Printer in the Treasury of the United States, to the credit of the appropriations for public printing, binding, and paper, respectively, as designated by him, and shall be subject to his requisition in the manner prescribed by law.

FOREMEN'S MONTHLY STATEMENTS.

SEC. 3819. The Foremen of Printing and Binding shall make out and deliver to the Congressional Printer monthly statements of the work done in their respective offices, together with monthly pay-rolls, which shall contain the names of the persons employed, the rate of compensation of and amount due to each, and the service for which it is due.

REPORT TO THE SECRETARY OF THE INTERIOR.

SEC. 3820. The Congressional Printer shall keep a true account of all paper received from contractors, and of all paper used in the Public Printing Office, and shall, at the end of each fiscal year, report to the Secretary of the Interior the amount of each class consumed in said office, and the works or publications in which the same was used.

REPORT TO CONGRESS.

SEC. 3821. The Congressional Printer shall, on the first day of each session, or as soon thereafter as may be practicable, report to Congress the exact condition, and the amount and cost of the public printing, binding, lithographing, and engraving; the amount and cost of all paper purchased for the same; a detailed statement of proposals made and contracts entered into for the purchase of paper and other materials, and for lithographing and engraving; of all payments made during the preceding year under his direction; of the amount of work ordered and done, with a general classification thereof, for each department, and a detailed statement of each account with the departments or public officers; a detailed statement of the number of hands employed in the establishment, and the time each has been employed; and such further information, touching all matters connected with the Printing Office, as may be in his possession.

ESTIMATES FOR CONGRESS.

SEC. 3822. The Congressional Printer shall also submit to Congress, at the beginning of each session, detailed estimates of the sums required for the support of the Government Printing Office.

OFFICIAL ADVERTISEMENTS.

SEC. 3823. The Clerk of the House of Representatives shall select in Virginia, South Carolina, North Carolina, Georgia, Florida, Alabama, Mississippi, Louisiana, Texas, and Arkansas, one or more newspapers, not exceeding the number allowed by law, in which such treaties and laws of the United States as may be ordered for publication in newspapers according to law shall be published, and in some one or more of which so selected all such advertisements as may be ordered for publication in said districts by any United States court or judge thereof, or by any officer of said courts, or by any executive officer of the United States, shall be published, the compensation for which, and other terms of publication, shall be fixed by said Clerk at a rate not exceeding two dollars per page for the publication of treaties and laws, and not exceeding one dollar per square of eight lines of space for the publication of advertisements, the accounts for which shall be adjusted by the proper accounting officers, and paid in the manner now authorized by law in the like cases.

Notification to heads of departments.—SEC. 3824. The Clerk shall notify each head of the several executive departments and each judge of the United States courts therein of the papers selected by him in accordance with the provisions of the preceding section, and thereafter it shall be the duty of the several executive officers charged therewith to furnish to such selected papers only, an authentic copy of the publications to be made as aforesaid; and no money appropriated shall be paid for any publications or advertisements hereafter to be made in said districts, nor shall any such publication or advertisement be ordered by any department or public officer otherwise than as herein provided.

SEC. 3825. The rates fixed in section thirty-eight hundred and twenty-three to be paid for the publication of the treaties and laws of the United States in the States therein designated shall also be paid

for the same publications in all the States not designated in that section.

In what papers to be printed.—That all advertising required by existing laws to
be done in the District of Columbia by any of the departments of the Government
shall be given to one daily and one weekly newspaper of each of the two principal
political parties, and to one daily and one weekly neutral newspaper: *Provided,*
That the rates of compensation for such service shall in no case exceed the regular
commercial rate of the newspapers selected; nor shall any advertisement be paid
for, unless published in accordance with section thirty-eight hundred and twenty-
eight of the Revised Statutes.

SEC. 2. All laws or parts of laws inconsistent herewith are hereby repealed.—21
Jan., 1881.

SEC. 3826. All advertisements, notices, and proposals for contracts
for all the executive departments of the Government, and the laws
passed by Congress and executive proclamations and treaties to be
published in the District of Columbia, Maryland, and Virginia, shall
be advertised by publications in the three daily papers published in the
District of Columbia having the largest circulation, one of which shall
be selected by the Clerk of the House of Representatives, and in no
others. The charges for such publications shall not be higher than
such as are paid by individuals for advertising in said papers, and the
same publications shall be made in each of the said papers equally as to
frequency: *Provided,* That no advertisement to any State, district, or
Territory, other than the District of Columbia, Maryland, or Virginia,
shall be published in the papers designated, unless at the direction first
made of the proper head of a department: *And provided further,* That
this section shall not be construed to allow a greater compensation for
the publication of the laws passed by Congress and executive proclamations and treaties in the papers of the District of Columbia than is
provided by law for such publications in other papers.

That hereafter all advertisements, notices, proposals for contracts, and all forms
of advertising required by law for the several departments of the Government may
be paid for at a price not to exceed the commercial rates charged to private individuals, with the usual discounts; such rates to be ascertained from sworn statements
to be furnished by the proprietors or publishers of the newspapers proposing to advertise: *Provided,* That all advertising in newspapers since the 10th day of April,
1877, shall be audited and paid at like rates; but the heads of the several departments may secure lower terms at special rates whenever the public interest requires
it.—20 June, 1878.

NOTE.—By statute of March 3, 1875, ch. 128, ∮ 1, vol. 18, p. 342, it is provided
"that hereafter the mail lettings for the States of Maryland and Virginia, and for the
District of Columbia, shall be advertised in not more than one newspaper published
in the District of Columbia, and at prices satisfactory to the Postmaster-General, not
exceeding the customary rates paid in the city of Washington for ordinary commercial advertisements"; and so much of this section as refers to the publication of

advertisements in newspapers was repealed by the act above mentioned.—See Rev. Stats., § 3941.

SEC. 3827. No payment shall be made to any newspaper published in the District of Columbia for advertising any other mail-routes than those in Virginia and Maryland.

> *Publication of laws in newspapers.*—SEC. 79. After the 4th day of March, 1875, no money shall be paid from the Treasury for the publication of the laws in newspapers. —Rev. Stat.

No advertisement without authority.—SEC. 3828. No advertisement, notice, or proposals for any executive department of the Government, or for any bureau thereof, or for any office therewith connected, shall be published in any newspaper whatever, except in pursuance of a written authority for such publication from the head of such department; and no bill for any such advertising or publication shall be paid, unless there be presented with such bill a copy of such written authority.

MISCELLANEOUS LAWS AND RESOLUTIONS.

Appropriations, new offices, etc.—SEC. 64. The Secretary of the Senate and the Clerk of the House of Representatives shall, as soon as may be after the close of each session of Congress, prepare and publish a statement of all appropriations made during the session, a statement of the new offices created and the salaries attached to each, and a statement of the offices the salaries attached to which are increased, and the amount of such increase.—Rev. Stats.

CONGRESSIONAL RECORD.

Debates of Congress.—SEC. 78. Until a contract for publishing the debates of Congress is made, such debates shall be printed by the Congressional Printer, under the direction of the Joint Committee on Public Printing on the part of the Senate.—Rev. Stats.

> *Number to be printed.*—That the Congressional Printer be directed to furnish 3,100 copies for the use of the Senate, and 7,250 copies for the use of the House of Representatives, of the *Congressional Record*, or of any such other like official report of the debates in Congress as may be hereafter authorized by law, either daily, as originally published, or in the revised form, without binding, or in bound volumes, or part in each form, as each Senator, Member, or Delegate receiving the same may elect.—*Con. Res.*, 4 June, 1874.
>
> *Resolved,* That the Congressional Printer be, and he is hereby, directed to keep a separate and exact account in detail of all expenditures for printing, mailing, and binding the *Congressional Record*, including specific statements of the cost of all machinery and material which may have been or shall be used for publication of said *Record*, commencing with its first publication at the Government Printing Office; and that he shall publish the amount thus yearly expended, in his next suc-

ceeding annual report, and each succeeding report, separately from the other disbursements of his office.—20 June, 1874.   See Sec. 3760, and amendments.

Postage on Record.—*Provided*, That the postage on each copy of the daily Congressional Record mailed from the city of Washington as transient matter shall be one cent.—23 June, 1874.

Clerk.—For one clerk of the first class, to keep the accounts of the *Congressional Record*, as required by joint resolution of Congress.—23 June, 1874.

Extracts from Congressional Record.—It shall be lawful for the Congressional Printer to print and deliver, upon the order of any Senator or Member of the House of Representatives, or Delegate, extracts from the *Congressional Record;* the person ordering the same paying the cost thereof.—3 Mar., 1875.

Distribution.—That the Public Printer be, and he is hereby, authorized and directed to forward, free of charge, one copy of the daily *Congressional Record* to each of our legations abroad ; commencing at the beginning of this session and continuing each day until the fourth day of March, eighteen hundred and eighty-one.—*Jt. Res.*, 18 Dec., 1880.

That the Public Printer be authorized to furnish the Chief Justice and each of the Associate Justices of the Supreme Court of the United States, and the clerk and marshal of the court, with a current copy of the daily *Congressional Record*, and at the end of each session a bound copy of the proceedings of Congress for such session.   And the Public Printer shall also furnish to the Official Reporter of the Senate five bound copies of the *Congressional Record* for each session.—*Jt. Res.*, 27 Jan., 1881.

The law of Feb. 8, 1881, directs the Public Printer to furnish the Secretary of the Senate and the Clerk of the House with copies of the *Congressional Record* to supply one copy each to the several National Soldiers' Homes and their branches.

Index.—That the Joint Committee on Printing be, and they are hereby, authorized and directed to make the necessary provisions and arrangements for hereafter issuing the index of the *Congressional Record* semi-monthly during the sessions of Congress, beginning with next ensuing session. That the Public Printer be, and he is hereby, directed to print and distribute the same number of copies of said semi-monthly index as he prints and distributes of the daily issue of the *Record*, and to the same persons and in the same manner.   That the Public Printer shall employ such person to prepare said index as shall be designated by the Joint Committee on Printing, who shall also fix and regulate the compensation to be paid by the Public Printer for the said work, and direct the form and manner of its publication : *Provided, however*, That the compensation allowed for preparing said semi-monthly index, including their compilation into a session index, shall not exceed the average total amount now allowed by the Joint Committee on Printing for compiling the session index.—*Jt. Res.*, 8 Feb., 1881.

OPINIONS OF THE ATTORNEY-GENERAL.

SEC. 383. The Attorney-General shall, from time to time, cause to be edited, and printed at the Government Printing Office, an edition of 1,000 copies of such of the opinions of the law officers herein authorized to be given as he may deem valuable for preservation in volumes, which shall be, as to size, quality of paper, printing, and binding, of uniform style and appearance, as nearly as practicable, with volume eight of such Opinions, published by Robert Farnham, in the year 1868. Each volume shall contain proper head-notes, a complete and full index, and such foot-notes as the Attorney-General may approve. Such volumes shall be distributed in such manner as the Attorney-General may from time to time prescribe.—Rev. Stats.

A digest of the opinions of the Attorney-General contained in volumes one to sixteen is authorized by the act of June 15, 1880.

ANNUAL REPORTS OF THE POSTMASTER-GENERAL.

SEC. 413. The Postmaster-General shall make the following annual reports to Congress: First. A report of all contracts for carrying the mails made within the preceding year. Second. A report of all land and water mails established or ordered within the preceding year, other than those let to contract at the annual letting. Third. A report of all allowances made to contractors within the preceding year above the sums originally stipulated in their respective contracts, and the reasons for the same, and of all orders made whereby additional expense is incurred on any route beyond the original contract price. Fourth. A report of all curtailments of expenses effected within the preceding year. Fifth. A report of the finances of the department for the preceding year. Sixth. A report of the fines imposed on and the deductions from the pay of contractors made during the preceding year. Seventh. A copy of each contract for carrying the mail between the United States and foreign countries. Eighth. A report showing all contracts which have been made by the department other than for carrying the mail. Ninth. A report on the postal business and agencies in foreign countries. Tenth. A report of the amount expended in the department for the preceding fiscal year. And the Postmaster-General shall cause all of such reports to be printed at the Public Printing Office, either together or separately, and in such numbers as may be required by the exigencies of the service or by law.—Rev. Stats.

COPIES OF PATENT CLAIMS.

SEC. 489. The Commissioner of Patents may print, or cause to be printed, copies of the claims of current issues, and copies of such laws, decisions, regulations, and circulars as may be necessary for the information of the public.—Rev. Stats.

SPECIFICATIONS OF PATENTS.

SEC. 490. The Commissioner of Patents is authorized to have printed from time to time, for gratuitous distribution, not to exceed 150 copies of the complete specifications and drawings of each patent hereafter issued, together with suitable indexes.—Rev. Stats.

LITHOGRAPHING AND ENGRAVING FOR PATENT OFFICE.

SEC. 492. The lithographing and engraving required by the two preceding sections shall be awarded to the lowest and best bidders for the interests of the Government, due regard being paid to the execution of the work, after due advertising by the Congressional Printer, under the direction of the Joint Committee on Printing; but the Joint Committee on Printing may empower the Congressional Printer to make immediate contracts for engraving whenever, in their opinion, the exigencies of the public service will not justify waiting for advertisement and award; or if, in the judgment of the Joint Committee on Printing, the work can be performed under the direction of the Commissioner of Patents more advantageously than in the manner above prescribed, it shall be so done, under such limitations and conditions as the Joint Committee on Printing may from time to time prescribe. —Rev. Stats.

CUSTODY AND DISTRIBUTION OF PUBLIC DOCUMENTS.

SEC. 497. The Secretary of the Interior is charged with receiving, arranging, and safe-keeping for distribution, and of distributing to the persons entitled by law to receive the same, all printed journals of the two Houses of Congress, and all other books or documents of every nature whatever, already or hereafter directed by law to be printed or purchased for the use of the Government, except such as are directed to be printed or purchased for the particular use of Congress, or of either House thereof, or for the particular use of the Executive or of any of the departments, and any person whose duty it shall be by law to deliver any of the same, shall deliver them at the rooms assigned by the Secretary of the Interior therefor.—Rev. Stats.

DAY'S WORK.

SEC. 3738. Eight hours shall constitute a day's work for all laborers, workmen, and mechanics who may be employed by or on behalf of the Government of the United States.—Rev. Stats.

LEGAL HOLIDAYS.

SEC. 993. The following days, namely: The 1st day of January, commonly called New Year's Day; the 4th day of July; the 25th day of December, commonly called Christmas Day; and any day appointed or recommended by the President of the United States as a day of public fast or thanksgiving, shall be holidays within the District, and shall, for all purposes of presenting for payment or acceptance, for the maturity and protest, and giving notice of the dishonor of bills of exchange, bank-checks, and promissory notes, or other negotiable or commercial paper, be treated and considered as is the first day of the week, commonly called Sunday, and all notes, drafts, checks, or other commercial or negotiable paper falling due or maturing on either of said holidays shall be deemed as having matured on the day previous. —28 June, 1870—*Sec. 993 Rev. Stat. relating to District of Columbia.*

That section 993 of the Revised Statutes of the United States relating to the District of Columbia be, and the same hereby is, amended by adding to the days therein declared to be holidays within the District the 22d day of February; and such day shall be a holiday for all the purposes mentioned in said section: *Provided,* That this act shall not apply to the 22d day of February, 1879.—31 Jan., 1879.

Resolved, That the employés of the Government Printing Office shall be allowed the following legal holidays, with pay, to wit: the 1st day of January, the 22d day of February, the 4th day of July, the 25th day of December, and such day as may be designated by the President of the United States as a day of public fast or thanksgiving: *Provided,* That the said employés shall be paid for these holidays only when the employés of the other Government departments shall be so paid: *And provided further,* That nothing herein contained shall authorize any additional payment to such employés as receive annual salaries.—*Jt. Res.,* 16 April, 1880.

That all employés of the Government in the city of Washington, District of Columbia, shall be paid for the fourth day of March (Inauguration Day) and the thirtieth day of May (Decoration Day), eighteen hundred and eighty-one, as for other days on which they perform labor.—*Jt. Res.,* 3 Mar., 1881.

TELEGRAPH LINES.

That the lines of telegraph connecting the Capitol with the various departments in Washington * * * be, and the same are hereby, placed under the supervision of the officer in charge of the public buildings and grounds. * * * And the Secretary or head of each executive department, and the Congressional Printer, are hereby authorized to detail one person from their present force of employés to operate the instruments in said departments and Printing Office, and each House of Congress may provide for the employment of an operator in their respective wings of the Capitol, at a compensation not exceeding $100 per month, during the sessions of Congress.—4 Feb., 1874.

Provided, That said lines of telegraph shall be for the use only of Senators, Members of Congress, judges of the United States courts, and officers of Congress and of the executive departments, and solely on public business.—7 Mar., 1874.

POSTAGE ON PUBLIC DOCUMENTS.

SEC. 13. That hereafter the postage on public documents mailed by any member of Congress, the President, or head of any executive department, shall be 10 cents for each bound volume, and on unbound documents the same rate as that on newspapers mailed from a known office of publication to regular subscribers; and the words "Public Document" written or printed thereon, or on the wrapper thereof, and certified by the signature of any member of Congress, or by that of the President, or head of any executive department, shall be deemed a sufficient certificate that the same is a public document; and the term "public document" is hereby defined to be all publications printed by order of Congress or either House thereof.—23 June, 1874.

SEC. 5. That it shall be lawful to transmit through the mail, free of postage, any letters, packages, or other matters relating exclusively to the business of the Government of the United States: *Provided*, That every such letter or package, to entitle it to pass free, shall bear over the words "Official Business" an indorsement showing also the name of the department, and, if from a bureau or office, the names of the department and bureau or office, as the case may be, whence transmitted. And if any person shall make use of any such official envelope to avoid the payment of postage on his private letter, package, or other matter in the mail, the person so offending shall be deemed guilty of a misdemeanor, and subject to a fine of $300, to be prosecuted in any court of competent jurisdiction.—3 Mar., 1877.

Penalty envelopes.—SEC. 29. The provisions of the fifth and sixth sections of the act entitled "An act establishing post-routes, and for other purposes," approved March 3, 1877, for the transmission of official mail matter, be, and they are hereby, extended to all officers of the United States Government, and made applicable to all official mail matter transmitted between any of the officers of the United States, or between any such officer and either of the executive departments of the Government, the envelopes of such matter in all cases to bear appropriate indorsements containing the proper designation of the office from which the same is transmitted, with a statement of the penalty for their misuse.—3 Mar., 1879.

INDIAN APPROPRIATIONS.

A tabular statement of the items paid out up to November 1st in each year of the appropriations made for the Indian Department for the fiscal year previously ending, each item being placed under the appropriation from which it was paid, in such manner as to show the disposition made of each appropriation and the amount unexpended of each; also, the itemized statement of the salaries and incidental expenses paid at each agency for the said year, and the appropriations out of which paid, and the number of Indians at each agency. * * * —3 Mar., 1875.

CONTRIBUTIONS FOR POLITICAL PURPOSES.

SEC. 6. That all executive officers or employés of the United States not appointed by the President, with the advice and consent of the Senate, are prohibited from requesting, giving to, or receiving from, any other officer or employé of the Government, any money or property or other thing of value for political purposes; and any such officer or employé who shall offend against the provisions of this section shall be at once discharged from the service of the United States; and he shall also be deemed guilty of a misdemeanor, and, on conviction thereof, shall be fined in a sum not exceeding $500.—15 Aug., 1876.

PUBLICATIONS OF GEOLOGICAL SURVEY.

The publications of the Geological Survey shall consist of the annual report of operations, geological and economic maps illustrating the resources and classification of the lands, and reports upon general and economic geology and paleontology. The annual report of operations of the Geological Survey shall accompany the annual report of the Secretary of the Interior. All special memoirs and reports of said Survey shall be issued in uniform quarto series, if deemed necessary by the Director, but otherwise in ordinary octavos. Three thousand copies of each shall be published for scientific exchanges and for sale at the price of publication; and all literary and cartographic materials received in exchange shall be the property of the United States, and form a part of the library of the organization; and the money resulting from the sale of such publications shall be covered into the Treasury of the United States.—3 Mar., 1879.

NATIONAL BOARD OF HEALTH.

SEC. 2. That the necessary printing of the National Board of Health be done at the Government Printing Office, upon the requisition of the secretary of the board, in the same manner and subject to the same provisions as other public printing for the several departments of the Government: *Provided*, That the cost of said printing shall not exceed the sum of $10,000 per annum.

SEC. 3. That the National Board of Health is hereby authorized and empowered to have printed and bound 10,000 copies of the report of the Board of Medical Experts created by former act of Congress, which report shall include the report of Doctors Bemiss and Cochran and Engineer Hardee upon the yellow-fever epidemic of 1878; 6,000 copies of the same to be furnished the House of Representatives, 2,000 copies to the Senate, and the residue to the National Board of Health: *Provided,* That the cost of publication and binding said report shall not exceed the sum of $7,500. And the said board is hereby authorized to pay Doctors Bemiss and Cochran and Engineer Hardee $10 per day, for the preparation of their said report, for the period of two months: *Provided,* That the same shall be completed and submitted to the board within that time.—1 July, 1879.

That there be printed and bound, under the direction of the National Board of Health, 6,000 copies of its annual report, with accompanying documents, and the board is hereby authorized to expend from the appropriation heretofore made for its use not to exceed the sum of $1,500 for the preparation of illustrations for the report; 1,500 copies of said report for the use of the Senate; 3,000 copies for the use of the House of Representatives, and 1,500 copies for the use of the National Board of Health.—1 Feb., 1881.

MEDICAL AND SURGICAL HISTORY OF THE WAR.

That there be printed at the Government Printing Office 5,000 copies of the first part of the Medical and Surgical History of the Rebellion, compiled by the Surgeon-General under the direction of the Secretary of War, and 5,000 copies of the Medical Statistics of the Provost-Marshal's Bureau, compiled and to be completed by Surgeon J. H. Baxter, as authorized by an act of Congress approved July 28, 1866, which also provides that the editions of both publications thus ordered shall be disposed of as Congress may hereafter direct.—*Jt. Res.,* 3 Mar., 1869.

> For the purpose of preparing for publication, under the direction of the Secretary of War, and of printing at the Government Printing Office, 5,000 copies of the first volume of the Medical and Surgical History of the Rebellion, compiled by the Surgeon-General; and for the purpose of preparing for publication under the direction of the Secretary of War, and of printing at the Government Printing Office, 5,000 copies of the Medical Statistics of the Provost-Marshal-General's Bureau, compiled and to be completed by Surgeon J. H. Baxter, $60,000: *Provided,* That the editions of both publications thus ordered shall be disposed of as Congress may hereafter direct: *And provided further,* That the necessary engraving and lithographing for these publications may be executed under the direction of the Secretary of War without advertisement.—28 July, 1866—Stats. at L., vol. 14, p. 310.

That of the 5,000 copies of the Medical and Surgical History of the War, authorized to be printed by joint resolution of Congress approved March 3, 1869, 2,000 copies shall be for the use of the House of Representatives, 1,000 for the Senate, and 2,000 for distribution by the Surgeon-General of the Army.—*Con. Res.,* 27 May, 1872.

SEC. 2. That 5,000 copies each of the second and third volumes be printed and bound by the Congressional Printer, to be distributed, with the first volume already printed, as may be hereafter directed by Congress.—8 June, 1872.

And the Congressional Printer is hereby authorized to print and bind 5,000 additional copies of the Medical and Surgical History of the War of the Rebellion; 1,000 of which shall be for the use of the Senate, 3,000 for the use of the House of Representatives, and 1,000 for distribution by the Surgeon-General of the Army.—3 Mar., 1877.

NOTE.—June 1, 1881. 10,000 copies of Parts I and II of Volume 2 and Parts I and II of Volume 1 have already been printed. There remain yet to be printed Part III of Volume 1 and Part III of Volume 2, as the series will probably consist of six books, two volumes of three parts each. No authority now exists for printing any greater number of copies than has been printed. Part III of Volume 2 is in hands of printer.

SURVEYS WEST OF THE 100TH MERIDIAN.

For engraving and printing the plates illustrating the Report of the Geographical and Geological Explorations and Surveys West of the One-hundredth Meridian, to be published in quarto form, the printing and binding to be done at the Government Printing Office, twenty-five thousand [thousand] *dollars.*—23 June, 1874.

That the following distribution shall be made of the Reports of the United States Geographical Surveys West of the One-hundredth Meridian, published in accordance with acts approved June 23, 1874, and February 15, 1875, as the several volumes are issued from the Government Printing Office, to wit: 950 copies of each to the House of Representatives, 250 copies of each to the Senate, and 800 copies of each to the War Department for its uses.—*Jt. Res.*, 4 May, 1876.

That the act entitled "An act making appropriations for sundry civil expenses of the Government for the fiscal year ending June 30, 1875, and for other purposes," approved June 23, 1874, be, and the same is hereby, amended by adding to the clause of said act relating to the engraving and printing of the plates illustrating the Report of the Geographical and Geological Explorations and Surveys West of the One-hundredth Meridian the following words: "and that 2,000 copies of the report shall be printed by the Congressional Printer," after substituting the word "dollars" in lieu of the concluding word of said clause.—15 Feb., 1875.

OFFICIAL RECORDS OF THE WAR OF THE REBELLION.

To enable the Secretary of War to begin the publication of the official Records of the War of the Rebellion, both of the Union and of the Confederate armies, the sum of $15,000. And the Secretary of War is hereby directed to have copied for the Public Printer all reports, letters, telegrams, and general orders not heretofore copied or printed, and properly arranged in chronological order.—23 June, 1880.

For continuing the preparation of the publication of the official Records of the War of the Rebellion, both of the Union and Confederate armies, and for the printing and binding, under direction of the Secretary of War, of 10,000 copies of a compilation of the official records, Union and Confederate, of the war of the rebellion, so far as the same may be ready for publication during the fiscal year, $40,000; and of said number 7,000 copies shall be for the use of the House of Representatives, 2,000 copies for the use of the Senate, and 1,000 copies for the use of the executive departments; and for the compensation of temporary clerks and other employés engaged thereon, the collection of such Confederate records as may be placed at the disposal of the Government by gift or loan, for rent of necessary offices, for fuel, stationery, and incidental expenses, $40,490; and the Secretary of War is authorized to negotiate with the legal representatives of the late Confederate Generals Bragg and Polk for the purchase of their private papers relating to the late war, and said Secretary shall report thereon at the next session of Congress.—16 June, 1880.

PRINTING AND BINDING FOR LIBRARY OF CONGRESS.

That the sum of $13,000, being the unexpended balance of the sum appropriated by the act approved December 15, 1877, for printing and binding for the Library of Congress, be, and the same is hereby, reappropriated, and may be expended for completing the new General Catalogue of the Library now in progress.—20 June, 1880.

ACTS OF CONTINENTAL CONGRESS.

That there be printed at the Government Printing Office, for the use of Congress, 5,000 copies of the resolves, ordinances, and acts of the Continental Congress and the Congress of the Confederation of the United States; 1,500 copies for the use of the Senate, 3,000 copies for the use of the House of Representatives, and 500 copies for the use of the executive departments.

SEC. 2. That said resolves, ordinances, and acts shall be taken from the journals and printed with a proper index, under the supervision of the Librarian of Congress.

SEC. 3. That the sum of $1,000, or so much thereof as may be necessary, is hereby appropriated, out of any money in the Treasury not otherwise appropriated, to defray the expense of making such work and index; the same to be disbursed under the direction of the Joint Committee on the Library.—3 Mar., 1877.

HAYDEN'S PUBLICATIONS.

Vols. 4 *and* 12.—That there be printed at the Government Printing Office 3,000 copies each of Volumes IV and XII of the final reports of the Geological and Geographical Survey of the Territories, in quarto form, with the necessary illustrations, 1,500 copies of which shall be for the use of the House of Representatives, 500 for the use of the Senate, 500 for the use of the Survey, and 500 for the use of the Smithsonian Institution; the illustrations to be made by the Public Printer, under the direction of the Joint Committee on Public Printing.—*Con. Res.,* 18 June, 1878.

Twelfth Annual Report.—That there be printed 10,000 copies of Professor Hayden's Twelfth Annual Report of the Geological and Geographical Survey of the Territories for 1878; 5,000 of which shall be for the use of the House of Representatives, 2,000 copies for the use of the Senate, 2,000 copies for the use of the Department of the Interior, and 1,000 copies for the use of the office of the Survey.—*Con. Res.,* 20 Dec., 1878.

Vols. 3, 8, *and* 13.—That there be printed at the Government Printing Office 3,000 copies each of volumes 3, 8, and 13 of the final reports of the Geological and Geographical Survey of the Territories, in quarto form, with the necessary illustrations; 1,500 copies of which shall be for the use of the House of Representatives, 750 for the use of the Senate, 375 for the use of the Survey, and 375 for the use of the Department of the Interior; the illustrations to be made by the Public Printer, under the direction of the Joint Committee on Public Printing.—*Con. Res.,* 25 Jan., 1879.

Atlas of Colorado.—That whenever the proper officer having charge thereof shall have received a sufficient number of orders for Professor Hayden's Atlas of Colorado, accompanied by the cost price thereof with 10 per cent. additional, to warrant, in his opinion, the expense of putting the plates to press, he shall cause an edition thereof to be published: *Provided, however,* That the number thus printed shall in no case exceed the number actually ordered and paid for in advance of said publication.—*Con. Res.,* 7 Feb., 1879.

That the Public Printer be, and he is hereby, directed to furnish 3,000 copies of the Atlas of Colorado by F. V. Hayden: *Provided,* The same can be supplied in sheets in every way equal in style and quality to the edition published by order of the Department of the Interior, for a sum not exceeding three dollars and fifty cents per copy: *And provided also,* That the necessary corrections be made in the same up to date; 800 copies of which shall be for the use of the Senate, 1,515 for the use of the House of Representatives, and 685 for the use of the Department of the Interior. And the sum of $10,500 is hereby appropriated for the purposes of this resolution.—*Jt. Res.,* 9 Feb., 1881.

Vols. 3, 4, 8, 12, *and* 13.—That there be printed at the Government Printing Office, for the use of the Department of the Interior, 1,500 copies each of volumes 4 and 12, and 1,200 copies each of volumes 3, 8, and 13 of the final reports of the Geological and Geographical Survey of the Territories, in quarto form, with the necessary illustrations, uniform with the edition ordered by Congress.—*Con. Res.*, 20 Mar., 1880.

Vol. 14.—That there be printed at the Government Printing Office, with the necessary illustrations, 5,000 copies of the Report on Zoology, being volume 14 of the final reports of the United States Geological Survey of the Territories, by F. V. Hayden; 2,800 copies of which shall be for the use of the House of Representatives, 1,200 for the use of the Senate, and 1,000 for the Department of the Interior.—*Con. Res.*, 17 April, 1880.

POWELL'S PUBLICATIONS.

Vol. 2, *Klamath Indians.*—That there be printed at the Government Printing Office 3,000 copies of the Report of the Geographical and Geological Survey of the Rocky Mountain Region, being volume 2, Contributions to North American Ethnology, in quarto form; 1,500 copies of which shall be for the use of the House of Representatives, 750 for the use of the Senate, 375 for the use of the Survey, and 375 for the use of the Smithsonian Institution.—*Con. Res.*, 25 Jan.,1879.

Vol. 3, *High Plateaus of Utah.*—That there be printed at the Government Printing Office 3,000 copies of the Report of the Geographical and Geological Survey of the Rocky Mountain Region, relating to the Geology of the High Plateaus of Utah, in quarto form, with the necessary illustrations and charts; 1,500 copies of which shall be for the use of the House of Representatives, 750 for the use of the Senate, 375 for the use of the Survey, and 375 for the use of the Smithsonian Institution; the illustrations and charts to be made by the Public Printer, under the direction of the Joint Committee on Public Printing.—*Con. Res.*, 25 Jan., 1879.

Vol. 2, *Henry Mountains.*—That there be printed at the Government Printing Office 5,000 copies of volume 2 of the geological series of the reports of the Geographical and Geological Survey of the Rocky Mountain Region, entitled The Geology of the Henry Mountains, with the necessary illustrations and charts; 3,000 copies of which shall be for the use of the House of Representatives, 1,000 for the use of the Senate, 500 for the use of the Department of the Interior, and 500 for the use of the Survey; the illustrations and charts to be made by the Public Printer, under the direction of the Joint Committee on Public Printing.—20 June, 1879.

Vol. 4, *Black Hills of Dakota.*—That there be printed at the Government Printing Office 2,000 copies of volume 4 of the geological series of the reports of the Geographical and Geological Survey of the Rocky Mountain Region, entitled Geology of the Black Hills of Dakota, with the necessary illustrations and charts; 1,000 copies of which shall be for the use of the House of Representatives, 500 for the use of the Senate, and 500 for the use of the Department of the Interior; the illustrations and charts to be made by the Public Printer, under the direction of the Joint Committee on Public Printing.—*Con. Res.*, 24 June, 1879.

Vols. 4 *and* 5.—That there be printed at the Government Printing Office 5,000 copies each of volumes 4 and 5, Contributions to North American Ethnology, uniform with the preceding volumes of the series, and with the necessary illustrations; 3,000 copies of which shall be for the use of the House of Representatives, 1,000 for the use of the Senate, and 1,000 for distribution by the Smithsonian Institution.— *Con. Res.*, 7 May, 1880.

Vols. 6, 7, 8, 9, *and* 10.—That there be printed at the Government Printing Office 6,000 copies each of volumes 6, 7, 8, 9, and 10 of the Contributions to North American Ethnology, uniform with the preceding volumes of the series, and with the necessary illustrations; 3,030 copies of which shall be for the use of the House of Representatives, 1,000 for the use of the Senate, and 1,970 for distribution by the Bureau of Ethnology.—*Con. Res.*, 2 Mar., 1881.

First Annual Report, Bureau of Ethnology.—That there be printed at the Government Printing Office 15,000 copies of the annual report of the Director of the Bureau of Ethnology of the Smithsonian Institution, with the necessary illustrations; 7,000 copies of which shall be for the use of the House of Representatives, 3,000 copies for the use of the Senate, and 5,000 for distribution by the Smithsonian Institution.—*Con. Res.*, 15 June, 1880.

Second and Third Annual Reports, Bureau of Ethnology.—That there be printed at the Government Printing Office 15,000 copies each of the second and third annual reports of the Director of the Bureau of Ethnology of the Smithsonian Institution, with the necessary illustrations; 7,272 copies of which shall be for the use of the House of Representatives, 3,000 copies for the use of the Senate, and 4,728 for distribution by the Bureau of Ethnology.—*Con. Res.*, 19 Feb., 1881.

REPORT OF COMMISSIONER OF FISH AND FISHERIES.

That there be printed 10,000 extra copies of the Report of the Commissioner of Fish and Fisheries for the year 1879; of which 2,000 shall be for the use of the Senate, 6,000 for the use of the House of Representatives, and 1,500 for the use of the Commissioner of Fish and Fisheries; the illustrations to be made by the Public Printer, under the direction of the Joint Committee on Public Printing; and 500 copies for sale by the Public Printer, under such regulations as the Joint Committee on Printing may prescribe, at a price equal to the additional cost of publication and 10 per cent. thereon added.—*Con. Res.,* 1 June, 1880.

That the Public Printer be, and he hereby is, instructed to print and stereotype, from time to time, the regular number of 1,900 copies of any matter furnished him by the United States Commissioner of Fish and Fisheries relative to new observations, discoveries, and applications connected with fish-culture and the fisheries, to be capable of being distributed in parts, and the whole to form an annual volume or bulletin not exceeding 500 pages. The edition of said annual work shall consist of 5,000 copies, of which 2,500 shall be for the use of the House of Representatives, 1,000 for the use of the Senate, and 1,500 for the use of the Commissioner of Fish and Fisheries. —*Jt. Res.,* 14 Feb., 1881.

REPORTS OF ENTOMOLOGICAL COMMISSION.

That there be printed, with necessary illustrations, at the Government Printing Office, 10,000 copies of the second report of the United States Entomological Commission on the Rocky Mountain Locust and other Injurious Insects; 5,000 copies for the use of the House, 3,000 copies for the use of the Senate, and 2,000 copies for the use of the Commission.—*Con. Res.,* 20 Mar., 1880.

That there be printed at the Government Printing Office, with necessary illustrations, 30,000 copies of the third report of the United States Entomological Commission; 7,000 copies thereof for the use of the Senate, 20,907 for the use of the House, and 2,093 for the Interior Department.—*Jt. Res.,* 26 Feb., 1881.

AMERICAN EPHEMERIS AND NAUTICAL ALMANAC.

That there shall be printed annually at the Government Printing Office 1,500 copies of the American Ephemeris and Nautical Almanac and of the papers supplementary thereto; of which 100 shall be for the use of the Senate, 400 for the House of Representatives, and 1,000 for the public service, to be distributed by the Navy Department.

SEC. 2. That additional copies of the Ephemeris and of the Nautical Almanac extracted therefrom may be ordered by the Secretary of the Navy for sale: *Provided,* That all moneys received from such sale shall be deposited in the Treasury to the credit of the appropriation for public printing.—*Jt. Res.,* 11 Feb., 1880.

COAST SURVEY REPORTS.

1878.—That there be printed 1,500 extra copies of the Report of Carlile P. Patterson, Superintendent of the Coast and Geodetic Survey, showing the progress made in said survey during the year ending June 30, 1878, for distribution by said Superintendent.—*Con. Res.*, 3 Mar., 1879.

1879.—That there be printed 3,000 extra copies of the Report of the Superintendent of the Coast and Geodetic Survey for the year ending June 30, 1879, for distribution by the said Superintendent.—*Con. Res.*, 29 May, 1880.

JEFFERSON'S DESK.

That there be printed 10,000 copies of the proceedings of the two houses of Congress upon the presentation to the United States by J. Randolph Coolidge and others of the desk upon which Thomas Jefferson wrote the Declaration of Independence ; 7,000 copies to be for the use of the House of Representatives and 3,000 copies for the use of the Senate.—*Con. Res.*, 7 May, 1880.

DISEASES OF SWINE.

That there be printed 50,000 copies of special report number thirty-four of the Commissioner of Agriculture, containing the reports of the veterinary surgeons appointed to investigate diseases of swine and infectious and contagious diseases incident to other classes of domesticated animals ; of which 30,300 copies shall be printed for the use of members of the House, 12,000 copies for the use of members of the Senate, and 7,700 copies for the use of the Commissioner of Agriculture.—*Jt. Res.*, 14 Feb., 1881.

Trichinæ in Swine.—*Resolved*, That there be printed at the Government Printing Office for the use of the Senate 4,300 copies of the letter of the Secretary of the Treasury transmitting, in response to a resolution of the Senate, copies of all documents touching upon trichinæ in swine.—*S. Res.*, 10 May, 1881.

REPORT OF COMMISSIONER OF EDUCATION.

That of the Report of the Commissioner of Education for eighteen hundred and eighty there be printed four thousand copies for the use of the Senate, eight thousand one hundred and eighty-one copies for the use of the House of Representatives, and twelve thousand eight hundred and nineteen copies for distribution by the Commissioner.—*Jt. Res.*, 23 Feb., 1881.

OPERATIONS OF LIFE-SAVING SERVICE.

That there be printed six thousand copies of the report of the operations of the United States Life-Saving Service for the year ending

June thirtieth, eighteen hundred and eighty, without the accompanying tables (except the one showing the location of stations), and with-out the accompanying reports on wreck ordnance, for distribution among the officers of our merchant marine, through the collectors of customs, under the direction of the Secretary of the Treasury.—*Jt. Res.*, 23 Feb., 1881.

REPORT OF COMMISSIONER OF AGRICULTURE.

That there be printed three hundred thousand copies of the Annual Report of the Commissioner of Agriculture for the year eighteen hun-dred and eighty; two hundred and fourteen thousand copies for the use of members of the House of Representatives, fifty-six thousand copies for the use of members of the Senate, and thirty thousand copies for the use of the Department of Agriculture.—*Jt. Res.*, 2 Mar., 1881.

LATE HON. E. W. FARR.

That there be printed twelve thousand copies of the memorial ad-dresses delivered in the Senate and House of Representatives upon the life and character of Honorable Evarts W. Farr, late a Representative from the State of New Hampshire, together with a portrait of the deceased; nine thousand copies thereof for the use of the House of Representatives and three thousand copies for the use of the Senate. And a sum sufficient to defray the expense of preparing and printing the portrait of the deceased for the publication herein provided for is hereby appropriated out of any moneys in the Treasury not otherwise appropriated.—*Jt. Res.*, 3 Mar., 1881.

REPORT OF DIRECTOR OF THE MINT.

That fifteen thousand copies of the report of the Director of the Mint on the annual production of gold and silver in the United States be printed; eight thousand for the use of the House of Representatives, three thousand for the use of the Senate, and four thousand for the use of the Treasury Department.—*Jt. Res.*, 3 Mar., 1881.

ANNUAL REPORT OF THE CHIEF SIGNAL OFFICER.

That there be printed for distribution by the War Department 10,000 extra copies of the annual report of the Chief Signal Officer for the fiscal year ending June 30, 1880.—*Con. Res.*, 3 *Mar.*, 1881.

TRANSPORTATION ROUTES TO SEABOARD.

For printing an edition of five thousand copies of the first volume of the report of the Committee on Transportation Routes to the Sea-board in eighteen hundred and seventy-four, four thousand dollars; two thousand copies for the use of the Senate, and three thousand copies for the use of the House of Representatives.—*Act of March* 3, 1881.

REPORT ON YELLOW FEVER.

That 500 copies of the report on yellow fever on the United States ship of war Plymouth, in 1878–'79, prepared under the direction of the Surgeon-General of the Navy, be printed and bound for the use of the Senate.—*S. Res.*, 5 *Jan.*, 1881.

REPORT OF SMITHSONIAN INSTITUTION.

That 15,560 copies of the report of the Smithsonian Institution for the year 1880 be printed; 2,500 copies of which shall be for the use of the Senate, 6,060 for the use of the House of Representatives, and 7,000 copies for the use of the Smithsonian Institution.—*Con. Res.*, 25 *Jan.*, 1881.

REPORT ON THE COTTON WORM.

That there be printed at the Government Printing Office 30,000 copies of the second revised edition, with necessary illustrations, of Bulletin No. 3 of the United States Entomological Commission, being a report on the cotton and boll worms, with means of counteracting their ravages; 10,000 copies thereof for the use of the Senate, 18,180 for the use of the House, and 1,820 for the Interior Department.—*Con. Res.*, 27 *Jan.*, 1881.

CONSULAR REPORTS ON COMMERCE, MANUFACTURES, ETC.

That there be printed and bound in one volume 50,000 copies of the three numbers issued by the State Department of Reports from the consuls of the United States on the commerce and manufactures, etc., of their consular districts; 35,000 of which shall be for the use of the members of the House of Representatives, and 15,000 for the use of the Senate.—*Con. Res.*, 23 *Feb.*, 1881.

APPROPRIATIONS FOR THE PUBLIC PRINTING, ETC.

For compensation of the Public Printer, three thousand six hundred dollars; for chief clerk, two thousand dollars; three clerks of class four; one clerk of class two; one clerk of class one; in all, thirteen thousand six hundred dollars.

For contingent expenses of his office, namely: For stationery, postage, advertising, traveling expenses, horses and wagons, and miscellaneous items, two thousand five hundred dollars.—*Act of March* 3, 1881.

To supply deficiency in the appropriation for public printing, for the public binding; and for paper for the public printing, including the cost of printing the debates and proceedings of Congress in the *Congressional Record*, and for lithographing, mapping, and engraving for both houses of Congress, Supreme Court, Court of Claims, Library of Congress, and departments, and for all necessary materials which may be needed in the prosecution of said work, four hundred thousand dollars.

To enable the Public Printer to pay for a hired horse lost while in the use of the Government Printing Office, through the fault of the driver, one of the employes of said office, two hundred and fifty dollars.

To pay for the use of telephones during the fiscal year eighteen hundred and eighty, ten dollars and eighty-four cents.

To pay the Public Printer balance due for printing for the Public Lands Commission, under the act of June sixteenth, eighteen hundred and eighty, four thousand four hundred and fifty-six dollars and twenty-six cents.—*Act of March* 3, 1881.

For the public printing, for the public binding, and for paper for the public printing, including the cost of printing the debates and proceedings of Congress in the *Congressional Record*, and for lithographing, mapping, and engraving for both houses of Congress, the Supreme Court of the United States, the supreme court of the District of Columbia, the Court of Claims, the Library of Congress, and the departments, and for all the necessary materials which may be needed in the prosecution of the work, one million seven hundred thousand dollars; and from the said sum hereby appropriated, printing and binding may be done by the Public Printer to the amounts following, respectively, namely:

For printing and binding for Congress, including the proceedings and debates, eight hundred and fifty thousand dollars; for the State Department, fifteen thousand dollars; for the Treasury Department, two hundred and ten thousand dollars; for the War Department, one hundred and twenty thousand dollars; for the Navy Department, fifty thousand dollars; for the Interior Department, two hundred and twenty thousand dollars; for the Department of Justice, ten thousand dollars; for the Post-Office Department, one hundred and fifty thousand dollars; for the Agricultural Department, eleven thousand dollars; for the Supreme Court of the United States, thirty-four thousand dollars; for the supreme court of the District of Columbia, one thousand dollars; for the Court of Claims, ten thousand dollars; and for the Library of Congress, nineteen thousand dollars.—*Act of March* 3, 1881.